Bohemond of Taranto

Bohemond of Taranto

Crusader and Conqueror

Georgios Theotokis

Pen & Sword
MILITARY

AN IMPRINT OF PEN & SWORD BOOKS LTD
YORKSHIRE – PHILADELPHIA

First published in Great Britain in 2020 by
PEN & SWORD MILITARY
An imprint of Pen & Sword Books Ltd
Yorkshire – Philadelphia

Copyright © Georgios Theotokis, 2020

ISBN 978-1-52674-428-9

The right of Georgios Theotokis to be identified as the author of this work has been asserted by him in accordance with the Copyright, Designs and Patents Act 1988.

A CIP catalogue record for this book is available from the British Library.

All rights reserved. No part of this book may be reproduced or transmitted in any form or by any means, electronic or mechanical including photocopying, recording or by any information storage and retrieval system, without permission from the Publisher in writing.

Typeset by Concept, Huddersfield, West Yorkshire, HD4 5JL
Printed and bound in England by TJ Books Limited, Padstow, Cornwall

Pen & Sword Books Ltd incorporates the Imprints of Aviation, Atlas, Family History, Fiction, Maritime, Military, Discovery, Politics, History, Archaeology, Select, Wharncliffe Local History, Wharncliffe True Crime, Military Classics, Wharncliffe Transport, Leo Cooper, The Praetorian Press, Remember When, White Owl, Seaforth Publishing and Frontline Publishing.

For a complete list of Pen & Sword titles please contact
PEN & SWORD BOOKS LTD
47 Church Street, Barnsley, South Yorkshire, S70 2AS, England
E-mail: enquiries@pen-and-sword.co.uk
Website: www.pen-and-sword.co.uk
or
PEN & SWORD BOOKS
1950 Lawrence Rd, Havertown, PA 19083, USA
E-mail: uspen-and-sword@casematepublishers.com
Website: www.penandswordbooks.com

To my Brigita –
for ever

Contents

List of Maps ix
List of Plates xi
Introduction 1
1. Early Life and Kin Dynamics 7
2. The Norman Invasion of the Balkans, 1081–83 19
3. The Norman Invasion of the Balkans, 1082–84 43
4. The Interlude Period, 1085–97 63
5. The Crusader – From Italy to the City 73
6. The Crusader – Conquering Antioch 89
7. Lord of Antioch 117
8. Back to Europe 141
Epilogue: Death and Heritage 159
Notes 167
Bibliography 187
Index 193

List of Maps

The area around Dyrrachium	32
The Albanian river system	45
The southern Balkans	51
The route of the First Crusade	100
The Middle East	132

List of Plates

Archangel Michael and Joshua, Church of St George Diasorites, Naxos island, southern Aegean Sea. A rare surviving example of a cross-in-square type of Byzantine church built and decorated in the second half of the eleventh century (probably in the early Komnenian period).

St George and St Demetrius, Church of St Anargyroi, Kastoria, western Macedonia, c.1160–80, depicted as typical mid-twelfth-century Byzantine cavalry officers.

Joshua, monastery of St Lucas in Veotea, central Greece, twelfth century, depicted as a Byzantine infantry soldier.

Battle scene between units of Byzantine and Arab cavalry from an illuminated manuscript, the 'Madrid Skylitzes', twelfth century.

Bohemond and Patriarch Daimbert of Pisa on their way to the Holy Land.

Battle scenes depicting Norman soldiers, Church of St Nicolas in Bari, eleventh century.

Mount Demirkazik (3,756m) in the Aladaglar mountains, Niğde Province, Turkey, part of the formidable Taurus mountains separating Anatolia from Upper Mesopotamia and Syria.

Aerial view of the castle of St George in Kephalonia, Ionian Sea, which was built by the Byzantines in the eleventh century.

The Via Egnatia in the river valley of the Skhumbi, resurfaced by the Italian military in 1940.

The medieval walls of Dyrrachium (modern Durrës).

The river Vjosë upstream from Tepelenë, Albania.

The mausoleum of Bohemond in Canosa di Puglia.

The tower of Bohemond in the castle of Ioannina.

Castle of St Marco Argentano.

Roman caltrops.

The liberation of Bohemond from his captivity by the Danishmendits. Image from the illuminated manuscript, Maître du Roman de Fauvel, 'Libération de Bohémond', 'Li rommans de Godefroy de Buillon et de Salehadin et de tous lez autres roys qui ont esté outre mer jusques a saint Loys qui darrenierem' (BnF 22495).

Introduction

We were sprung from poor and obscure parents, and leaving the barren fields of the Cotentin and homes ill supplied with the means of existence, we set out for Rome, and it was not without great difficulty and much alarm that we passed beyond that place. Afterwards, by God's aid, we got possession of many great cities.

[Orderic Vitalis, *Ecclesiastical History*, vol. II, p. 369]

The Aims and Scope of the Book

Bohemond of Taranto was a man of boundless ambition and inexhaustible energy; he was, in the words of Romuald of Salerno, 'always seeking the impossible'. If he failed, however, to conquer the Byzantine empire and establish his own great eastern empire, he did succeed in founding the most enduring of all the states in the Latin East. He proved to be one of the most remarkable warriors in medieval Mediterranean history, coming from a family of 'soldiers of fortune', the Hautevilles, who managed to establish a powerful principality in Italy and seriously threaten the Byzantine empire's very existence.

Remarkably very few monographs have been devoted to this *chevalier d'aventure* (Jean Flori) and Ralph Yewdale published the only one in English more than a century ago, in 1917. Since then, Jean Flori has published a modern, although dense and difficult to read, examination of Bohemond's life and career in French. This was supplemented, in 2008, by an updated and compelling biography of the Norman in Italian by Luigi Russo. Yet the aim of this book is to write about 'the great son of Guiscard' as a warrior – in a sense, minimising his political and diplomatic 'machinations' or his contribution to the holy war in the Middle East and focusing instead on his military achievements in Italy, Sicily, the Balkans, Anatolia and the Middle East.

Bohemond was famous for being one of the most experienced officers in the crusader army and the undisputed leader because he 'knew' the enemy. He had fought in Italy and Sicily against the local Lombard and Arab levies, while he was the second-in-command (later to become the leader) of the Norman armies that invaded Byzantine Illyria twice in three decades to face the multi-cultural armies of the Byzantine emperor Alexios Komnenos, comprising Greek, Armenian and Turkish troops. Therefore, because medieval commanders have in general received little credit for their strategic understanding, I want to focus on Bohemond's career as:

- **a strategist**: analysing his war-plans in different operational theatres (Italy, Balkans, Middle East) and examining which strategy he follows – annihilation, exhaustion or attrition? I will attempt to elucidate the degree to which one can characterise the Norman – and more specifically Bohemond's – strategies in Italy, Sicily and the Balkans as 'Vegetian'.
- **a tactician**: studying Bohemond's deployment and employment of troops in actual fighting against different enemies in different operational theatres. How well does he adapt his battle-tactics to those of the enemy? How well does he 'know' the enemy (reconnaissance, diplomacy, espionage, etc.)? How suitable were these tactics for the warfare in each region?
- **a trans-cultural warrior**: How typical a 'Norman' warrior was Bohemond? While the many 'cultures of war' that emerged in the medieval world shared some basic characteristics, what is more broadly comparable are the processes or dynamics that shaped military cultures around the world. More specifically, in this monograph I will explore those dynamics and the cultural patterns they produced by focusing on Bohemond's military career in regions that were hotly contested in the Middle Ages – the Italian Peninsula, Sicily and the opposite Adriatic coast, and the Middle East.

The Norman Expansion out of Normandy

In his monumental *The Making of Europe*, Robert Bartlett wrote, 'one of the more striking aspects of the expansionary activity of the tenth to thirteenth centuries was the movement of western European aristocrats from their homelands into new areas where they settled and, if successful, augmented their fortunes'. He was referring to the medieval aristocratic expansion from the core of Europe's old 'Carolingian lands' into its periphery – eastern and southern Europe and, of course, the Middle East. Men of Norman descent became lords in England, Wales, Scotland and Ireland, in southern Italy and Sicily, in Spain and Syria. One Norman adventurer became lord of Tarragona and a Poitevin family attained the crown of Cyprus.

However, what were the reasons behind this migration of these 'medieval warriors' to the Mediterranean in the first half of the eleventh century? One factor would have been pilgrimage. Although the religious importance of Santiago de Compostela in Galicia, northwestern Spain, is indisputable, Italy was the crossing point of every major pilgrimage route leading to the Holy Land. Furthermore, religious visitors could perform their pious duty at the Sanctuary of Monte Sant'Angelo sul Gargano in northern Apulia, and the Normans appear as pilgrims in two of the three relatively different versions mentioning the coming of the Normans to Italy around the year 1000.

Another contributing factor to the Norman migration would have been the overpopulation of Normandy. In the last speech that Orderic Vitalis puts into the mouth of Robert Guiscard in July 1085, we read: 'We were sprung from poor and obscure parents, and leaving the barren fields of the Cotentin and homes ill supplied with the means of existence, we set out for Rome ... Afterwards, by God's aid, we got possession of many great cities.' Similar accounts underline the fact that the division of the family patrimony was a serious issue in eleventh-century Normandy and that customs of inheritance dashed the aspirations of many younger sons to acquire a piece of land for themselves.

The driving force behind the expansion of the 1020s–50s, however, was the political and social disturbances in many parts of northern France after the breakdown of Robert II's regime in 1034. In fact, there seems to be a link between periods of particular disturbance in the duchy of Normandy and periods of expansion in Italy. For example, the period of the growing power of Rainulf of Aversa (second half of 1030s) and the establishment of the Normans at Melfi (1041) were preceded by the troubled reign of Richard III (1034–35) and the minority years of William II.

Finally, recent studies have dashed the myth of this being a period of a purely Norman 'invasion' of southern lands. Italian sources and charter evidence contain numerous references to newcomers from other parts of France.[1] In the last twenty years it has become clear that approximately one in three of the 'invaders' were of non-Norman origin and, more specifically, from Normandy's neighbouring regions including Brittany, Anjou, Maine and Chartres, or even from further south, like Burgundy and Champagne.

The Normans in Italy, Eleventh Century

The Normans are first attested in southern Italy in early 999, when a group of Norman pilgrims came to the support of the local population in

Salerno who were being attacked by marauding Arab raiders from the emirate of Sicily. Several other Normans became involved in the revolt of Melus of Bari against Byzantine rule in Apulia in the years 1017–18. As a direct result of this impromptu military involvement, other Normans arrived in Italy, no longer as pilgrims but as mercenaries recruited by local Lombard princes. By the end of the 1020s the numbers of men under the command of Rainulf, the future (after 1030) count of Aversa, swelled following the death of Duke Robert II of Normandy in 1035 and the minority years of his son William. Yet they were still not the main players in the political insurrection against Byzantine authority in Apulia; rather they were taking the side of the highest bidder.

The Norman establishment in Aversa, north of Naples, in 1030 and in Melfi, in the Apulian-Campanian borders, in 1041 would have profound long-term socio-political consequences for the area. In fact, the Normans were only 500 strong when they established themselves in Melfi, being heavily outnumbered by their enemies. In the short term, however, the Byzantines reacted sharply and confronted the united Lombard-Norman forces in two pitched battles at Olivento (17 March 1041) and Ofanto (4 May 1041), followed by a third at Montepeloso in early autumn. Although the Normans emerged victorious, at this early stage of their expansion into Italy these newcomers were still divided, with the two most powerful groups being those in Aversa and Melfi, with other smaller bands operating independently in the Capitanata and northern Campania. Finally, the Norman victory over the papal army led by Leo IX at Civitate in 1053 firmly established the Normans in southern Italy by opening the way for further conquests in every direction.

In 1059 at Melfi Robert Guiscard made peace with Pope Nicholas II, to whom he swore an oath of fealty. Robert was invested as duke of Apulia and Calabria, while Richard, count of Aversa and son of Rainulf, was acknowledged as prince of Capua, having captured that city in the previous year. Robert Guiscard's crowning achievement on mainland Italy was the conquest of the Byzantine capital Bari after a prolonged siege between 1068 and 1071, during which he did his best to exploit the internal divisions of the local inhabitants.

The fertile and strategically important island of Sicily was conquered over a period of more than thirty years from the first invasion in 1061, followed by the conquest of Palermo in 1071–72. However, the three major pitched battles in this operational theatre that took place in the first decade of the Norman expansion reveal the weaknesses of the Norman leaders, Robert Guiscard and his brother Roger, in managing the invasion of an island so far from their bases on the Italian mainland. In no case were the Normans able to put into the field more than a few hundred mounted horsemen, while every winter the mounting casualties had to be replaced by shipping in fresh troops from Calabria and Apulia. Finally, in order to diminish the numerical superiority of their enemies and take full advantage of the mobility of their cavalry, they chose relatively broken, hilly or marshy terrain, that was also dominated by a river or an uphill castle, as in the battles of Castrogiovanni (1061) and Cerami (1063) in the heart of the island.

An Introduction to the Narrative Sources

The basic primary sources for the Norman expansion in Italy and Sicily, and their invasions in the Balkans, include mainly those authors who wrote in Latin, including Amatus of Montecassino, William of Apulia and Geoffrey Malaterra, and the sole author who wrote in Greek, Anna Komnena. The former is the author of the earliest of the three substantial narrative accounts of the conquest of southern Italy by the 'peoples beyond the Alps' in the eleventh century. *The History of the Normans*[2] was probably completed shortly after the last event mentioned, the death of Richard I, hence around 1078/9. William of Apulia wrote a poem in hexameters ('epic verse') about *The Deeds of Robert Guiscard*,[3] probably between 1096 and 1099, although the poem is not exclusively concerned with the life of the duke of Apulia and Calabria. William seems to have been a member of Roger Borsa's court and was probably a layman, although his full identity remains elusive. He was obviously well informed about the Byzantine Empire, but his contemporary sources remain difficult to identify. Geoffrey Malaterra is the third chronicler to commemorate the conquest of Italy and Sicily by the Normans, and indeed the only one whose focus is Roger Hauteville. Malaterra notes that he was a 'newcomer' to the region, and that he almost certainly had come to Sicily sometime after 1091 at the request of Count Roger, who wished to re-establish the power and influence of the Latin Church on the island. His *The Deeds of Count Roger of Calabria and Sicily and of his Brother Duke Robert Guiscard* was completed in the closing years of the eleventh century.[4]

Anna Komnena, one of the most important and influential historiographers of Byzantine literature, was the first-born child of Emperor Alexios I Komnenos. She was born on 1 December 1083 and at the age of 8 was betrothed to Constantine Doukas, the son of the deposed emperor Michael VII Doukas. A highly educated princess, Anna may have started compiling her *Alexiad*[5] after the death of her husband Nicephorus

Bryennius in 1137, but it seems more likely that she waited for her brother John (Emperor John II, reigned 1118–43) to pass away in 1143. Therefore, the work was completed within five years, since we understand that the fourteenth of her fifteen books was finished in 1148. Anna's position in the imperial court brought her into close contact with many leading figures of the empire, including her father, Emperor Alexios I Komnenos, her uncle and governor of Dyrrachium, George Palaeologus, her husband and trusted senior official Nicephorus Bryennius, her grandmother and regent Anna Dalassena, Empress Irene, and Tatikios, who was Alexios' representative to the Latin Armies of the First Crusade. Her high position would have allowed her access to imperial archives and state correspondence. She also gathered useful information from eyewitnesses, as she herself describes: 'My material [...] has been gathered [...] from old soldiers who were serving in the army at the time of my father's accession, who fell on hard times and exchanged the turmoil of the outer world for the peaceful life of monks.' Finally, she was an eyewitness herself in a number of events at which 'most of the time [...] we were ourselves present, for we accompanied our father and mother. Our lives by no means revolved round the home.'[6]

Chapter 1

Early Life and Kin Dynamics

A Portrait of Bohemond

Now the man [Bohemond] was such as, to put it briefly, had never before been seen in the land of the Romans, be he either of the barbarians or of the Greeks (for he was a marvel for the eyes to behold, and his reputation was terrifying). Let me describe the barbarian's appearance more particularly – he was so tall in stature that he overtopped the tallest by nearly one cubit, narrow in the waist and loins, with broad shoulders and a deep chest and powerful arms. And in the whole build of the body he was neither too slender nor over weighted with flesh, but perfectly proportioned and, one might say, built in conformity with the canon of Polycleitus. He had powerful hands and stood firmly on his feet, and his neck and back were well compacted. An accurate observer would notice that he stooped slightly, but this was not from any weakness of the vertebrae of his spine but he had probably had this posture slightly from birth. His skin all over his body was very white, and in his face the white was tempered with red. His hair was yellowish, but did not hang down to his waist like that of the other barbarians; for the man was not inordinately vain of his hair, but had it cut short to the ears. Whether his beard was reddish, or any other colour I cannot say, for the razor had passed over it very closely and left a surface smoother than chalk; most likely it too was reddish. His blue eyes indicated both a high spirit and dignity; and his nose and nostrils breathed in the air freely; his chest corresponded to his nostrils and by his nostrils ... the breadth of his chest. For by his nostrils nature had given free passage for the high spirit which bubbled up from his heart. A certain charm hung about this man but was partly marred by a general air of the horrible. For in the whole of his body the entire man shewed implacable and savage both in his size and glance, methinks, and even his laughter sounded to others like snorting. He was so made in mind and body that both courage and passion reared their crests within him and both inclined to war. His wit was manifold and crafty and able to find a way of escape [lit. 'handle'] in every emergency. In conversation he was well informed, and the answers he gave were quite irrefutable. This man who was of such a size and such a character was inferior to the Emperor alone in fortune and eloquence and in other gifts of nature.[1]

This lengthy and intimate portrait is undoubtedly the best description of Bohemond's physical appearance that has been saved for posterity, written down some eight-and-a-half centuries ago by the Byzantine princess Anna, the eldest child of the Emperor Alexios Komnenos (r. 1081–1118). She delivered this description of her father's nemesis in Book XIII, one of the last books of her monumental historical and biographical text, written around the year 1148 and named the *Alexiad* after her father. But although Bohemond appears in Anna's work as early as Book IV, by the time the historian evidently thought it was time for her to deliver this detailed picture of her villain-hero, the Norman had already submitted to her father's envoys on the outskirts of the Illyrian port-city of Dyrrachium (modern Durrës in Albania).

What immediately follows the portrait of Bohemond is the famous *Treaty of Devol* (Diabolis), drawn up in September 1108 between the Norman and Alexios, under the terms of which 'second pact' [following Bohemond's formal submission to Alexios in 1097], 'I [Bohemond] shall become the liege-man of Your Highnesses [Alexios and John Komnenoi].'[2] Therefore, in this contest between the two great antagonists, Anna leaves no doubt as to who eventually triumphed over whom, and through her desire to magnify her father's political and, more importantly, military success over this imposing barbarian in the eyes and ears of her audience, she ingeniously chose to place the physical description of the Norman count immediately after his defeat and surrender to the true hero of her work, her father.

It is not until he becomes a crusader in the summer of 1096 that Bohemond draws Anna's virulent attacks; after that, no colours are too dark for painting him! However, he is not the only westerner to incur the princess's sarcastic, derogatory or downright hateful comments. The Latin peoples of the West, who are called indiscriminately Latins, Franks or Celts, are all 'barbarians' as far as she is concerned. Anna ascribes to them numerous unpleasant attributes: they are 'shameless [ἀναίσχυντον] and reckless [ἰταμόν]', but they are also 'greedy of money [ἐρασιχρήματον]', and 'immoderate in everything they wish', and this – naturally – made them 'unstable and easily led'.³ This implies that the Franks would change sides even during battle to serve the highest bidder, thus discarding any previous agreements with former allies.⁴

Nevertheless, Anna admits on several occasions that the Franks were brave and daring, though untamed and undisciplined, especially when on horseback.⁵ Their impetuous nature and lust for battle and bloodshed, along with other characteristics like their 'hot-headedness [θερμότατον]' and 'eagerness [ὀξύ]' for glory which made them 'uncontrollable [ἀκάθεκτον]', all of these bear down to one of the three distinct components of ethnicity in the Middle Ages; the first two were the idea of a nation's common descent (usually going back to a mythical figure), followed by a shared language, but I will not elaborate on these two here; the third one was that each people had its own distinct characteristics, both physical and mental, and this is a fundamental idea behind the formation of the notion of the 'invincibility' on the battlefield of the Frankish and Norman nations.⁶

In the Middle Ages there was a widespread belief that physical appearance was transmitted by heredity, which in turn was determined by climactic and geographical factors. In fact, Isidore of Seville's *Etymologiae* (written in the early seventh century AD), the first work of 'universal knowledge [*summa*]', was the standard medieval work of reference for the creation and sustenance of ideas relating to the character of races: 'The Saxon people ... are accomplished in strength and agility. Whence they were named [i.e. from *saxosus*, 'stony'], because they are a hard and very powerful kind of people, standing out above the other piratical tribes.'⁷ Two centuries earlier, Vegetius' *Epitoma Rei Militaris* (written in the early fifth century) was the first Roman military treatise that offered a view of foreign warriors, in which the division of the Roman army's recruits was geographical rather than sociological:

> Or with what success would their [the Romans'] small size have been opposed to the prodigious stature of the Germans? The Spaniards surpassed us not only in numbers, but in physical strength. We were always inferior to the Africans in wealth and unequal to them in deception and stratagem. And the Greeks, indisputably, were far superior to us in skill in arts and all kinds of knowledge.⁸

The aforementioned ideas were adopted and elaborated by later medieval historians contemporary with the Norman expansion in the south, such as Orderic Vitalis, Geoffrey Malaterra and Amatus of Montecassino.⁹ Yet these stereotypical views of the 'characters' of nations have a much older origin, as they follow the same principle outlined by Tacitus in his *Germania* (first century AD) and Hippocrates on his climatic theory of human nature (around 400 BC).[10]

Geoffrey Malaterra promoted the introduction of clichés about Norman prowess that were universally accepted by his Latin contemporaries. He, along with William of Apulia, did his utmost to elaborate the Italo-Norman 'warlike nature', with characteristics such as energy (*strenuitas*), fierceness or martial spirit (*fierte*), boldness (*hardiesce*) and valour (*vaillantize*)[11] playing a fundamental role in shaping the identity of these newcomers to Italy.[12] Two examples from the Norman campaigns in the Balkans between 1081 and 1083 portray the Norman clichés of valour and boldness in facing great danger:

> His [Robert Guiscard] army did not consist of more than ten thousand troops, but he relied more on the valour than on the numbers of his soldiers to strike the enemy with terror, in his invasion of Greece renowned for its warlike character since the times of Adrastus and Agamemnon.[13]

> For the duke [Robert Guiscard] was extraordinarily bold and determined in military matters, and this was abundantly clear to many of the army, even if all the rest kept it quiet. It could in particular undoubtedly be realized from this fact; that he dared to undertake a war with only a small force against so populous an empire and an emperor so well provided with troops, against so many thousands of enemies, and he expected to defeat them. (Those who were present during this affair have testified that he had with him no more than 1,300 fully armed knights).[14]

Equally significant for the Norman invaders was their resourcefulness, as adaptation to the new geo-political environment in Italy proved crucial for their Mediterranean expansion in the eleventh century, literally matching the term 'soldiers of fortune'. William of Apulia sets the tone here:

> Although he [Robert Guiscard] knew the bravery of his soldiers, he wanted no rash undertakings. Not only had he been told of the vast numbers of the enemy but he knew nothing of the sort of men they were. So he sensibly counselled his people to be cautious, and prepared for every possible eventuality.[15]

In direct relation to their resourcefulness, the Normans are often depicted as crafty and opportunistic, seeking the perfect opportunity to desert their former allies in order to achieve their goals by 'any means', chivalric or unchivalric:

> But, realising how stingy the prince of Capua was, they [the Normans] abandoned him and changed sides to enter the employ of the prince of Salerno. He received them as was fitting, because their military reputation had already made them extremely well known throughout Apulia, and particularly since they had deserted the prince his enemy and joined him. Their loyalty to him was encouraged with generous gifts.[16]

Writing about the Norman invasion of the island of Sicily in the early 1060s, Malaterra further notes that: 'Seeing their enemies facing their army on the other shore and no prospect of doing anything, Count Roger resorted as was his custom to cunning proposals, as if he had read, "What is to be done? Success falls to the crafty weapons."'[17]

But what particularly distinguished the Normans in the military 'arena' of medieval European warfare was their *strenuitas* – energy in the field – which is a characteristically Norman quality that differentiated them from their 'effeminate' enemies, like the Greeks and the Lombards:

> In this province there is a city called Coutances, and in its territory there is a village named Hauteville; called thus not so much because of the height of any hill upon which it is situated, but rather, so we believe, as an omen predicting the extraordinary fortune and great success of the future heirs of this village, who with the help of God and their own dynamism [*strenuitas*] raised themselves step by step to the highest of ranks.[18]

Therefore, coupled with the power of Divine Providence and Fortune, which are ever-present in all contemporary historical accounts of Norman expansion, it was their energy that guided them out of their ancestral places in northern France and into southern Italy. And in the Latin accounts of the time, this process of military expansion in Apulia resembles more of a 'conquest' of a woman than territorial aggrandisement – Apulia is depicted as a beautiful and fertile woman who stood defenceless and ready to be grabbed by her powerful new masters: the Hautevilles and their companions-in-arms.[19]

Finally, the aggressiveness of the Normans was epitomised by their natural inclination to dominate other peoples and lands. In referring to the *avidas dominationis*, the eleventh-century historian Malaterra was undoubtedly influenced by the idea of the *libidem dominandi* ('lust for domination') which Sallust, the Roman politician and historian (86–35 BC), associated with the tyrannical regimes of the Athenians and the Spartans of the fifth century BC.[20] Hence, we read in Malaterra's *Deeds*:

> For the natural and customary inclination [*mos incitus*] of the sons of Tancred was always to be greedy for domination [*avidas dominationis*], to the very utmost of their powers. They were unable to put up with anybody in their vicinity holding lands and possessions without being envious and immediately seizing these by force and rendering everything subject to their authority.[21]

To return to Anna Komnena and her character portraits of the Normans, they loom so large in her eyes during their campaigns in the Balkans (1081–84) and then in the First Crusade that she seems to 'see a Norman in every Westerner'. Nonetheless, there is another important figure that dominates the *Alexiad* from the middle of Book I to the middle of Book VI: Bohemond's father Robert. In fact, he is so important that our princess describes his character and appearance twice in her work:

> This Robert was a Norman by birth, of obscure origin [τύχην ἄσημος], with an overbearing character [γνώμην τυρρανικός] and a thoroughly villainous soul [ψυχήν πανουργότατος], he was a brave fighter [χεῖρα γενναῖος], terrible [δεινότατος] in his assaults on the wealth and power of great men; in achieving his aims absolutely inexorable, diverting criticism by incontrovertible argument.[22]

Anna puts emphasis on Robert's humble status, compared to the noble and high-born heroes in her work, both Alexios Komnenos and Constantine Doukas (the son of Emperor Michael VII, reigned 1071–78). She carries on with the same admiration for the Norman leader's qualities as we saw in the case of Bohemond, confirming that he was a brave and formidable fighter, although cunning and overbearing. In fact, Anna's emphatic use of the 'thoroughly villainous soul' serves as a frequent reminder of the unstable and rapacious nature of the man. Then she winds up her description by confirming the rich endowments of *fortune* and *nature* in Robert, that resulted in him being 'a slave to no man, subject to none of all the world', which seems to astonish Anna since Robert was of such an obscure origin.

But the Norman warrior that surpasses Robert Guiscard in greed, treachery and dishonesty was none other than his son Bohemond, the *fons et origo malorum* of the western knights and a 'a living model of his father's character in audacity, bodily strength, bravery and untameable temper'.[23]

These derogatory comments on Bohemond's character come from the closing paragraphs of Book I of the *Alexiad*, when the princess is writing about the Norman invasion of Byzantine Illyria in the summer of 1081. During that campaign, in which Bohemond had been assigned the role of second-in-command, he was sent along with a reconnaissance force to the northern Greek coast to prepare the ground for the main invasion force that was about to sail from Otranto. In this first conflict with the Byzantines Bohemond has, indeed, no distinguishing feature as he is portrayed merely as his father's son. But from 1097 onwards, when he arrives in Constantinople with the rest of the crusaders, and up until the Treaty of Devol in 1108 and his death soon afterwards, he is always there as the anti-hero in Anna's work.

The princess is scornful about Bohemond's motives in joining the First Crusade: a desire to improve his fortunes, and some sort of irrational ambition to become *Grand Domestic* or even emperor. She even writes about Bohemond having an 'ancient grudge' against her father.[24] Therefore, by the time the Norman count swore an oath of allegiance to Alexios in the imperial palace, thus becoming a liege-man of the emperor, Anna – writing much later and with the benefit of hindsight – already knew that he would break his promises, because, like all the other Latins, he was 'unstable' and 'most cunning [πανουργότατος]'. However, as was the case with Anna's portrayal of Robert, she is even-handed enough to deliver a fair assessment of Bohemond's good qualities: he was, indeed, brave and eager to win victories in the battlefield, energetic, a very capable tactician, and 'skilled above all men in the art of sieges, even surpassing the famous Demetrius Poliorcetes'.[25]

'Buamundus Gigas': Early Life and Kin Dynamics

Let us begin with the baptismal name of the man, which was not, as one would expect, Bohemond. That was just a sobriquet, derived – according to the Norman historian Orderic Vitalis – from the Latin *Buamundus*, the name of a mythical Gigas (giant) about whom we know nothing, and originally given to the future count by his father because he was abnormally large at birth.[26] He was, rather, baptised Mark, possibly because he was born at his father's castle of San Marco Argentano in Calabria. Yet the symbolism of that name is also palpable, given in honour of Mark the Evangelist, whose symbol was the winged lion – a figure of courage and monarchy in most European, African and Asian cultures for millennia; the name Marcus – very popular in Italy, southern France and Spain around AD 1000 – is also a masculine patronym of pre-Christian Roman origin that refers to Mars, the Roman god of war. Sadly, we can only speculate about the year of Bohemond's birth according to the dates of the marriage of his father Robert to his first wife Alberada, sometime between 1050 (the year of the marriage) and 1058 (the year of the divorce on grounds of consanguinity).

Robert Guiscard's divorce from Alberada on the grounds of consanguinity, a pretext that was widely used in the Middle Ages, proved to be an adept political move that boosted Robert's career in Italy on an unprecedented scale; in other words, Alberada's repudiation, and the subsequent demotion of her first-born son Bohemond to the status of a bastard, formed part of a well-thought-out plan conceived by Robert to advance his alliances in the region. Therefore, it would be best to pause at this point, and take the narrative back to the coming of Robert to Apulia, and elaborate on the political and military instability he entered upon his arrival in southern Italy in the late 1040s, in order to understand the kin dynamics of the Hautevilles in the region in the middle of the century.[27]

Throughout the 1040s the power of the Normans in Apulia grew steadily with every passing campaigning season, following the Lombard-Norman decisive victories over the Byzantine field armies at Olivento (17 March 1041), Ofanto (4 May 1041) and Montepeloso (3 September 1041). Coupled with their establishment in the fortress-town of Melfi in the Apulian-Campanian borders early in 1042, an event with long-term geo-political consequences for the *status quo* in the region, news of such triumphs found their way beyond the Alps, thus causing the tide of immigration southwards to swell:

> They talked of the fertility of Apulia and of the cowardice of those who lived there. They advised them to carry with them only what was necessary for the journey; for they promised that once there they would find a wise patron, under whose leadership they would gain an easy victory over the Greeks ... All of them were greedy for gain.[28]

The fact, however, that many territories in the north and west of Apulia surrendered to the Normans of Melfi does not necessarily imply that this came as a result of their numerical strength, or was part of a well-prepared plan. By the mid-1040s the exact number of the Normans in Apulia is not known, because of the meagre information from the sources, but estimates indicate that they would not have exceeded a few hundred (perhaps as many as five hundred), based on their operational role, their casualty rates and recruiting from parts of France, and the political divisions within their ranks that prevented them from establishing a coherent political identity.[29] It was during this period of socio-political upheaval in the South that, sometime in 1046, two young men appeared in southern Italy within a few months of each other. Each was, in his own way, to achieve greatness; they were Richard, later to become prince of Capua, and Robert Hauteville, soon to earn the cognomen *Guiscard* (the 'Cunning').

For Robert, the welcome which awaited him at the court of his half-brother Drogo in Melfi was distinctly unenthusiastic, not to say strained. Drogo Hauteville was the second son of Tancred of Hauteville and his first wife Muriella, and he was one of the twelve Norman leaders who first came to Apulia. He managed to get elected leader of the Apulian Normans on 3 February 1047, following the death of his elder brother William 'Iron-Arm', after beating Peter of Trani – another senior Norman leader – for the succession. Drogo held the support of Guaimar IV, the Lombard prince of Salerno (r. 1027–52), and was astute enough to marry Guaimar's sister Gaitelgrima in early 1047, a marriage alliance which significantly advanced his political standing in the region. Therefore, when Robert – Drogo's brother from his father's second wife Fressenda – arrived in the midst of this political confusion in southern Italy, Drogo refused to give him any territory of his own. The Norman leader may not have had enough land to give away anyway; nevertheless, he made sure to get rid of this young newcomer by sending him to take possession of the as-yet-unconquered Calabria, in the heel of Italy.

Robert quickly realised that his future looked bleak in this mountainous and desolate region of Calabria, and he soon rode off to serve the Lombard Prince Pandulf IV of Capua (d. 1049/50) as a mercenary in his wars against Guaimar IV of Salerno. Following Pandulf's death, Guiscard returned to his brother in desperate search of a fief. Drogo, who had just finished campaigning in Calabria, handed Guiscard command of the strategic Calabrian fortress of Scribla, near Cosenza on the river Crati. In this hostile and distinctly uninviting land, being handed a fortress-town that was hot, dry and rank with malaria would have felt more like a curse than a blessing to young Robert.[30] Dissatisfied with his predicament, Guiscard moved his base to the castle of San Marco Argentano, another strategic location further up the river Crati, and the birthplace of his future son Bohemond.

Soon after his move to San Marco Argentano, Robert married his first wife, the Norman Alberada De Macon, known in Italy as Alberada of Buonalbergo. She was the daughter of Reginald I, count of Burgundy, also known as Renaud I De Macon (Raynald I), Baron of Buonalbergo, and his wife Alice of Normandy. This was a highly rewarding alliance between a family which was establishing itself, the Buonalbergos, and an ambitious young knight who desperately sought different ways to advance his standing in Italian politics. This marriage brought Robert two things he really needed: a band of two hundred knights, and an heir.[31] Both came at just the right time.

Robert quickly rose to prominence. He fought with distinction commanding the left division of the Norman troops in their victory over the allied Papal-Lombard army at the Battle of Civitate-sul-Fortore, in northern Apulia, on 17 June 1053. Civitate was a turning point in the future of the Normans in Italy who, following the outcome of the battle, were able to solidify their legitimacy in the process of expanding further south into the heel of Otranto, in Calabria and, soon enough, to the Muslim-held island of Sicily. Not only that, it was the first major victory for Robert Guiscard, who would eventually become the undisputed leader of the Normans in Italy and Sicily.

Eventually, it would be the changing patterns of succession in the Hauteville kin that would further Robert's career. Just as the middle of the eleventh century was the turning point in the Hautevilles' succession process, it was also around that time when we notice a change from horizontal inheritance among siblings to vertical inheritance between themselves and their children. Therefore, when Drogo died in 1051 he was succeeded, following a brief interregnum, by his younger brother Humphrey rather than by his only known son Richard, who was probably born shortly before his death.[32] But it would be Humphrey who would attempt to establish vertical succession within the Hauteville kin-group, thus pushing aside his two younger brothers from Muriella, Geoffrey and Serlo. This radical reconception of Hauteville dominance in the region would backfire for Humphrey when, shortly before his death in 1057, he put forward his infant son Abelard (d. 1082) as a future count, under the guardianship of Robert. The outcome was what we would have expected from such an opportunistic warrior-leader like Guiscard: he promptly claimed the countship for himself.

It was unfortunate for the first three Hauteville brothers that they did not live long enough to see their children come of age. However, Guiscard's enduring rule in southern Italy lasted for another quarter of a century, giving Robert the chance to provide for his sons and therefore to inaugurate a new period of vertical inheritance in Apulian politics. Yet Guiscard took further steps to consolidate his authority in the region immediately after he claimed power in Apulia: Alberada of Buonalbergo was put aside on the grounds (or, rather, the pretext) of consanguinity, probably in early 1058. She would end up marrying Richard, son of Drogo Hauteville and Robert's nephew, with whom she later had a son named Robert. What is important to emphasise, however, is that this move did not mean the exclusion of the Buonalbergo kin from Guiscard's faction, as the latter's charters confirm, while the duke's first-born, Bohemond, would remain very much present in his father's plans until the end.[33]

After divorcing Alberada, Guiscard married Sigkelgaita (1040–90), the daughter of Guaimar IV of Salerno and younger sister of Gaitelgrima, the wife of both Hauteville brothers Drogo and Humphrey. Sigkelgaita had been a member of one of the most powerful and influential Lombard kin groups, and her brother Gisulf II had succeeded his father Guaimar as prince of Salerno (1052–77). It is needless to point out Guiscard's conspicuous diplomatic strategy in marrying into this powerful Lombard kin.[34] As Petrizzo has argued, Sigkelgaita represented for Robert a direct link to her father's rule, as she repeatedly appeared as someone whom Guiscard had systematically associated with his reign, therefore lending him some sort of legitimacy in southern Italy.[35] And this need to secure Lombard support was also reflected, of course, in prioritising Sigkelgaita's offspring over Bohemond.

Nevertheless, as I mentioned earlier, while regional politics may have dictated the putting aside of Bohemond from the inheritance line, he was never ostracised from his father's court as a potential threat or banished under the stigma of being a bastard.[36] In fact, there is ample proof that Bohemond was very much trusted by his father, who recognised his military prowess and the loyalty of the army and the nobles to his face. On the other hand, Guiscard's son from Sigkelgaita, named Roger, had on his side the legitimacy of his mother's kin, which brought with it the crucial alliance with the Lombard aristocracy of the region. One can easily sense why rebellion was to be expected in that political climate although, surprisingly, it did not come from Bohemond. When Guiscard was taken seriously ill in early 1073, Sigkelgaita, fearing her husband's death, held a baronial assembly in Bari to proclaim her thirteen-year-old son Roger as Guiscard's heir. Robert's nephew, Abelard of Hauteville, was the only baron to actively oppose the election, as he regarded himself to be the lawful heir.[37]

Unfortunately, the primary sources provide scarce information about Bohemond's early career in Italian politics prior to his participation in his father's ambitious invasion of the Balkans between 1081 and 1084. A mention in the *Breve Chronicon Nortmannicum* of Guiscard's 'first-born' son being defeated by the aforementioned Abelard near Troia in northern

Apulia in 1079 has been discounted.[38] However, it is easy to imagine that by the time Bohemond was dispatched, along with an elite force ferried on fifteen ships, on a reconnaissance mission to capture Corfu and Avlona in early May 1081, he must have already 'earned his spurs'. This suggests that Guiscard had kept his eldest son close despite having put aside his mother.

Chapter 2

The Norman Invasion of the Balkans, 1081–83

He [Bohemond] was, in very truth, like the pungent smoke which precedes a fire, and a prelude of attack before the actual attack. These two, father and son, might rightly be termed 'the caterpillar and the locust'; for whatever escaped Robert [Guiscard], that his son Bohemond took to him and devoured.

[Anna Komnena, *Alexiad*, I. xiv]

The decade that followed the Norman conquest of Bari in 1071 can be seen as an era in which relations between the Normans in southern Italy and Byzantium disintegrated rapidly. Although it was their victory at the Battle of Civitate in 1053 over the allied army of Pope Leo IX (papacy, 1049–54) that opened the way to the Apulian Normans for major conquests in all directions, including Capua, Salerno, Capitanata, Apulia and Calabria, the siege of Bari was to prove the most ambitious and decisive military operation Robert Guiscard and his men had yet undertaken in the Italian Peninsula. The task of dislodging the Byzantines from Bari must have seemed a daunting task, not only because the city was the largest, wealthiest and most important port-city of the southern Adriatic, and the seat of the general of the Byzantine province of Longobardia (or what was left of it), but also because the major weakness of the Normans at this stage was their lack of experience in conducting siege and naval warfare.[1]

The siege of Bari went on for two-and-a-half years, between August 1068 and April 1071, a clear sign of Guiscard's decisiveness and (financial) ability to keep large numbers of troops in the field for long periods. Amatus of Montecassino mentions two attempts by the Byzantines to relieve the city with shipments of supplies and money, one in 1069 and another in early 1071, both of which proved inadequate to support the defenders for long.[2] During the siege, however, a Norman fleet was scattered by a Byzantine squadron off Brindisi, to the south of Bari, sometime in 1070. Yet it is striking that no armies reminiscent of the 1038–41 massive expedition against Sicily were dispatched by the imperial government and, despite Kekaumenos' famous writing in the late 1070s that the fleet constituted 'the glory of Romania', the Byzantine navy had, by now, all but disappeared from the Adriatic and the Ionian Seas.[3]

To better understand this, we need to appreciate the basic strategic considerations (or interrelated factors) that determined the empire's strategic thinking and planning: (1) the position of the empire in the wider geostrategic context of the Balkans, Asia Minor and the Middle East; (2) the economy and manpower of Byzantium in relation to warfare; and (3) the Byzantine cultural approach to warfare that prioritised the use of diplomacy, the paying of subsidies, and the employment of stratagems, craft, wiles, bribery and 'other means' to deceive the enemy and bring back the army with as few casualties as possible.[4] Bearing these in mind, therefore, we can understand the sad reality the emperors in Constantinople had to face with their finite resources available in each area at any given time, and the limited ability of the state to move adequate reinforcements from one place to another to deal with an external threat.

Hence, it should not come as a surprise to see that the same factors that raised Asia Minor to the top of the strategic priorities of the emperors also downgraded Italy to a secondary (or, better, tertiary) theatre of operations for the Byzantine governments (one exception is Constantine IV's reign in the seventh century). Because it was only when the East had been pacified that the Byzantines were able to concentrate their efforts in any other region, it is crucial for the reader to fully appreciate the timing of the Norman aggression in Italy and in Byzantine Illyria, which came at a period (1070s) of increasing geo-political and social tensions for the empire in both Anatolia and the Balkans.

The Geopolitical Background of the Norman Invasions: Central and Western Anatolia

The outcome of the Battle of Manzikert on that fateful day in August 1071 ushered in an element of chaos in the geo-political history of the Byzantine Empire in the 1070s. Although not the military disaster it was once thought to have been, the political consequences of Alp Arslan's victory and the capture of Romanus IV far outweighed the actual losses in the battlefield.[5] For modern historians, however, the real cause behind the disintegration of Byzantine power in Anatolia was the ambitions of the Norman renegade mercenary leader, Roussel de Bailleuil, who sought to profit from this instability and establish his own statelet in the northeastern Anatolian Plateau. The key milestones for the future of central

Anatolia were the two imperial campaigns to subdue him, in 1073 and 1074. These campaigns, combined with the multiple civil wars of 1077–81, would eventually transform Byzantine politics in the region into a game of aligning Turkish interests from which the Byzantines would emerge as the great losers.

The real challenge for the empire in the aftermath of Manzikert lay in the mad scramble for power in Constantinople, in which the army commanders deserted their posts in Asia Minor, leaving the countryside open to the Turkomans. With the Doukas family in the capital using the Varangian Guard to declare Romanus Diogenes deposed, the new regime – headed by the *kaisar* Ioannes and his sons Andronikos and Constantine – tonsured the Empress-regent Eudokia (*c.* 1021–96) and proclaimed her son Michael as sole emperor. The Doukas' next step was to dispatch an army under Constantine Doukas against Romanus Diogenes, when they learned that the latter had been released from Turkish captivity and was collecting taxes in northeastern Anatolia. Romanus' defeat in battle forced him to retreat to Cappadocia, and then to Cilicia, where he spent the winter of 1071/72 under the protection of the *dux* of Antioch. Yet another defeat in the following spring (1072) compelled the former emperor to appeal for help to the Seljuks, while the government of the Doukas had already acquired the services of the Frankish mercenary leader Crispin and his followers. In the end, the lack of reinforcements and hope forced Romanus to surrender. He was cruelly blinded on 29 June 1072.

What came to add to the socio-political unrest in Anatolia in the aftermath of Manzikert was Roussel de Bailleuil's attempt to create a realm for himself in Asia Minor. Frankish warriors from Italy first appear as individual mercenaries in the service of the Byzantine state as early as 1047, and they are to be found in every major operational theatre in the Balkans and in Anatolia throughout the 1050s and 1060s, fighting – probably on horseback – alongside regiments of the elite Varangian Guard.[6] Roussel de Bailleuil was, perhaps, the most (in)famous of the Franks to have been employed by Constantinople. He was Roger Hauteville's principal lieutenant in Sicily, who won the day for the Normans at the Battle of Cerami in June 1063.[7] The next mention of Roussel comes in 1071 during Romanus IV's fatal campaign that culminated at Manzikert, where Roussel's contingent numbered around five hundred men. Then, he followed the 'treacherous', 'greedy' and 'violent' nature that characterised all Frankish and Norman warriors according to Anna Komnena, as we saw before, and he rebelled against his paymasters.

Roussel's rebellion is described in detail by two contemporary historians, Attaleiates and Bryennius.[8] The Frank sought an opportunity to break with the government in Constantinople when he was ordered to take part in an imperial campaign to pacify Anatolia in 1073, which was led by Isaakios Komnenos (Alexios' elder brother); already by 1071 the Komnenoi had forged ties with the ruling Doukas family by marrying their eldest son Isaakios to Helene, the cousin of the Georgian-born wife of the Emperor Michael VII (r. 1071–78), Martha (whom the Greek sources call 'Maria of Alania'). This expeditionary force included some four hundred Frankish horsemen under Roussel who, under the pretext of protecting one of his men who had been mistreated by Byzantine officers, split with the main body of the imperial forces in Ikonion. Isaakios was, eventually, defeated and captured by the Turks close to Kaisarea, prompting many modern historians to speculate what would have happened if the Byzantine commander had had Roussel's elite heavy cavalry unit at his disposal. My impression is that Isaakios would have achieved little in terms of strategic and battlefield manoeuvrability, because the Turkish horse-archers would have easily kept out of reach of the Frankish lances, as the crusaders would learn to their horror a quarter of a century later.[9] What is certain, however, is that Isaakios' army was the last Christian army that would march across Asia Minor to Kaisarea – in the heart of the Anatolian Plateau – until the coming of the First Crusade.

What seems to have been far more disruptive for the Doukas regime was the severing of links between the capital and the towns and villages in Galatia and Lykaonia, in the western and northwestern Anatolian Plateau, where the mercenary leader was now collecting taxes and selling protection to the locals. An expedition was dispatched against Roussel in the spring of 1074 under the *kaisar* Ioannes, who had also brought with him Varangian and Frankish units. But they were defeated at the famous Battle of the Zombou Bridge over the Sangarios river, with the imperial Franks deserting to Roussel before the battle.

The Frankish captain then attempted something unimaginable: to take his troops – by now numbering some three thousand in all – and march to Constantinople, in the vain hope that the people of the city would open the gates to him. His illusions were soon dashed, and he simply delighted himself in burning Scutàrion (modern Üsküdar), on the opposite Asian coast, to demonstrate the regime's impotence. Sometime at the end of 1074 Roussel even tried to create his own 'puppet-emperor' by proclaiming the captive *kaisar* Ioannes as the legitimate ruler of the empire, in an attempt to provide political cover to his aggression; this tactic would be adopted by Robert Guiscard seven years later.

The growing power of Roussel's forces caused the Doukas regime to seek a strong counterweight, which at that time only the Turks could provide. Hence, the chief minister of the imperial government took the fateful decision to hire a Turkish marauder in Bithynia, one Artuk (usually identified with Abu Sa'id Taj ad-Dawla Tutush, the younger brother of the Seljuk Sultan Malik Shah I).[10] The Turks defeated Roussel's forces at the Battle of Sophon (1074/75) by applying their typical steppe tactics of feigned flight while picking off the Franks with their arrows from a safe distance,[11] an outcome that confirms my last point about Isaakios Komnenos' defeat by the Turks the previous year. Both Roussel and *kaisar* Ioannes were taken prisoner, although Roussel was swiftly ransomed by his wife sometime in early 1075. Henceforth, the Byzantines would hire Franks to fight Turks and Turks to fight Franks.

As Roussel resumed his operations in the Armeniakon theme, he carried on with his collection of taxes and the selling of protection to the locals. The Doukas regime now gave the task of capturing Roussel to Nicephorus Palaeologus, who in 1075 led a considerable force of Byzantine and Georgian troops, around six thousand strong, against the Franks, but his men deserted him after he failed to pay them on time. Then it was Alexios Komnenos' turn to appear on the political scene at the young age of 20. The Komnenian writers magnify Alexios' capture of Roussel, probably in 1076, but the actual events were less glamorous: Artuk had treacherously arrested Roussel and delivered him to Alexios at Amaseia, where the latter simply took him as a prisoner back to the capital.[12] Although it took about three years to suppress this uprising that had significantly undermined imperial authority in large swathes of the Anatolian Plateau, this period marks the definitive loss of central Asia Minor to the Turks.

The Turkish forays into Asia Minor were not perceived as a serious threat to the empire's hold in the region until the middle of the 1060s. In 1067 Attaleiates mentions a Turkish attack across the Euphrates onto the territory of Melitene, an attack that managed to put the defenders of the city to flight and even threaten Kaisarea, hence marking the beginning of the Turkish penetration of Cappadocia and of the central Anatolian highlands.[13] Surely, Romanus IV Diogenes' campaigns of the years 1068–71 should be viewed as an attempt to plug the gap in the empire's eastern frontiers and, if possible, reverse these developments.

The number of Seljuk and Turkoman bands arriving in the central Anatolian plateau increased dramatically after 1071–72, although there are no traces of permanent establishment in major towns; rather, they remained in rural areas where they formed profitable coalitions with members of the local aristocracy. Isaakios Komnenos' defeat and capture by the Turks close to Kaisarea in 1073, followed by Alexios' pursuit of his brother's captors in a northwesterly direction as far as Ankara, old capital of Galatia and the Boukellarion theme, and the ambush – soon after Isaakios' release – of the two Komnenoi brothers by a band of two hundred Turks outside Nicomedia (less than 100km east of Constantinople), clearly show that the invaders had opened the way to Bithynia and the Marmara Sea through the southwestern parts of the Anatolian plateau from Cappadocia to Lycaonia, Phrygia and the Upper Meander and Sangarios river valleys. Yet between 1073 and 1076 Roussel's Franks posed a more immediate threat to the Doukas regime, especially in view of Roussel's proclamation of *kaisar* Ioannes as 'emperor'.[14]

The critical phase for the permanent establishment of Turkoman bands in western Asia Minor roughly coincides with the years between the revolt of the *dux* of Anatolikon Nicephorus Botaneiates in June 1077 and the revolt of Alexios Komnenos in April 1081. Undoubtedly this is a period of massive Turkish involvement in Byzantine internal conflicts and power struggles, during which the Turks sought the opportunity to make money and gain privileges and land. Botaneiates' revolt against the Doukas regime brought to the political forefront the sons of Qutlumush, the Seljukid prince who had struggled unsuccessfully against his cousin Alp Arslan at the Battle of Damghan (1063) for the throne of the Great Seljuk Empire.[15]

Following Qutlumush's death in 1064, his eldest son Suleiman fled with his three brothers into the Taurus mountains in eastern Anatolia. Sadly, the sources provide little information about how they reached Bithynia around the middle of the 1070s. Nevertheless, from the outset of Botaneiates' revolt, it is clear that both Michael VII and Nicephorus were keen to employ the Turkish warriors roaming in northwestern Asia Minor, and Suleiman b. Qutlumush and his men played a crucial role in these negotiations. According to Attaleiates, it was God's providence that turned Suleiman to agree to an alliance with the rebel general, and it is likely that Botaneiates promised Suleiman a strategic town as a seat of his ever-extending power in the region: Nicaea.[16]

Suleiman's Turks were also involved in the seditious movement of the *dux* of Dyrrachium Nicephorus Bryennius (the Elder), an important commander in Diogenes' army at Manzikert, who – around the same time as Botaneiates – had risen against Michael VII, having the support of the Byzantine army's regiments in the Balkans. Bryennius continued his revolt even after Botaneiates was crowned Emperor in March 1078, and after failed negotiations the young Alexios Komnenos was dispatched against him. Interestingly, Alexios sought a significant force of two thousand horse-archers from 'the Turkish chieftains residing in Nicaea' (i.e. Suleiman and his brother Mansour) [17] to take part in an expedition that would culminate in the Battle of Kalavrye, by the Halmyros river in Thrace, where the rebel army was broken and Bryennius was captured.[18]

Two more revolts followed Kalavrye, but both of them were crushed by the up-and-coming *Domesticus of the Scholae* of the West, Alexios Komnenos. Another veteran of Manzikert, Nicephorus Basilakes, brought up the armies of Dyrrachium and Bulgaria and some Franks from Italy, to Thessaloniki, only to be defeated by a cunning trick by Alexios. Two years later, in the autumn of 1080, Nicephorus Melissinos, another general who had remained loyal to Michael VII and had been exiled by Botaneiates to the Aegean island of Kos, decided to raise an army of Turks from western Asia Minor and march to Constantinople. Melissinos was married to Alexios' elder sister Eudokia, hence the former's refusal to face him in a pitched battle when ordered to by Botaneiates. Between the autumn of 1080 and the spring of 1081 Melissinos seized control, with Turkish aid, of what remained of Byzantine Asia Minor and proclaimed himself emperor. However, following the successful seizure of the throne by his brother-in-law Alexios Komnenos on 1 April 1081, he submitted to him, accepting the title of *kaisar* and the office of the governor of the second largest city of the empire, Thessaloniki.

The Geopolitical Background of the Norman Invasions: the Balkans

After the crossing of the frozen Danube by tribal groups of Patzinaks in the winter of 1046/47, followed by more groups in the next winter, they were implanted by the imperial government in lands along the main road that ran from Niš to Sardica (modern Sofia). Yet the bitter struggles that ensued with the imperial government between 1048 and 1053 clearly show that the 'pacification' of these nomads was not a straightforward matter. A thirty-year peace treaty agreed in 1053 eventually recognised the settlement of these independent Patzinak groups between the Haemus mountains and the lower Danube.

Both parties to the treaty seem to have been content with the status quo, with the exception of a military intervention by Isaac I Komnenos (r. 1057–59) in the summer of 1059 against a Hungarian invasion of

Sardica that included Patzinaks from the Paristrion.[19] Nevertheless, in 1072, barely a year into the reign of Michael VII, a Patzinak rebellion flared up in the Paristrion. The main reason behind this upheaval, in such a crucial period for the empire following the disaster at Manzikert the year before, was the decision taken by the chief minister Nicephoritzes, to cease both the annual subsidies and the 'gifts' dispatched to the 'mixobarbaroi'[20] and the Patzinaks of the Paristrion on the basis of the agreed peace of 1053, apparently in an attempt to replenish the cash-strapped treasury.

The minister's reaction to this local uprising in the Paristrion was sharp: he dispatched his confidant, the *vestarches* Nestor – a native of the northern Balkans – to restore order. However, Nicephoritzes' handling of the situation in the capital, which would have involved plenty of back-stage slander, caused Nestor to abandon his orders and side with the rebels. Following the appearance of a new Patzinak leader, Tatrys or Tatous, who showed himself willing to challenge the loose Byzantine supremacy over the Paristrion, Nestor – apparently in coordination with the Patzinak chieftain – directed his forces against the capital, probably in the summer of 1074.[21] At the same time, allied Patzinak groups ravaged Macedonia and Thrace before returning to Paristrion, which for the first time is referred to in the Byzantine sources as 'the land of the Patzinaks'.[22] This rebellion marks a watershed in the sense that after 1074 the Patzinaks of the region were no longer ruled over by Byzantine *strategoi* (generals/governors), but by their own elected leaders.[23] This situation must have drawn some unsettling parallels in the capital with the Battle of Ongal (AD 680), which led to the establishment of the first Bulgarian state that stretched from the Dniester river to the Balkan mountains.

As Nestor and Tatous were taking full advantage of the political turmoil in Anatolia, a dispute over grazing fields north of the Danube between Patzinaks and Uzes reached boiling point in 1077/1078. Subsequent movement of Patzinak tribal groups to the south of the Danube created a sort of domino effect in the sense that this population pressure may have encouraged the Patzinak elites in Paristrion to launch a new round of pillaging in Thrace. To make matters worse (for the Doukas regime), these Patzinak groups actively participated in the multiple civil wars of 1077–81, offering their services to Nicephorus Bryennius in 1077/78 and to the Paulician insurgent Lecas in 1078/1079, while they were also contacted by Nicephorus Basilakes with the promise of imperial gold.[24] Certainly several Patzinak groups played a key role as 'hired guns' (or bows) in many revolts and attempted coups during this brief but turbulent period, and peace was only restored in Paristrion in the autumn of 1080.[25]

Around the same period as the Patzinak rebellion of 1072, turmoil was brewing in another corner of the Balkans. The name Duklja (Greek: *Diokleia* (Διοκλεία)) describes the entire region of the Adriatic littoral, between the theme of Dyrrachium in the south and the town of Kotor in the north (roughly corresponding to modern Montenegro), which had been inhabited by a predominantly Serb population since the first Slavic settlements in the region around AD 600. Duklja became independent from Byzantine suzerainty in 1042/43, under Stefan Vojislav (d. 1043), and his son Michael (r. 1046–81) made peace with the empire, thus earning himself the title *protospatharios*.[26]

Michael was very well aware that the greatest threat to Duklja was from Byzantium, and therefore he embarked upon a perilous military intervention in Macedonia; in 1072, when an important Slavic landholder in Skopje named George Vojteh revolted against Byzantium, Michael dispatched two armies to support the rebel and his followers, one under his son Constantine and another under a general named Petrilo. At the beginning things went well for the rebels in the autumn of 1072, when Constantine was crowned *tsar* of the Bulgars at Prizren and Petrilo conquered Ohrid in the heart of Macedonia. Successive Byzantine punitive expeditions, however, managed to inflict some disastrous defeats on the Dukljan armies, and even managed to capture Constantine late in 1072 or early in 1073; he remained in Byzantine captivity until 1078.

To counterbalance the power and influence of Byzantium in the region, Michael sought allies on the opposite side of the Adriatic Sea. In 1077 he turned to Pope Gregory VII (papacy, 1073–85), who had already crowned Zvonimir as king of Croatia two years earlier, in return for his oath of fealty. Rome's expanding influence in the western Balkans must have given the Byzantines plenty of reasons to be concerned, especially following Gregory VII's despatching of a crown to Michael of Duklja in 1077, whom he addressed thereafter as 'king of the Slavs'.[27] Furthermore, some sources suggest that Michael also aimed to raise the bishopric of Bar in southern Duklja, until then under the jurisdiction of the Orthodox archbishop of Dyrrachium, to an archbishopric directly under the Pope.[28] After his coronation Michael also quickly entered into diplomatic relations with another rising power in Italy – the Normans – by marrying his son and heir Constantine Bodin (ruled, 1081–1101) to the daughter of the Norman governor of Bari.[29]

The Prelude to the Invasion

Following the successful outcome of three major siege operations against Salerno (1076), Naples (1077) and Benevento (1078), Robert Guiscard's political and diplomatic breakthrough came with his reconciliation with Pope Gregory VII at the conference at Ceprano in June 1080.[30] The Norman duke had been excommunicated twice by Gregory, in Lent 1075 and again in February 1078, mainly because of Norman incursions into territory under papal overlordship, on which the new Pontiff took a much firmer stance than his appeasing predecessor, Alexander II (papacy, 1061–73). Yet politics in Italy depended upon a third party that, theoretically, regarded southern Italy as part of its *imperium* – the German emperors. As relations between Gregory VII and the German emperor Henry IV (r. 1056–1105) broke down after 1075, on account of Henry's involvement in the election of the archbishop of Milan (1075), the situation deteriorated even further when Henry declared Gregory deposed at Worms, with the Pope retaliating by excommunicating him in the spring of 1076.

The worse the diplomatic relations between Rome and Germany, the more susceptible Gregory became towards reconciling with Guiscard. Loud has emphasised that the relationship between the papacy and the Normans in this period was essentially a practical one, in which one side (the Pope) offered legitimacy and the other (the Normans) provided military muscle while otherwise paying very little attention to papal denunciations.[31] For Gregory, who lacked the services of a standing army, the risk of a possible alliance between Henry and Guiscard was one not worth taking. Following Gregory's second excommunication of Henry in March 1080, after which he also declared him definitely deposed, the Pontiff's alliance with the Normans became paramount. Peace with Gregory VII, after six years of almost continuous strife between them, left the Norman duke free to consider his most ambitious plan to date: his campaign against the Byzantine Empire.

Since Robert's time historians have ascribed the attack on Byzantium in 1081 to the Norman duke's mounting ambition for the imperial crown. In the words of Anna Komnena: 'But this Robert was for ever aspiring at further increase of power, and because he had visions of the Roman Empire, he alleged as pretext his connection with the Emperor Michael, as I have said, and fanned up the war against the Romans.'[32] Considering the immense influence of Byzantine culture, language, state organisation and economic prosperity on the everyday lives of the peoples of Italy

(Lombards, Greeks, Arabs or Normans) in the eleventh century, we can understand why Guiscard would have hatched plans to transfer an army across the Adriatic, especially in such a critical period for Byzantine history, as we saw before.

Then Anna adds to Robert's motives that: 'the Emperor Michael [VII Doukas] for some inexplicable reason betrothed this despot's daughter (Helen by name) to his son, Constantine'. Attempts to establish marriage alliances between the emperors in Constantinople and Robert Guiscard go back to the reign of Romanus IV Diogenes, when the latter had sought to agree on a treaty of alliance – sealed with a royal marriage – sometime in 1071; no doubt, Romanus would have looked for the provision of elite Norman mercenaries to defend against the Turkoman invaders of Anatolia, similar to Alexios Komnenos' letter to Robert of Flanders requesting military assistance in 1091, while trying to minimise Norman aggression on both sides of the Adriatic.[33] Talks with Guiscard reopened under the Doukas regime, and a treaty was ratified in August 1074 by a marriage alliance between Michael's son Constantine and Guiscard's daughter Helen. In 1078, however, following Nicephorus Botaniates' usurpation of the throne, Guiscard's daughter was swiftly dispatched to a convent.

Even though Robert would not have needed to look very hard for a pretext to invade the Byzantine Empire, while preparations were in full swing during the summer of 1080 the deposed emperor Michael VII made his appearance at the Norman court. Although the man pretending to be Michael was, certainly, an impostor and this whole episode was an elaborate hoax, it provided Guiscard with a convenient pretext to justify his campaign as a 'restoration mission', for which he also acquired the backing of Rome.[34] Yet if we set this pretext aside, modern historians have suggested three deeper reasons for the Norman invasion of Byzantium in 1081:[35] (a) Guiscard would have wished to punish the empire for harbouring and providing aid to Norman aristocrats in Apulia who opposed Robert's rule; (b) as the Norman expansion in Italy was stagnating, Robert's power, which rested on his ability to hand out booty and land to his vassal lords, would have been threatened, hence the opening of another theatre of war in the Balkans presented a lucrative option, in an operation that evokes parallels to the Norman invasion of England in 1066. Finally, (c) if we look beyond the exaggerated statement of a twelfth-century historiographer that Guiscard had planned 'to make Bohemond emperor of the Byzantine Empire, and himself ruler of a great Mohammedan empire',[36] the establishment of a Norman principality for Bohemond on the opposite side of the Adriatic would, certainly, have looked like an enticing plan in the 1070s, especially if we consider the latter's career in the Levant in the aftermath of the First Crusade.

The Invasion: Phase One (1081–82)

> Not being satisfied with the soldiers who had followed his fortune from the beginning, and were experienced in war, he [Guiscard] recruited and equipped a new army, without any distinction of age. But he collected all, under age and over age, from all over Lombardy and Apulia, and pressed them into his service.[37]

After designating his son Roger Borsa as heir to his dukedom, Robert Guiscard ordered his fleet to sail from the port-city of Otranto sometime in late May 1081. But as the sources vary widely in their estimates of the size of Guiscard's army, twentieth-century historians have come to read pre-modern estimates of numbers of armies with a pinch of salt. The reason is that the estimates of those ancient or – in our case – medieval chroniclers who reported on major geo-political events like campaigns or battles would have been affected by five factors:[38] (a) their inherent tendency to exaggerate; (b) their reliance on oral testimonies, which always bears the risk of inflation and/or miscalculation; (c) the time when the chronicler is writing their work; (d) their experience in military matters (a dismounted knight may be counted as infantry by an inexperienced chronicler); and, finally, (e) their biases and sympathies.

Anna Komnena reports that the Norman expeditionary force was made up of some thirty thousand men, with 150 ships of all types to ferry them to the opposite Illyrian coast, with – more or less – two hundred men and horses onboard each of the ships. Anna's estimate of the Norman army seems, in my view, to be an exaggeration based on hindsight (Anna wrote the *Alexiad* in the mid-1140s) to glorify her father's ultimate success over the Normans against all odds. Malaterra's figure of '1,300 knights' is surely closer to the truth, and it probably describes the elite core of the Norman expeditionary force – the knights, contrary to the rest of the Norman army that formed, according to Geoffrey, a 'poorly armed mob'. Other sources, such as Orderic Vitalis, put the figure at no more than ten thousand men, Peter the Deacon notes fifteen thousand men, and Romuald of Salerno talks about seven hundred horsemen – a much more plausible figure.[39]

Before embarking on his journey across the Adriatic, however, the sources say that Guiscard dispatched his second-in-command, Bohemond, along with a small force ferried on fifteen ships, which would have carried perhaps between 2,000 and 2,500 men and horses, in an advance mission to capture Corfu and Avlona.[40] That operation would have been launched several weeks in advance of the main invasion force, perhaps as early as the beginning of the sailing season in March. Yet Bohemond did not carry out all his objectives because, according to Malaterra, he decided to bypass Corfu and await his father's larger army before attempting to seize the island. Corfu's fortifications must have been considerable, and the castles [*castra*] well-fortified and maintained; hence Bohemond would have appreciated that his advance party was completely ill-equipped for such an undertaking. Then, in her typical anti-Norman style of writing, Anna describes Bohemond's landing and march along the opposite Illyrian coast: '[he] fell like a thunderbolt, with threats and irresistible dash upon Canina, Hiericho (Oricum), and Valona, and seized them, and as he fought his way on, he would ever devastate and set fire to the surrounding districts'.

The strategic significance of the aforementioned targets cannot be overstated: Avlona (with its protected gulf that offers an excellent point of disembarkation), Canina and Oricum were the three most important fortresses of the southern coastal approaches to the port-city of Dyrrhachium, and therefore of great strategic value for Norman operation in the Balkans. Furthermore, Ahrweiler has pointed to the strategic importance of Corfu for the defences of the empire's western naval approaches in the eleventh century, highlighting the existence of a substantial naval base on the island, which, along with bases in Dyrrachium, Kephalonia and Naupactus further south, controlled the western maritime frontiers of the empire in the second half of the eleventh century.[41] Yet these bases had been left all but deserted around the third quarter of the eleventh century, following the dramatic decline of the Byzantine navy in that period, although Corfu remained the capital of the administrative office of the *duke-katépanô* and it retained its strategic importance throughout the Komnenian period (1081–1180).

After sailing from Otranto in late May, the main Norman army under Robert Guiscard targeted the island of Corfu and its capital Koryfo, 'a city strongly furnished with both natural and man-made defences'. Malaterra reports that the army landed and immediately undertook the siege of the key fortress-town of Cassopolis-Cassiope, a *castrum* in the northeast of the island that dominated the straights between Corfu and the opposite Illyrian coast, before marching south to attack the Corfiot capital. But sadly, none of the sources provides any details about the course of the

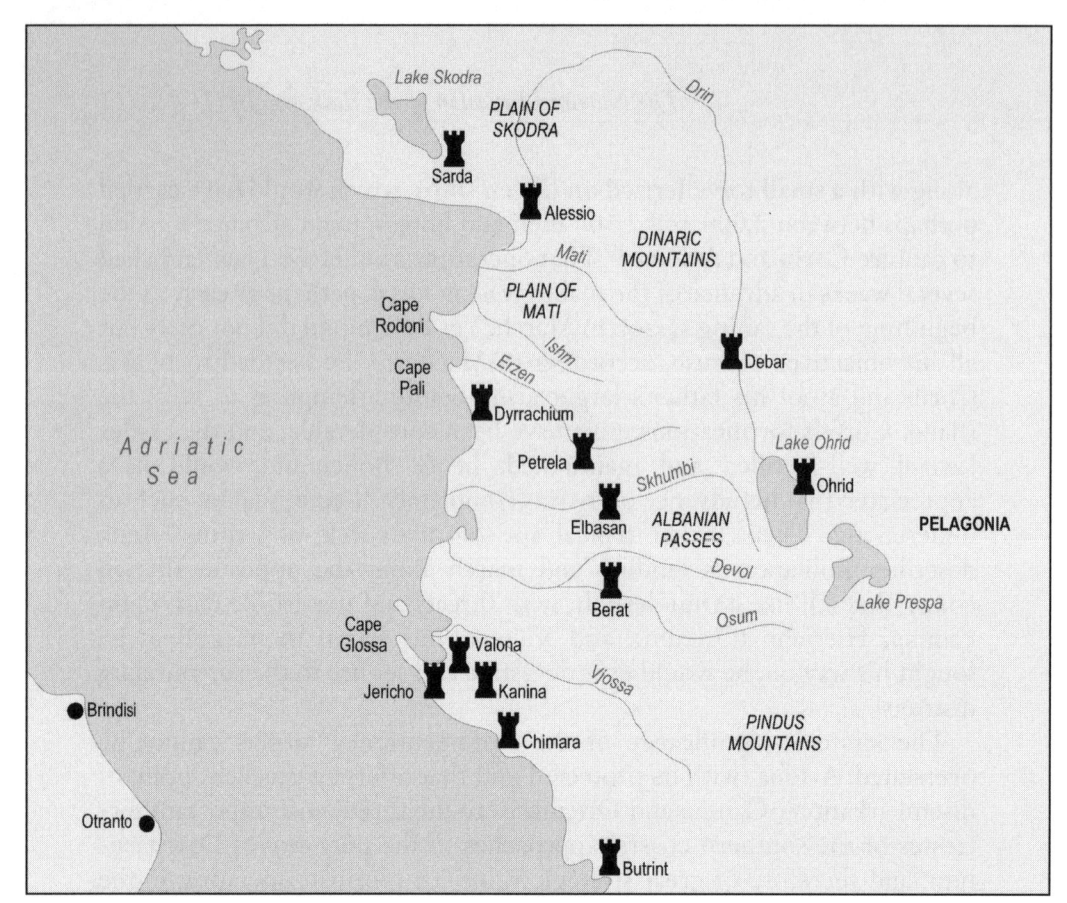

The area around Dyrrachium.

siege of either Cassiope or Koryfo.[42] The only thing we know is that the defenders of the island's capital soon capitulated and paid tribute to the Norman duke, who later resumed his operations, ferrying his army across the straits of Corfu to Avlona.

After disembarking at Avlona sometime in early June, Guiscard headed to Butrint (ancient Buthrotum), some 3km from the straits of Corfu, where he joined forces with the advance party led by Bohemond. A decision was made to march north against Dyrrachium, with Robert assuming command of the fleet and Bohemond taking the land route with the elite part of the army. The conquest of this major port-city on the southern Adriatic was paramount if the Normans wanted to secure a foothold in the southern Balkans: Dyrrachium was the starting point of the ancient *Via Egnatia*, one of the two most strategically important military roads in the Balkans that linked Constantinople with Europe and Italy through Thessaloniki and Adrianople (modern Edirne).[43] Yet this operation got off to an ominous start as the Norman fleet encountered a major storm that sank a large number of ships at Cape Glossa, in today's region of

Cheimara at the tip of the Avlona gulf. The sources are silent about the exact number of casualties and the number of vessels taken out of action, but the fact that Guiscard decided to remain at Glabinitza, to the south of Cape Glossa, for a week to allow his troops to recuperate shows how badly his fleet was battered by the elements.[44]

Meanwhile, the newly crowned emperor was kept up-to-date regarding the whereabouts of the Norman invaders, and his response was swift and ingenious; first, he raised the bishopric of Corfu and Paxoi to the status of a metropolis, in an apparent attempt to boost the morale of the local population. Then he replaced the governor of Dyrrachium with his faithful friend and brother-in-law George Palaeologus, a wise move considering that the previous governor, a man named Monomachatus, is repeatedly accused by Anna Komnena of secret and treacherous dealings with Guiscard, accusations that are confirmed by William of Apulia.[45] Additionally, Alexios was intent on creating trouble on Guiscard's rear in Apulia, first by releasing Guiscard's rebellious nephew Abelard, one of the ringleaders of many rebellions against the duke's rule in Apulia, from his 'comfortable' exile in Constantinople; he also attempted a political rapprochement with the German emperor Henry IV, whose relations with Rome had broken down following his excommunication by Gregory VII in March of that year. In fact, it is clear from the letter dispatched by Alexios to Henry, quoted in Book III of the *Alexiad*, that Abelard was, by that point, acting as an agent of German and Byzantine interests in Apulia.[46]

Furthermore, two landmark political decisions taken by Alexios in these early months of his reign were to have long-lasting implications for the empire's foreign policy concerning two powerful players in the region, the Venetians and the Seljuks. In order to disrupt Guiscard's communications with Apulia, Alexios needed a war fleet of his own. Yet by the third quarter of the eleventh century it was obvious that the Byzantine naval units available were not up to the task. Hence, we have Alexios' immediate decision to call for his vassal and old ally, the maritime republic of Venice. The *Doge* Domenico Silvio (ruled, 1070–84) did not hesitate to send a large squadron to the rescue of Dyrrachium in exchange for, as Anna Komnena tells us: 'some rewards that were pledged, others granted at once. All their desire would be satisfied and confirmed by *chrysobulls*, provided they were not in conflict with the interests of the Roman Empire.'[47] Nevertheless, extensive trading privileges would not have been enough for the Venetians to risk dispatching a war-fleet so far away from their metropolis.

Although the relationship between the *Serenissima* and Byzantium may have been affected by centuries of close political relationship from as far back as Justinian's expeditions against the Ostrogoths in the second half of the sixth century, it was based more firmly on realism! Trade was the most significant factor that brought these two parties together, and for a good reason: Constantinople and the Byzantine ports of the eastern Mediterranean were the treasure houses of Venetian trade, and the Venetians quickly adapted to the larger role of middlemen between East and West. On top of that, a small but influential percentage of Dyrrachium's population derived from Amalfi and Venice, traders who had settled many decades ago at the starting point of the ancient Via Egnatia that led to Constantinople.[48] The deeper motive, therefore, that prompted both parties' common interest to keep the Adriatic Sea clear of rival naval activity was geography and trade routes![49] Voyages to and from Venice, both up and down the Adriatic, were invariably made along the Balkan coast, and the sea-routes south of the Strait of Otranto lay inshore of Corfu, Kephalonia and Zante, all of which had their main medieval harbours on their east coasts; to secure these sea-routes that formed the lifeline of its trade with the empire, Venice had to prevent any enemy naval activity that threatened to disrupt the flow of goods to and from its ports. By the summer of 1081 the Normans posed just such a threat to the *Serenissima*.

When Alexios usurped the throne in April 1081, the Byzantine Empire was gravely threatened by the incursions of her aggressive Turkish neighbours. It is impossible to draw any concrete conclusions about the political role of Suleiman b. Qutlumush and his Turks or, indeed, of any other Turkmen warrior groups in western Asia Minor during the years 1078–81, but we can say that the military situation in western Asia Minor around 1080 had become increasingly precarious for the empire. And although the Turks were still unable to take fortified towns by themselves, by the time Alexios took the throne the key city of Nicaea was under firm Turkish control.[50] Therefore, very soon the new emperor was forced to take firm action against Turkish incursions into imperial territory in Bithynia. Anna reports ambushes and night-time raids by small detachments on small boats (the term used is ἀκατίοις) attacking enemies who were lingering near the shores, in an apparent attempt to force the Turkish bands to withdraw further inland; the Byzantines' inability to launch any major offensive to dislodge these groups from Bithynia is also palpable.[51]

Alexios was quick to appreciate the long-term danger posed by the expansionist lordship of Suleiman b. Qutlumush in and around Nicaea.

Therefore, it became his top priority to secure his flanks before embarking on a campaign to tackle the more pressing danger of the Norman invasion in the western Balkans. It was the raids against the Turks, datable to April/May 1081, that prepared the ground for the conclusion of a peace treaty, including the formal recognition of a borderline along the Drakon river, in exchange for Suleiman's promise to cease his attacks and to provide military assistance when asked. Alexios may have been treading a fine line in relying on a Turk to ensure the stability of a region so close to the capital while he was planning a campaign far away in Dyrrachium. Yet in the summer of 1081 Alexios turned to a man with whom he had dealt before, and whom he trusted more than any Byzantine official in the capital.[52] Suleiman's help would eventually prove decisive in the summer of 1081, and again in the winter of 1082/83.

Led by Robert and Bohemond, the Norman army turned out in the vicinity of the city of Dyrrachium on 17 June 1081, setting up their camp in the 'ruins of the city formerly called Epidamnus', probably the ruins of the city of Dyrrachium, devastated by the catastrophic earthquake of the second half of the fifth century.[53] The task of imposing an effective blockade of the city would have seemed daunting because of the topography of the site where medieval Dyrrachium was built. The city dominated the tip of a long and narrow peninsula which ran parallel to the coast but with a marshy and swampy lagoon separating it from the mainland. There were also two fortified outposts situated on the opposite mainland area, both of them centred around two churches, one dedicated to St Nicholas and the other to the Archangel Michael.[54] And although little is known about the eleventh-century fortifications of the city, mainly because of later use during the late Byzantine and Ottoman periods, Anna points out the formidable defences of medieval Dyrrachium:

> The walls were flanked by towers standing up above it all around and rising as high as eleven feet, which were ascended by a spiral stair and strengthened by battlements. Such was the appearance and the defence of the city. The thickness of the walls was remarkable, in fact so great was its width that more than four horsemen could ride abreast on it quite safely.[55]

The mountain passes to the east of Dyrrachium were dominated by smaller *castra*, which are identified in the *Alexiad* as those of Diabolis and Mylos; the former, probably associated with the Devol valley, lay near Lake Ohrid. Because Dyrrachium was approachable only from the north and the northeast, the Normans could deploy their siege-engines and the bulk of their forces only on these two sides, thus being unable to completely surround the city. Their *helepoleis* (multi-storey wooden siege towers fitted with stone-throwing catapults and drawbridges that were protected from fire by layers of hides) failed to have any impact on the city's fortifications, nor did they sap the morale of the defenders, who made repeated sorties to burn down these machines. And while the siege dragged on without any significant breakthrough, an unknown number of Venetian warships arrived in the waters off the Gulf of Dyrrachium sometime in July or August.[56]

The inevitable clash between the two fleets is reported by historians from both sides, although they provide contradictory accounts of the events. Anna Komnena[57] describes the arrival of the Venetian fleet at the promontory of Pallia, the northern extremity of the Dyrrachium peninsula, but then she notes that once the Venetians 'had viewed Robert's fleet fitted out with every species of military instruments, they lost heart for the war'. Whether it was genuine fear that prevented the Venetians from attacking the Norman fleet moored off Dyrrachium, or whether it was simply a clever ruse to refuse battle in anticipation of the clash that was to follow the next day, we will never know. Guiscard's initial reaction to the appearance of the Venetians was to dispatch Bohemond to force them to acclaim himself and the man posing as Emperor Michael, which the Venetians, unsurprisingly, promised they would do the following day. Instead, during the night they feverishly prepared their ships for battle and the following morning the Normans woke up to find that their enemies had formed a 'sea-harbour' (πελαγολιμένα) – a defensive formation where the biggest and strongest vessels were tied tightly together in the form of a closing crescent, sheltering the smaller and more vulnerable vessels inside their formation.

The battle that followed the Venetian rebuff of Bohemond's mission – Anna, probably wishing to taunt the Norman, writes that they poked fun at his ginger beard – was ferocious and at one point even Bohemond found himself in great danger when the ship he had embarked on was sunk. The Venetians eventually routed the Norman fleet, which landed inshore and suffered a second major defeat by a sortie party led by Palaeologus. The triumph was celebrated in the capital with great pomp as the Venetian ambassadors were received by Alexios 'with great honour', and 'as was natural, [he] bestowed many benefactions upon them, and then dismissed them with a large gift of money for the Doge of Venice and his subordinate magistrates'.

Geoffrey Malaterra,[58] on the other hand, produced an account of the day's events that portrays the Venetians as a cunning enemy. After attacking the Norman fleet immediately after their arrival in Illyrian waters, there followed a ferocious naval battle that lasted until sunset, and 'with their strength exhausted, the Venetians promised to give in and asked for a truce until dawn, when they would make a treaty with the duke on his terms'. But while the exhausted Normans recuperated in their ships during the night, the Venetians erected wooden towers in the ships' main masts and made their vessels lighter and more manoeuvrable. By sunrise, the Normans had a nasty surprise when they realised the reorganised Venetian squadron was ready to attack them; soon the Norman fleet was scattered and the naval blockade of Dyrrachium was lifted, while a land sortie by a detachment from the city attacked the Norman land forces, making effective use of Greek Fire.

The disaster in the waters off Dyrrachium must have dealt a severe blow to Guiscard's fleet and, no doubt, to his prestige as a commander of an invasion force. To that end, Norman communications and supply routes with the Italian mainland would have been severed, while William of Apulia reports that 'the islands [Corfu and Paxoi?] which had previously paid tribute to Robert rose in fierce revolt when they heard of the damage which his ships had suffered, and acclaimed the emperor'.[59] Despite Robert Guiscard's determination to press on with the siege of the city, the menacing presence of the allied Byzantino-Venetian fleet, combined with effective sorties by Palaeologus' men, the lack of provisions and the inevitable spread of disease made the situation desperate in the Norman camp.

Alexios left the capital around mid-August, heading to Dyrrachium, where the Normans had resumed the siege. His first order to muster reinforcements was dispatched to his trusted military commander and recently appointed *Grand Domesticus of the West*, Armenian-born Gregory Pakourianos, who set out from Adrianople to link up with the emperor. Next we find Alexios in Thessaloniki sometime in early September 1081; advancing via the Egnatia, he arrived in the vicinity of Dyrrachium on 15 October, pitching his camp on the banks of the river Charzanes (modern Erzen river, 12km east of the city).[60]

Before his arrival at Dyrrachium, the emperor had dispatched a reconnaissance party of two thousand Turkopole (lit. 'sons of Turks', i.e. Christianised descendants of the Seljuks) mercenaries, an elite body of lightly armed mounted archers, to reconnoitre Robert Guiscard's camp. This incident is described only by William of Apulia but it is of great importance for the history of transcultural warfare in the Balkans because it marks the first recorded case when large bodies of Norman (i.e. from the 'military culture' of western Europe) and Turkish (i.e. from the 'military culture' of the Central Asian Steppes) warriors clashed. William's description of the reaction of both troops to this encounter is fascinating:

> Although a large number [of Normans] had already been wounded by arrows from the Turks whom Basil commanded, all resolved rather to die in battle than to retreat in cowardly fashion from the Greeks. Drawing up their ranks as best they could, they turned towards their enemies. The Turks were terrified by the sight of their enemies turning on them, resisting fiercely and striking hard. They fled, and Basil was unable to prevent this. He himself was captured as he fled.[61]

There are two elements to take from William's short description: first, the stereotypical description of the bravery, boldness and manliness of the Norman warriors, who preferred to die than to surrender to the 'effeminate' and 'cowardly' Greeks or, in this case, their Turkish mercenaries. Then there is the tactical reaction of the Normans encountering the typical steppe tactics of mounted archers. As was the case with most steppe armies, Turkish armies applied tactics intended to exploit their mobility and their abilities with the bow, usually by staying out of reach of their opponents' weapons. They applied 'hit-and-run' tactics in waves, and showered the enemy with arrows by employing the famous 'Parthian shot'. At Dyrrachium William implies that the Normans sustained high numbers of casualties until they eventually resorted to grouping together into a tight tactical body of troops to bring the fight to their enemies, i.e. denying them their two main tactical advantages: their mobility and their use of the bow. The tactical reaction of the Normans had the desired effect on their enemies who, 'terrified by the sight', beat a hasty retreat.

Anna Komnena's invaluable description of Alexios' war-council on the eve of the Battle of Dyrrachium provides us with a glimpse of the conflicting views about the best way to defend the city against the besieging Norman army.[62] The most sensible view was put on the table by the more experienced officers, led by Palaeologus, who had been hastily summoned from the besieged city; they backed the idea of a blockade of the Norman camp that would eventually lead the invading army to seek terms owing to hunger and disease. In fact, this summarises everything that the authors of the Byzantine military manuals of the tenth century recommended about getting to know one's enemy and the terrain, and avoiding battle unless all opportunities were on one's side.[63] Yet Alexios seems to have been drawn to the calls by the younger, 'hot-headed' officers, led by Constantine Porphyrogennitus, the son of the former emperor Constantine X Doukas (r. 1059–67), and brother of Michael VII (r. 1071–78), who urged the emperor to take the field against the invaders, probably raising issues of pride and honour against the 'barbarian' duke, although nothing of the sort is mentioned by Anna.

We read in the *Alexiad* that the emperor's intention was to surprise the Normans by launching a night attack against their camp from two directions: the east and the north. But during the night of 17/18 October Guiscard was probably alerted to the Byzantine plans and he quickly resorted to crossing the marshy lagoon and deploying his army on the opposite mainland, close to the chapel of St Theodore. He therefore managed to outwit the emperor by moving closer to the Byzantine camp, thus evading a surprise Byzantine two-pronged attack, possibly coupled with a sortie by the city's defenders. But the stage was now firmly set for a pitched battle.

Having deployed his army between Alexios' camp and the Dyrrachian lagoon, with the sea to the right, the Norman duke arranged his troops into three divisions: retaining command of the centre, he entrusted the left wing to his son Bohemond, and the right wing – the one closer to the sea – to 'Amiketas' (probably Amicus II of Molfetta and Giovenazzo). The sources are silent about the composition of each of these divisions, but I believe that Robert would have held his elite heavy cavalry with him in the centre, probably behind a screen of heavy infantry for better protection against enemy missiles, as Duke William of Normandy had done at Hastings fifteen years before. The rest of the infantry levies, including any archers (if, indeed, there were any), and the lighter and less experienced cavalry would probably have been placed on the wings of the Norman formation.

The response of the emperor to seeing the Normans in battle array on the morning of 18 October was to arrange his battle-lines accordingly and prepare for the inevitable clash that was about to follow. Alexios maintained command of the centre of the Byzantine army facing Guiscard's division, while his trusted Pakourianos was put at the head of the left wing, closer to the sea, and *kaisar* Nicephorus Melissinos was in charge of the right wing. We know from Anna[64] that the emperor marched against the Normans with an army that was jumbled together from different parts of the empire, including 300 men from Choma, a contingent of the Varangian Guard estimated to be around 1,500–2,000 strong, the tagma of the *Excubitae*, his personal household of the *Vestiaritae*, a unit of Frankish mercenaries, a corps of 2,000 Turkopoles, some 2,800 heretic Manichaeans, and units from Macedonia, Thrace and Thessaly. Alexios also called for his imperial ally, the Dukljan župan Constantine-Bodin, son of Michael who had died sometime in 1081. Sadly, though, we know next to nothing about the composition of the three main divisions of the imperial army at Dyrrachium.

The first stage of the battle was opened by the Norman duke, whose first move was to order a unit of his elite cavalry, probably from his own division, to march against the Byzantines and apply their feigned retreat tactics. Alexios was diligent enough to have the Varangian Guard deployed in front of the rest of the infantry in the centre, probably projected at some distance but by no means isolated from the rest of the army, as their operational role was to receive the enemy attack which was to come from the heavy cavalry; the emperor would, no doubt, have been aware of the English hatred for the Normans over the conquest of their homeland. As the Norman mounted units were attempting to create confusion in the Byzantine centre, Alexios ordered his archers and peltasts to advance and repel the enemy charge. Meanwhile, Guiscard and his elite knights were swiftly covering the distance between the two armies before an anticipated charge against the Byzantine centre. The wings of the Norman army were also advancing, so as not to leave the wings of the centre exposed to enemy attacks; Amiketas' mounted and infantry units attacked the exposed left flank of the Varangian Guard exactly at the point where it met with Pakourianos' division on the left (by the sea). This attack against the Varangians soon escalated/developed into a clash that further involved units from the Byzantine centre and left, who rushed to support their beleaguered comrades who were putting up a stiff resistance. As a result, Amiketas' attack broke up into a disorderly retreat, with the Norman mounted and infantry troops 'throwing themselves into the sea up to their necks and when they were near the Roman and Venetian ships begged for their lives – but nobody rescued them'.

At this point Anna intersects an incident with Guiscard's wife Sigkelgaita who, appalled by the cowardice of her husband's soldiery, made an attempt to prevent the retreat from escalating into a full-blown rout of the Norman army:

> And now, as rumour relates, directly Gaita, Robert's wife (who was riding at his side and was a second Pallas, if not an Athene) saw these soldiers running away, she looked after them fiercely and in a very powerful voice called out to them in her own language an equivalent

to Homer's words, 'How far will ye flee? Stand, and fight like men!' And when she saw they continued to run, she grasped a long spear and at full gallop rushed after the fugitives; and on seeing this they recovered themselves and returned to the fight.[65]

Anna's fascinating portrait of Sigkelgaita builds an image of a 'valkyrie-like' woman who defied the stereotypic gendered roles some twenty years before the crusades made warlike women a more visible phenomenon in a military expedition. Patricia Skinner notes that Anna depicted the Lombard Sigkelgaita as both wife and warrior, and at the same time plays with gender to create an army of 'effeminate' Normans who need a woman as a 'masculine role-model' to make them fight. In fact, Anna overturns an insult more commonly used by western authors against the Byzantines by using Sigkelgaita – a non-Norman – as the means with which to make her point in reversing the common perception of the Normans as invincible warriors.[66]

In the meantime, Guiscard's and Bohemond's divisions were advancing against the imperial army at a steady pace and they were by now involved in skirmishing with Alexios' and Melissinos' troops respectively, although the sources do not mention any tactical breakthrough at this stage. The incident that tipped the scale in favour of the Normans was the apparent disobedience (Yewdale's 'rashness') of the Varangians who, by breaking ranks and charging in pursuit of the retreating Normans of Amiketas' right wing, became separated from the main body of the imperial army and, as a result of Guiscard's swift decision to order an attack (probably by spearmen) on their right wing, they were eventually cut to pieces; the few survivors sought refuge in the nearby church of the Archangel Michael, where they were all burned to death by the Normans, who set the church alight. Although it has recently been suggested that the Varangian 'rashness' may have come as a result of an 'all-out attack' order that the rest of the army simply failed to follow,[67] this case proves beyond doubt that even a heavily armed, well-trained and disciplined unit fighting on foot could not withstand/repel a sustained heavy cavalry attack unless it is itself supported by units of archers and cavalry. Once losing the cover of their supporting units, thus leaving their flanks exposed to enemy attacks, their encirclement and eventual annihilation becomes inevitable, as with the Saxon attacks downhill at Hastings in 1066, or the encirclement of the seven hundred Swabian heavy infantry at Civitate in 1053.

The Battle of Dyrrachium reached its climax after the annihilation of the men of the Varangian Guard. With the loss of such an elite unit of heavily armed infantry, whose tactical role was to work as a 'buffer' against the Norman cavalry, Alexios found himself in a position where his division in the centre became exposed to enemy cavalry attacks from the front and left flank. Guiscard was quick to appreciate the great opportunity he was landed with, and he immediately threw his elite knights into the ongoing mêlée. The impact of the cavalry attack on the morale and discipline of the Byzantine army was decisive. Some units did stand and fight courageously, but many of their comrades abandoned the fight and ran away, with the entire front soon disintegrating rapidly.

The outcome of the Battle of Dyrrachium was, beyond any doubt, a strategic disaster for the Byzantine emperor and, according to some modern historians, it has been dubbed 'a defeat far more severe than that at Manzikert'.[68] The reason behind this is that there was now a real danger that the Normans would press on to Thessaloniki and Constantinople, and Alexios, 'dusty and bloodstained, bareheaded, with his bright red hair straggling in front of his eyes',[69] seemed incapable of stopping them. He had lost as much as a quarter of his army, including the 2,000-strong contingent of the Varangian Guard, and his reputation as a general had taken a battering. Yet Alexios was undoubtedly a good tactician, who was badly let down by his troops during the pursuit of the beaten enemy right wing. This was a cardinal sin in the Byzantine tactical manuals of the tenth century, the authors of which put great emphasis on rigorous battle discipline ($\tau\acute{\alpha}\xi\iota\varsigma$) and strict regulation of the pursuit of a retreating foe.[70]

Chapter 3

The Norman Invasion of the Balkans, 1082–84

Alexios wept to have been defeated by an enemy inferior both in numbers and in wealth. He himself was wounded and retired. The man who had vainly hoped to celebrate a spectacular triumph was forced instead to make a tearful and inglorious return.

[William of Apulia, IV, p. 53]

Following his crushing defeat on the outskirts of Dyrrachium, Alexios Komnenos would probably have spent the winter season somewhere in the region of Ohrid (most likely at the castle on the northeast shore of Lake Ohrid), as severe winter conditions would have impeded his orderly retreat to Thessaloniki through the high mountains of Epirus or western Macedonia. Yet the emperor made the necessary arrangements for the city of Dyrrachium to resist the Norman siege for as long as possible. He entrusted the citadel to the empire's Venetian allies, thereby acknowledging their important role in the defence of the city. The defence of the lower city was assigned to a native Albanian who bore the title of *komeskortes* (Greek *Κομισκόρτης*; a corruption of '*komes tes kortes*'),[1] proving beyond doubt the reliance of the Byzantine authorities on local populations to provide support and manpower in cases of great military necessity. On top of that, the Latin sources confirm that the rest of the castles in the Dyrrachium region capitulated shortly after the battle. Then, on 21 February 1082, the lower city of Dyrrachium was betrayed to the Norman duke by one of the leading men of the city, a certain nobleman of Venetian origin called Domenico to whom – according to William of Apulia – the defence of a principal tower was delegated.[2]

The Invasion: Phase Two (October 1081–April 1082)

With the western gateway to the Egnatia and the entire Illyrian littoral under his control, Robert Guiscard undertook the next phase of his invasion of the Byzantine Empire. With the advent of spring, the Norman army left Illyria and marched eastwards towards Ohrid and Thessaloniki. The Illyrian highlands east of Dyrrachium would have presented an almost insurmountable hurdle to an invading army marching from west to east, mainly due to the almost unbroken mountain chains that run in a north–south direction. Nonetheless, three river valleys would have worked as natural highways through these mountain ranges and on to Lake Ohrid: from north to south they are the Shkumbin, which originates in the eastern Valamara mountains and accommodated the ancient Via Egnatia; the Devol, which has its source in the modern Greek-Albanian border region, and which, after initially flowing to the northeast towards Lake Prespa, abruptly turns west towards central and western Albania; and the Aoös (Greek: Αώος) or Vjosë (Albanian), a river in northwestern Greece and southwestern Albania that has its source in the Pindus mountains of northern Epirus.

The Norman duke seems to have marched inland from the Illyrian littoral without encountering any significant opposition. However, Malaterra points out that Guiscard deviated from the route he was expected to follow towards Ohrid and Thessaloniki – the Via Egnatia through the river valley of the Shkumbin. Instead, he turned south towards the western Macedonian city of Kastoria. Although it is impossible to be sure about Guiscard's motives for this strategic decision, we can only speculate that he might have wanted to have his army's flanks covered from enemy attacks. He would have known that Kastoria was an important imperial city and a major trading centre, while his intelligence would have informed him about the presence of a contingent of three hundred Varangians in the city's citadel – probably a regiment detached by Alexios while on his way to Dyrrachium the previous October. Following a brief siege, the outnumbered defenders surrendered the city to the Normans in March or early April 1082.[3]

It was at this crucial time for the empire that Byzantine diplomacy carried the day, only to confirm once again the old maxim that 'you [the general] should not endanger yourself and your army if it is not of utmost need or if you are not to have major gains'.[4] The agile manoeuvring of Komnenian diplomacy followed the principle of activating a network of alliances to avoid the costly and laborious process of going to war with neighbouring peoples, or to compel an invader to withdraw its forces from one's territory. In his work widely known as *De Administrando Imperio* (written between 948 and 952), Emperor Constantine VII (r. 944–59 as senior emperor) details to his son and heir – and privileged readers of the

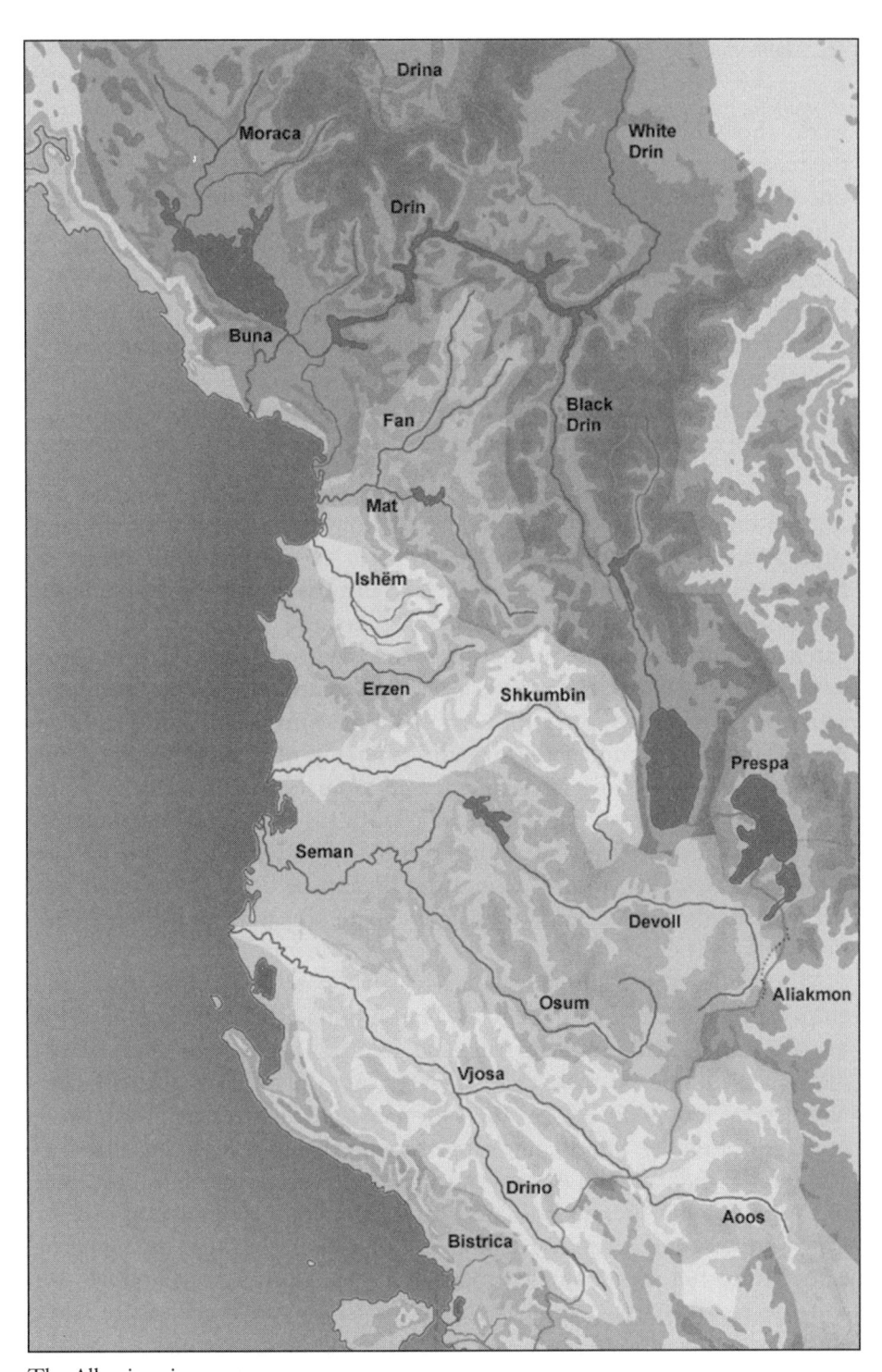

The Albanian river system.

work – how this system of alliances could threaten a potential enemy from the rear; as this was more frequently seen on the Danube front, Constantine evokes the example of the Bulgars, the Magyars and the Patzinaks:

> So long as the Emperor of the Romans is at peace with the Patzinaks, neither Russians nor Turks can come upon the Roman dominions by force of arms ... for they fear the strength of this nation [Patzinaks] which the emperor can turn against them while they are campaigning against the Romans. For the Patzinaks, if they are leagued in friendship with the emperor and won over by him through letters and gifts, can easily come upon the country both of the Russians and of the Turks.[5]

Anna Komnena leaves no doubt as to how well the aforementioned strategy worked for Alexios. As the emperor set in motion the gears of Byzantine diplomacy that had worked so effectively for him some eight months before with the Turks and the Venetians, in April 1082 he dispatched another embassy to the German emperor Henry IV, promising lavish gifts and a royal marriage. Meanwhile, imperial agents were also active in stirring up yet another rebellion against Guiscard's rule in Apulia, most likely under the overall leadership of the duke's rebellious nephew Abelard, who had been released from his comfortable exile in Constantinople the previous summer.[6] With his dominions in Apulia in turmoil, a German army marching south to Italy, and a terrified Pope Gregory VII writing to him requesting his return, Robert Guiscard was left with no alternative but to make immediate preparations for his departure back to Italy.

Meanwhile, sometime in the early spring of 1082, the Byzantine emperor had established the city of Thessaloniki as the rallying point for his troops who had retreated from the area of Dyrrachium in the aftermath of the battle. At that stage, however, not only did he lack sufficient numbers of troops to engage the Normans, but his treasury was also – practically – empty. Drastic measures were needed to reverse this dire situation in the Balkans, and Alexios quickly rose to the occasion by resorting to the unpopular measure of confiscating precious ecclesiastical objects from various churches in the capital; I should point out that the emperor enjoyed the full support of the patriarch Eustathius Garidas (1081–84) and the residential synod of twelve bishops, and so the measure went ahead with no serious protests.[7] The amount of cash collected would have enabled Alexios to hire crack troops to fight against the advancing

Normans, thus explaining Anna's reference to an unknown number of Seljuk troops that were attracted to Byzantine service at the time.[8]

The Invasion: Phase Three (April 1082–November 1083)

Robert Guiscard's departure from the Balkans marks a significant turning point for the Norman invasion of the Byzantine Empire, despite the fact that virtually no troops were taken back to Italy. It might be expected that once the leader and mastermind of the entire operation had to return to his base some 500km away in Apulia, leaving his army in hostile territory and in the middle of a military expedition overseas, this move would have disastrous ramifications for the course and outcome of the campaign. However, Guiscard seems to have found a less experienced yet equally bold, adventurous and highly ambitious young knight to take over from him: his son Bohemond.

As the Norman army resumed its operations in May 1082, Anna Komnena becomes virtually our only source for the whereabouts of Bohemond and his men in the southern Balkans. The Norman army advanced in a southwesterly direction from western Macedonia towards Epirus and its capital city, Ioannina. An obvious reason for this change in the strategic objectives of the campaign would have been the Norman leader's inexperience in being in command of the siege of a city with such formidable defences as those of Thessaloniki. Ralph Yewdale has also suggested that Guiscard may have anticipated having his Italian affairs resolved quickly, so as to be back in Greece before the end of the campaigning season of 1082, and therefore he ordered his son to simply consolidate the Norman positions in Greece and neutralise any remaining Byzantine garrisons to the southwest of the Via Egnatia. The Vlach populations of these regions – especially in central Greece – and their cooperation with the Normans would have also played a key role in Bohemond's decision to turn south to Epirus and Thessaly.[9] Nevertheless, risking another pitched battle with Alexios would have been out of the question at this stage of the campaign. However, the situation in Italy was far more serious than Guiscard had expected, and he would be unable to resume the leadership of his expeditionary army before 1084.

Convinced of the inability of the Byzantine emperor to come to their rescue, the defenders of Ioannina quickly capitulated in order to avoid any retribution and pillaging by the Normans. Almost immediately after taking Ioannina, Bohemond ordered improvements to the city's curtain walls and the building of a second – 'most strong' (ἐρυμνοτάτη) – acropolis. We read in the *Alexiad*: 'He made a survey of the walls and recognising that the citadel was in a dangerous condition, he not only hastened to restore it as far as was possible, but he even built a second very strong one in another part of the walls where he thought it would be of more use.'[10] Bearing strong similarities to the stone castles and towers (keeps; also known as *donjons* in France) that proliferated in Normandy, France, England, Catalonia, Apulia and Calabria in the third quarter of the eleventh century,[11] this impressive round keep would have dominated the citadel of the castle of Ioannina at 12.5m in height, with a diameter of 7.75m and a solid 2.5m-thick wall. Known locally as the 'Tower of Bohemondus', it is one of the few substantial remaining structures of the city's pre-Ottoman fortifications.

The emperor's belated arrival at Ioannina in late May, at the head of an army of mercenaries he had collected during his stay at Thessaloniki, did little to raise the morale of the people of the Epirotic capital. Outnumbered, and with the crashing defeat at Dyrrachium the previous October still looming large, Alexios seemed determined to engage the Normans in another pitched battle soon after his arrival in the outskirts of the city.[12] Yet he appears to have learned a valuable lesson from his previous experience against the Normans because, according to Anna, he dispatched reconnaissance parties to harass the Norman camp and gather intelligence about their numbers and the fighting capabilities of their leader, Bohemond.[13] On top of that, as Anna explains, Alexios was quick to appreciate that 'the first onset of the Frankish cavalry upon their opponents was quite irresistible', and for that reason 'hit upon a new device. He had wagons built, smaller and lighter than the ordinary ones, and four poles fixed to each; in these he placed heavy infantry so that when the Latins came dashing down at full gallop upon the Roman phalanx, the heavy-armed infantry should push the wagons forward and thus break the Latins' line.' In fact, these were more likely to have been two-wheeled carts rather than four-wheeled wagons, apparently to improve manoeuvrability, thus bearing great similarities to what came to be known a century later in northern Italy (mainly in Milan) as a *plaustrella*; they were used by Milanese forces against Frederick Barbarossa at the Battle of Legnano in 1176.

Alexios' tactical decision to use obstacles to disrupt the Norman cavalry charge not only demonstrates his experience in fighting against an army of western heavy cavalrymen, which would have been hard-earned during the conflict against Roussel de Bailleuil in Anatolia in the mid-1070s, but it also falls into line with the advice given in Leo VI's *Taktika* (*c.* 900) when coming up against 'Frankish' cavalry on rugged and difficult ground.[14] Yet the author of this military treatise also emphasised that: '[generals] who wanted to assault these people [Franks] ... did not line *their own troops up* for a pitched battle against them. Instead, they proceeded against them with well-planned ambushes and sneak attacks, or else they delayed combat and kept putting it off.'[15] Astonishingly, it would take two more defeats in the field of battle for the emperor to adhere to this advice.

As on the eve of the Battle of Dyrrachium, Anna notes that Bohemond was somehow informed about the Byzantine stratagem to impede the charge of his knights with wagons, and he swiftly 'adapted himself to the changed circumstances'; his answer was to split his forces and launch an assault against the flanks of the imperial army in a pincer move. The Byzantines were caught completely by surprise, and their disorderly retreat suggests that either they had no heavy cavalry at all, or that that unit was simply swept away by the Norman knights, who then immediately turned and attacked the infantry.

The next clash between the two armies is poorly placed chronologically and geographically, and Anna's confused account gives the impression that it took place just a few days after the first Norman victory at Ioannina. But it would have required several weeks of forced marching for Alexios to withdraw his surviving forces, first to Ohrid and then to Thessaloniki, in order to regroup and replace as many casualties as possible; therefore, the emperor would have had the chance to seek another battle with the Normans only in the middle of June at the earliest. Meanwhile, Bohemond did not remain idle; leaving Ioannina, he headed southwest towards the Epirotic coastal city of Arta, on the Amvrakikos Gulf.[16] The reason behind Bohemond's advance against Arta remains unknown, but this is the first time the city is attested in the Byzantine sources,[17] despite the existence of several churches from the ninth and tenth centuries, while its medieval castle was built much later, in the early thirteenth century, under the family of Komnenos-Doukas who ruled the Despotate of Epirus.[18]

The emperor's battle-plan for the second clash with the Normans was, once again, to disrupt their heavy cavalry charge, which had proved irresistible so far. This time, however, instead of using carts, Alexios adopted an ancient stratagem of throwing hundreds of four-spiked implements called caltrops (τρίβολοι) over the battleground to lame the enemy's horses.[19] These were apparently tied together with strings so that they could be recovered even when hidden in grass. In addition, the emperor reinforced the first line of his infantry with peltasts deployed immediately behind them, who were supposed to add to the mayhem caused by the caltrops by showering the Norman cavalry with javelins. The main idea behind the Byzantine plan was to thwart the initial Norman cavalry charge, before 'the left and right wings were to fall upon them in a vehement charge' in an attempt to envelop them.

Alexios' plan may have had the potential to win him the battlefield that day but, as Anna tells us: 'my father's plans ... did not escape Bohemond. For this is what happened: whatever plans my father made against him in the evening, the Frank knew by the morning.' Whether the Norman leader had, once again, been informed about the Byzantine plan of action, or if he simply made an 'educated guess' based on good reconnaissance of the battlefield, we will never know. Bohemond eventually directed his heavy cavalry against the Byzantine flanks, in a repeat of the tactics that won him the day at Ioannina just a few weeks before. Outnumbered and demoralised by their last defeat at the hands of the Normans, the soldiers of the imperial army 'turned their backs to the Latins and had not even the courage to look them in the face again'.

Following the disorderly retreat of his army, Anna desperately tries to present her father as a heroic figure who, despite the great disaster that had just befallen the empire:

> remained undaunted in hand and heart and offered brave resistance, wounding many and sometimes too being wounded himself ... But on comprehending his unquestionable danger, he deemed it his duty to save himself, so as to be able to fight once again against his conqueror, and prove himself a very formidable opponent who would not allow Bohemond to reap a complete victory.

Our historian makes it clear that her father had a sacred duty to save the empire from the menace of the Norman yoke, hence it would have been rash and futile ($μάταιον$) to thrust himself into certain danger or even death. William of Apulia observed that since Alexios was cognisant of the ever-changing outcomes of *bellum*, the emperor nonetheless returned to the fray and began to secure victories, to the point that the poet even declared Alexios 'has exercised manly [*virilis*] battle against the Normans'.[20] Alexios eventually succeeded in escaping his pursuers and returned to Constantinople, leaving the burden of further operations to his trusted officer Gregory Pakourianos.

Taking full advantage of Alexios' absence in the capital, Bohemond enjoyed a free rein on the Greek mainland.[21] From Arta he marched northeast towards Skopje and the surrounding regions of the two Polovoi,

The southern Balkans.

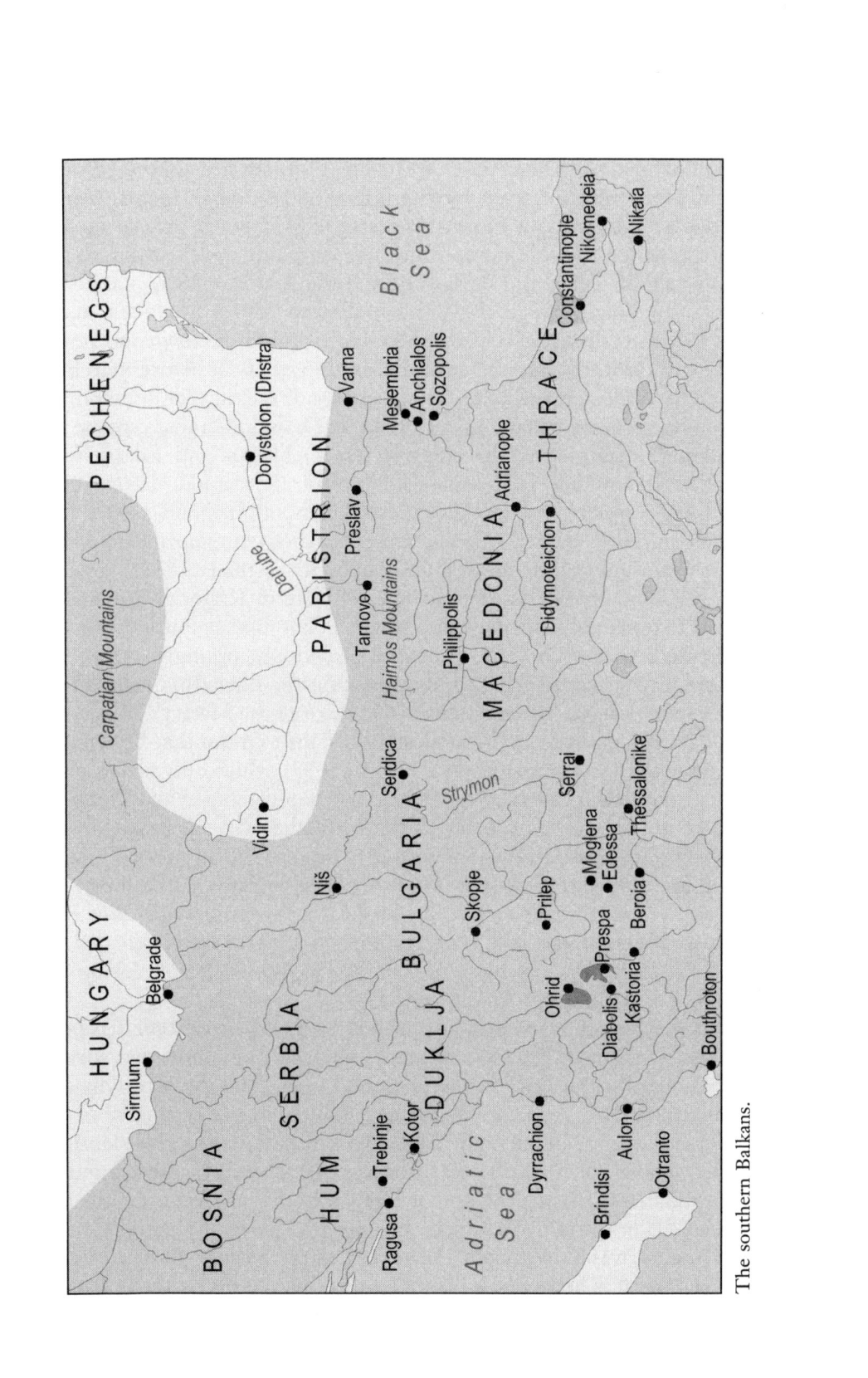

south of Skopje, and Ohrid to the west. The Norman siege of the castle of Ohrid was repelled, however, forcing Bohemond to march against Ostrobus, east of modern-day Florina in western Macedonia, where he was again compelled to withdraw. From there he plundered Verroia, Servia (a town south of Verroia), Edessa (Vodena) and Almopia (Moglena, east of Edessa), reaching through the Vardar valley to Aspres Ekklesies, about 40km to the northwest of Thessaloniki. He captured the town and stayed there for about three months until the autumn of 1082, before marching back to the Via Egnatia and the city of Kastoria. It is clear that Bohemond's plan was to secure the main military road to Thessaloniki that crossed the Macedonian countryside: the cities of Ohrid, Florina and Edessa were located exactly on the Via Egnatia, while Verroia, Servia and Almopia controlled its southern approaches. Nevertheless, Bohemond lacked the numbers and the necessary siege equipment to even contemplate launching a siege operation against the second largest city of the empire.

Because of the cold and damp winter climate in Kastoria, Bohemond decided to transfer his winter camp some 200km further south to the dry and fertile fields of Thessaly, in central Greece. According to Anna, the Norman leader arrived with all his troops on the outskirts of the Thessalian capital Larissa 'on the festival of St George the Martyr'. This comment has been taken by many modern historians to mean that Bohemond was on the outskirts of the city by 23 April (1083), which only makes sense if we assume that the Norman spent the winter somewhere between Kastoria and Larissa – probably in the Thessalian city of Trikala, some 65km to the west of Larissa – and moved to besiege the capital of Thessaly only in the early spring of 1083. A more plausible date that has been put forward for Bohemond's arrival in Larissa is 3 November (1082), a date which commemorates the consecration of a cathedral dedicated to St George in Lydda, southeast of today's Tel Aviv in Israel, during the reign of Constantine the Great (305–37).[22]

The hill where the medieval fortifications of Larissa were built has been inhabited for four millennia, and many important buildings that survive today date from the Ancient Greek period, including the acropolis and the ancient theatre. Although much more limited in size compared to the ancient city, Larissa in the high Middle Ages must have had a substantially fortified citadel, because the seat of the general (*strategos*) in command of the military-civilian province of Greece (*theme of Hellas*; established between AD 687 and 695), which encompassed parts of Central Greece and Thessaly, was moved from Thebes to Larissa in the second half of the tenth century.[23] The citadel was besieged for three years by the Bulgarian tsar Samuel before surrendering in AD 982. Yet surprisingly little archaeological evidence has survived from the medieval fortifications of the city, perhaps because these were destroyed during the civil conflicts and raids of the turbulent fourteenth century or during the early Ottoman period.[24]

The defence of Larissa was entrusted to an experienced officer named Leo Kephalas. He was a man whom Alexios trusted not to surrender the city all too easily to the Normans, as had happened at Kastoria and Ioannina; he was the son of Alexios' *doulos* (lit. 'slave'; more likely to mean 'dependent'),[25] and he was later appointed military governor (*katepano*) of Abydos in the Hellespont (*c*. 1086).[26] Leo managed to resist the besiegers for around six months before the blockade began to take its toll on the morale of the population. Although Anna gives no details about the course of the siege, she notes that her father once again made use of the 1081 agreement with Suleiman b. Qutlumush of Nicaea, and requested a large number of mercenary troops to fight against the Normans; he eventually received an elite force of seven thousand men under a certain Kamyres. Meanwhile, sometime in the winter of 1082/83, Alexios' trusted general Pakourianos was dispatched to Thessaloniki, along with the patriarch of Jerusalem, Euthemius, to attempt to broker a deal with Bohemond.[27]

Alexios left the capital for Larissa sometime in the early spring of 1083, and he would have arrived in the region of Thessaly after a few weeks, pitching his camp at Trikala, some 65km west of Larissa. Anna's narrative of the events that followed illustrates a radical change of strategy on the part of Alexios about how to defeat Bohemond's army; ultimately, he came to appreciate that '[generals] who wanted to assault these people [Franks] ... did not line *their own troops* up for a pitched battle against them. Instead, they proceeded against them with well-planned ambushes and sneak attacks, or else they delayed combat and kept putting it off.'[28] A detailed reconnaissance of the battle-ground was paramount for any ambush to be effective, hence Alexios' order to get hold of a local man to ask questions about the topography of Larissa and its vicinity. By that stage of the Norman invasion of the Balkans, it had become obvious that the Byzantine emperor had given up any idea of facing the Norman army in a pitched battle for the fourth time. Yet it would not be until much later in her narrative, in Chapter XIII of the *Alexiad* on Bohemond's campaign of 1107–08 and the Treaty of Devol, that Anna condemned the purposeful provocation of an enemy into battle or armed conflict as bad generalship:

> The general (I think) should not invariably seek victory by drawing the sword; there are times when he should be prepared to use finesse

> ... and so achieve a complete triumph. So far as we know, a general's supreme task is to win, not merely by force of arms; sometimes, when the chance offers itself, an enemy can be beaten by fraud.[29]

The Byzantine emperor decided to make use of the feigned retreat tactics that had worked so effectively for the Norman army at the Battle of Dyrrachium. We read about Alexios' simple but brilliant battle-plan in Anna's account of the war-council the night before the first engagement with the Normans; he instructed his closest officers to take command of his forces and – critically – of his personal standards, and to arrange their battle lines 'in their usual manner followed in former engagements'. The plan was to attack the Norman army head-on and then pretend to retreat in disorder, just as in the previous clashes in Ioannina and Arta, to lure the Norman knights into a trap set up by the emperor at a specific location somewhere to the east of Larissa.[30] Anna is also keen to show that her father had ordered a thorough reconnaissance of the terrain both to the east and west of Larissa, because of his decision to take advantage of a slight depression on the ground close to an unidentified place called 'Allage', where he would have been able to crouch down with his elite unit in order to keep out of sight of the advancing Normans.

The Byzantine strategy worked as planned. The following morning Bohemond ordered his knights to open the battle with a full-frontal cavalry charge against the centre of the Byzantine formation, where he could clearly make out the imperial standards; these would have been prominently displayed as part of the trap set by Alexios the previous day. The Normans swallowed the bait and swiftly went after the retreating imperial units, with Bohemond dividing his cavalry forces into two main divisions, one led by himself and the other by the second-in-command, the count of Brienne. After pillaging the largely undefended Norman camp with his small band of elite troops, Alexios then dispatched a small force of mounted archers and peltasts to harass the pursuing Normans and tempt them to turn around and engage them. His advice on how to engage the Norman knights illustrates the level of familiarity of the Byzantines, and especially of Alexios Komnenos, with the fighting tactics of the eleventh-century 'Frankish' knight:

> [Alexios ordered his men] not to start a close fight, but rather aim at the horses from a little distance and direct showers of arrows upon them ... For every Frank is invincible both in attack and appearance when he is on horseback, but when he comes off his horse, partly due to the size of his shield, and partly to the long curved peaks of his

shoes and consequent difficulty in walking, then he becomes very easy to deal with and a different man altogether, for all his mental energy evaporates, as it were.[31]

While the mounted archers and peltasts sent by Alexios played havoc with the Norman knights of the count of Brienne's pursuing cavalry, Bohemond seems to have withdrawn from the battle after the first charge, because the messengers whom Brienne sent to him with the news found him eating grapes on a little island in the 'Salabrias' river (modern Pineiós). This small detail gives us a hint about the date of the event, which probably took place in late July, since Bohemond would not have been able to eat grapes in May or June.

The final defeat of the Normans took place the following morning in a narrow and marshy area on the outskirts of Larissa. Once Bohemond 'realized the craftiness and the victory won by guile he was naturally, indeed, furious with the Emperor', but he did not take the bait this time. Although Alexios dispatched a small contingent of elite 'Turkish and Sarmatian' mounted archers to lure the Normans out of their encampment, they were routed and driven down to the river. Next, Anna refers to a small unit of elite Norman cavalry who chose to occupy a neighbouring height, and they defended their ground effectively, managing to kill around five hundred of the imperial troops sent to clear them out. Meanwhile, Bohemond decided to cross the river early in the morning and to 'find a swampy place in the neighbourhood of Larissa and a tree-covered plain between two hills which ran out into a very narrow pass (this is called a "kleisoura"'), ... he entered by the pass and fixed his palisades there'.[32] Clearly aware of the difficult position his army was in, the Norman leader planned to make his defence in the aforementioned wooded pass between two mountains, forcing the enemy to attack them through the narrow pass in order to minimise the numerical advantage of the imperial forces. Alexios, however, was experienced enough not to fall for Bohemond's clever strategy. We read in the *Alexiad*:

> The Emperor gave strict injunctions to this man [Michael Doukas] not to let all the troops enter the mouth of the 'kleisoura'; but to leave the mass of them outside in squadrons, and to pick out a few of the Turks and Sauromatians [Patzinaks] who were skilled archers and allow these to enter, and to command them to use no weapon but their arrows. These entered and made cavalry attacks on the Latins, and the men outside, burning for a fight, vied with each other as to who should enter the mouth.

Bohemond's tactical response was to order his troops to form a solid shield-wall to fend off the enemy showers of arrows. As we will see in the following chapter, this battle experience would prove invaluable fourteen years later at the Battle of Doryleum, where, during the first stage of the battle, the crusaders found themselves completely enveloped by the Seljuk cavalry, and Bohemond ordered them to close their ranks and hold the line. Eventually, panic spread in the Norman ranks when Bohemond's standard-bearer was killed while fending off Alexios' mounted archers. Bohemond now decided to retreat, abandoning his expedition in Greece, after the defeat at Larissa and the loss of his camp and supplies; he withdrew his army west to Trikala, and from there to Kastoria.

With most of the Greek mainland restored to Byzantine rule before the end of the summer of 1083, Bohemond was becoming aware of his inability to sustain this campaign any longer. An incident involving his most trusted officers also confirmed the low morale in the Norman camp; the emperor tried to set the Norman aristocrats and senior officers against their leader by contacting them with promises of lavish gifts, high court titles and a warm welcome for any deserters to the imperial army. Bohemond realised that his best course of action would be to install the count of Brienne in Kastoria, and retreat to the Adriatic port of Avlona, which he reached in early August 1083.

Before the emperor was free to pack up and return to the Queen of Cities in triumph, he had to deal with the Norman garrison in Kastoria. Anna is, once again, our only source for the siege of this strategic Macedonian city by her father's armies.[33] Aware that conventional siege machines like the *helepoleis* were having little impact on the city's formidable defences, Alexios came up with an ingenious plan. The city is situated on a promontory on the western shore of Lake Orestiada, and the emperor dispatched a number of elite troops under his trusted officer George Palaeologus, the former governor of Dyrrachium, in small vessels to launch an attack on the city from the lake, while at the same time the emperor would attack from the land and attempt to draw the attention of the defenders towards him while Palaeologus' party would be climbing the walls almost undetected. The plan worked flawlessly, and Brienne's followers deserted to the emperor *en masse*, while the count of Brienne himself was made to swear never to take up arms against the empire again.

In this way ended the siege of Kastoria, probably around the end of October or early November 1083. As for Bohemond, we only know that he was able to join his father at Salerno soon after Henry IV had withdrawn his armies from Italy around May 1084,[34] and it seems likely therefore that he chose to spend the winter of 1083/84 in Illyria, no doubt reluctant to risk a passage of the Adriatic in mid-winter. Finally, an unknown number of Venetian ships recaptured the lower city of Dyrrachium from the Normans, although the defenders of the citadel put up a hearty resistance and denied the Venetians the glory of taking back the entire city for the empire. Avlona was also captured shortly after Bohemond's departure, while the local population of Corfu rebelled against the Norman rule, with only the citadel remaining firmly in Norman hands.[35]

The Invasion: Phase Four (November 1083–July 1085)

While Bohemond was trying to keep alive the Norman campaign in Greece, Robert Guiscard had his hands full in Apulia. From the scarce information available in the primary sources it is difficult to assess the extent of the Norman nobles' Apulian revolt, or to identify the ringleaders; they may have included Guiscard's rebellious nephew Abelard, his half-brother Hermann and his other nephew Geoffrey of Conversano, but this is mere speculation. Moreover, there were insurrections in the Capitanata region, in northwestern Apulia, and – crucially – in the capital, Bari. Suppressing the rebellion took Robert some fifteen months, from his landing at Otranto in April 1082 to the storming of Hermann's Apulian castle at Cannae in July 1083.

In the meantime, the German emperor Henry IV and his imperial army had established themselves on the outskirts of Rome by the early months of 1082, imposing a blockade on the 'Leonine City' (the part of Rome surrounded by the Leonine Wall, built by Pope Leo IV in the mid-ninth century). One of Henry's key allies in his Italian campaign was Jordan I of Capua (d. 1091), the eldest son and successor of the Norman prince Richard I of Capua, and the nephew of Robert Guiscard. Jordan exchanged his alliance with Pope Gregory VII for an investiture of his lands by the German emperor, a change of heart that was arbitrated by Jordan's chief adviser, the abbot of Montecassino, Desiderius of Benevento. Jordan of Capua had always been a destabilising player for Robert Guiscard's interests in Italy, and he would go as far as to support Bohemond's succession over Roger Borsa after the duke's death in Greece in 1085.

Once Hermann's castle at Cannae had been reconquered, Guiscard's next step was to launch a campaign against Jordan of Capua, sometime in the second half of 1083. It was only after he had dealt with the threat from Jordan, early in 1084, that he was free to march against the German army besieging Rome. His arrival could not have come at a more critical point, as Henry's forces had finally forced themselves into the city of Rome in

March 1084 and had trapped the Pope inside Castel St-Angelo. The duke's army arrived on the outskirts of the Eternal City in late May 1084, by which time the German emperor had withdrawn his forces from the city following the coronation of the anti-Pope Clement III in St Peter's basilica on 24 March. Guiscard in turn forced his way into Rome and his army eventually became embroiled in street fighting with the people of Rome, who had become incensed by the excesses of the Pope's Norman allies. Gregory VII was compelled to withdraw to Monte Cassino, and later to Guiscard's castle of Salerno.

The Norman duke must have been anxious to resume his military operation across the Adriatic as soon as possible, to relieve his beleaguered garrison troops in Corfu and Dyrrachium. Sadly, the primary sources are even more silent about the numbers and consistency of the Norman army in 1084 than they were for the 1081 campaign. However, we can speculate about the size of the Norman expeditionary force, if we consider William of Apulia's information about the numbers in Guiscard's army that marched against Henry IV in May 1084: some six thousand knights and thirty thousand foot-soldiers.[36] The critical question is how many of these troops actually took part in the Norman invasion of the Byzantine Empire four months later. The only answer we can give is that Guiscard's expeditionary army would have been much smaller compared to the numbers he had mustered to quash his rebellious barons and march to Rome.

According to William of Apulia, the Norman duke took his army across the Adriatic in some 120 ships.[37] This provides another vital clue in trying to assess the numbers of the Normans because, bearing in mind that the duke had twenty-five warships at his disposal in the subsequent naval engagements with the Venetian fleets, this gives us around eighty to ninety transport vessels available to ferry the bulk of the Norman army to Illyria. Even if all of them were specially modified horse-transport ships – highly unlikely in my view, considering that the average capacity of each ship was fifteen horses – this would give us a number of 1,275 horses carried from Italy.[38] Furthermore, bearing in mind the maximum capacity of 108 men in a tenth-century Byzantine warship (*dromōn*), which would surely not have been the case for the Norman transport ships, this would give us a maximum of 9,180 men. Yet even after these contentious calculations, a realistic estimate of the numbers in Guiscard's army has to be narrowed down by at least a third.

The Norman duke sailed from Brindisi to Avlona sometime at the end of September or the beginning of October 1084, mobilising his four sons, namely Bohemond, Roger Borsa, Robert and Guy.[39] Roger and Guy were dispatched to Avlona before the main expeditionary force sailed, their task being to capture the city and link up with Guiscard's force close to the castles of Oricum and Canina, just like three years before. However, ferocious storms kept the Normans at bay in Butrint, unable to sail to the relief of the Norman garrison in the citadel of Corfu castle. After spending two months lingering in frustration, Guiscard was finally able to take his army across to the island of Corfu in early December, landing at the northern port of Cassiope, just as he had done in 1081. To his surprise, he found a joint Venetian-Byzantine fleet poised to offer battle.

Anna portrays the Norman duke as eager to pick up the gauntlet thrown down by the allied fleet, although it is doubtful whether he would have been able to avoid being intercepted by the allies if he had chosen to return to Avlona. Although we lack significant details about the first naval encounter, we know that the Venetians managed to rout the Norman fleet.[40] Three days later the allied fleet attacked the Normans once more, only this time they made the grave mistake of overestimating the losses sustained by the Normans, and dispatched their envoys to the doge in Venice to announce the news. With the small and fast Venetian ships sent back home, the Normans attacked their enemies in earnest, after having their ships made much lighter the day before, catching them completely off guard and overwhelming them.

Anna Komnena reports around thirteen thousand Venetian casualties, which is surely an exaggerated figure, although it reflects the serious blow to Venice's prestige, and some two thousand five hundred prisoners, who were probably sent back to Avlona.[41] But the most appalling incident in her narrative on the naval engagements between the two fleets is her description of the harrowing fate that befell the Venetian prisoners in Norman custody; this is, no doubt, another attempt by the princess to paint a dark portrait of the Norman duke as a cruel barbarian:

> After this signal victory Robert in a fit of harshness treated many of the prisoners most cruelly, for he had the eyes of some gouged out, the noses of others cut off, and some he deprived of their hands and feet, or both. About the rest he sent word to their fellow-countrymen that whoever wanted to ransom a friend for a price might come without fear.

But there was a precedent in the duke's actions in the waters off Corfu. By mutilating some of the Venetian prisoners, Guiscard was sending a powerful message to the emerging naval power of the *Serenissima* never to launch another naval campaign against him. A similar approach was followed by Guiscard's brother Roger after the Battle of Misilmeri (1068), in the final stages of the Norman expansion in Sicily, when a small Norman army led by Roger crushed a much more numerous Muslim army from Palermo, and hardly any Muslims survived to bring the news to the inhabitants of the Sicilian capital. Instead, the Normans used a gruesome method of psychological warfare, supposedly writing notes with the blood of the dead Muslim soldiers and attaching them to carrier-pigeons before releasing them back to Palermo. As Malaterra reports: 'When the people of Palermo heard the news, the whole city was shaken: the tearful voices of the children and women rose up through the air to the heavens.[42]

Following the defeat of the allied Venetian-Byzantine fleet off the northeastern coast of Corfu, Guiscard was now free to relieve the Norman garrison at Corfu castle, before having to return to his base on the Illyrian mainland because of the onset of winter. He set up his winter quarters on the banks of the river Glycys (modern Acheron) on the Epirus coastline, with himself and his elite cavalry pitching camp further south at Vonitsa, on the southern coast of the Amvrakikos Gulf. However, both William of Apulia and Anna Komnena write about an outbreak of famine and disease that decimated the Norman army.[43] This disease, which may have been either dysentery or malaria, would have been caused by the unsanitary conditions in the Norman camp and by the wet climate in the area of the Glycys and the Amvrakikos Gulf. The spread of the disease must have had a hugely demoralising effect upon the Norman troops, especially if we consider the fact that even Bohemond asked to return to Italy for treatment.

The onset of spring gave a new impetus to the demoralised Norman leader to expand his operations further south. In the early summer of 1085 Robert Guiscard sent his son Roger Borsa, in command of a small force of elite troops, to Kephalonia in an attempt to capture the island's capital, Hagios Georgios. This major change in the Norman plans can be explained by the shifting of the strategic objective of the campaign from Dyrrachium to the much more lucrative target of the southern Greek cities of Athens, Corinth and Thebes. These were three of the wealthiest cities in the empire because of their prosperous silk industry, and they were targeted again during the 1147–49 Norman expedition in the Ionian and Aegean Seas, when the Normans sacked the cities and transferred all of the silk workers back to Palermo.[44] This may explain Guiscard's decision in the summer of 1085 to capture the island of Kephalonia, the seat of the civilian governor (*krites*) of the Theme of Kephalonia, which comprised the islands of the Ionian Sea. He would have to have control of the Ionian islands before even contemplating a naval operation against Corinth, Athens and Thebes through the Gulf of Corinth. But his plans were cut short almost immediately.

Roger Borsa's repeated attempts to storm the castle of Hagios Georgios proved unsuccessful, and Robert Guiscard himself arrived to take command of the operations just a few weeks later in June. We have two slightly different versions of what happened as the duke landed at the promontory of Atheras, in the northwest of the island.[45] According to the *Alexiad*, he arrived in a single galea at the promontory of Atheras, while the rest of his army remained on the opposite Epirus coast in battle positions. Before he even managed to reach his son, Guiscard was stricken 'by a violent fever'. William of Apulia tells us that the duke, after sending his son to besiege the town of Hagios Georgios, returned to Vonitsa to take his entire army across the sea and march against the island's capital. He embarked for Kephalonia, but 'before he managed to see the castle fortifications [of Hagios Georgios] he went down with fever'.

Robert Guiscard died on 17 July 1085, after suffering from an intense fever for six days, in an area which still recalls the Norman duke's name in the form of 'Fiskardo' (former Panormus). Anna gives a last description of the Norman duke, as a befitting and dispassionate 'epitaph' to her father's great foe:

> Now Robert, as rumour insisted and many said, was a most exceptional leader, quick-witted, good-looking, courteous in conversation, ready too in repartee, loud-voiced, easily accessible, very tall in stature, his hair always close-cut, long bearded, always anxious to maintain the ancient customs of his race. He preserved his perfect comeliness of countenance and figure until the end, and of these he was very proud as his appearance was considered worthy of kingship, he showed respect to all his subordinates, more especially to those who were well-disposed towards him. On the other hand he was very thrifty and fond of money, very business-like and greedy of gain, and, in addition to all this, most ambitious; and since he was a slave to these desires, he has incurred the serious censure of mankind ... For all acknowledge Robert's bravery, remarkable skill in warfare and steadfast spirit; and he was a man who could not be conquered easily but only with extreme difficulty, and after a defeat he seemed to rise again with renewed vigour.[46]

Chapter 4

The Interlude Period, 1085–97

The duke's widow Sigkelgaita and his son Roger, who was at that time also present among the Bulgarians, and the other barons carried out his funeral ceremonies with the proper honours, not undeservedly. They brought his body back across the sea and buried it at Venosa. Freed by the departure of its enemies, Greece rejoiced in peace. [However] the whole of Apulia and Calabria were in confusion. For the brothers Roger and Bohemond quarrelled among themselves, both seeking the ducal office, and many people sought their own advantage, looking to profit first from one and then from the other.

[Geoffrey Malaterra, III. 41–2]

The Successor of the 'Terror Mundi'[1]

Guiscard's sudden death while he was on campaign in Greece not only brought an abrupt halt to what had been, more or less, a personal expedition, but also inevitably introduced an element of chaos into Norman politics in southern Italy. Immediately following the announcement of his death to his troops in Kephalonia, William of Apulia notes the fear and panic that overran everyone who had embarked on that perilous operation across the Adriatic and Ionian Seas, a consequence no doubt of the psychological impact of losing a great leader while on campaign and in hostile territory:

> While Roger [Borsa] was thus absent visiting his camp [in Epirus], the men in the other camp [Kephalonia] became absolutely panic-stricken, and abandoned all hope of escape, thinking that life and safety were to be denied them. If all the Greeks, Persians and Arabs [*gens Agarena*] had attacked them, and all the peoples of the world flocked together, armed themselves, and came upon them while they were themselves unarmed, they could not have been more afraid than they were now. The death of this one man made all these people fearful. Those who, when the duke had been alive, were accustomed to defeating innumerable peoples were now, once he was dead, afraid to resist [even] a few.[2]

As mentioned in the previous chapter, Roger Borsa had been mobilised to participate in his father's second expedition against Byzantium in 1084–85, along with his other brothers, Bohemond, Robert and Guy. Bohemond was afflicted by either dysentery or malaria during the Norman army's stay in their winter camp on the Epirotic coastline, with his condition deteriorating to the point that he had to return to Italy to receive medical treatment sometime in the early spring of 1085. With the biggest threat to his succession recovering back in Italy, Borsa had to act fast to secure what he felt was rightfully his. First, though, he had to ensure the loyalty of the army deployed in Kephalonia and Epirus, and William of Apulia leaves no doubt as to where the army's loyalty lay: 'They [the Norman leaders] all promised that they were ready to serve him [Roger Borsa] faithfully as they had served his father, and then they begged him to help them to return across the sea.'[3]

After returning to Italy to bury his father in the Church of the Holy Trinity at Venosa, Borsa also had to win over the support of his father's vassals in Italy. And for that he could rely on a close relative who, over the last thirty years, had developed an enduring and mutually rewarding relationship with his father: Guiscard's younger brother Roger Hauteville. Petrizzo has emphasised the key role played by Roger at this pivotal moment in the history of the Norman dukedom in Italy, as his decades-long and enduring bonds of fealty to his elder half-brother, combined with his growing political and military power during the prolonged process of conquering the island of Sicily from the Muslims, which would last until 1091, transformed the Norman count into a 'king-maker' (or, more accurately, a 'duke-maker') and, crucially, established the vertical inheritance for overlordship in the Hauteville clan.[4] To put it in a nutshell, Roger Hauteville found it too difficult, owing to his preoccupations in Sicily, to claim his brother's lands in Italy, but his political moves and support held the key to the vertical (from father to son) rather than horizontal (between brothers) succession in the dukedom that would see Roger Borsa acclaimed duke in September 1085, in spite of the opposition from the disinherited Bohemond. Malaterra spells out in no uncertain terms the decisive role Roger Hauteville played in the events, along with his 'reward' for supporting Borsa over Bohemond:

> Roger was eventually made duke with the help of his uncle Count Roger of the Sicilians who, while his brother was still alive, had promised that he would do this. All the *castella* of Calabria in which up to now Count Roger held only a half share were granted to him by his nephew in full ownership, and handed over to him.[5]

The Rebel

As I explained in the first chapter of this book, it was because of astute political reasons that Guiscard chose to repudiate his first wife Alberada of Buonalbergo in favour of Sigelgaita, the daughter of Prince Guaimar IV of Salerno, thus automatically demeaning Alberada's son Bohemond to the status of a bastard. Yet it would be a mistake to assume that Bohemond was therefore ostracised from the political scene of Norman Italy. As Alberada remained an acknowledged spouse of Guiscard and for that reason part of the extended Hauteville clan, Bohemond's paternity and his right to be fully associated with his father were also never challenged.[6] Bohemond was very much trusted by his father, who saw in him a capable and charismatic military leader who also enjoyed the loyalty of the army. Borsa, in contrast, had not been seriously tested on the battlefield, but he had on his side the legitimacy of his mother's kin, the Lombard princes of Salerno, and his uncle's promise of political support.

One can easily appreciate the serious threat Bohemond posed to his half-brother, and the likelihood of a rebellion being mounted by him and his followers would have been high during the closing months of 1085. But any military insurrection that disrupted the smooth transition of power in Apulia would have been unsound and foolhardy, and could potentially have led to a full-blown civil war. However, for the first two years after Guiscard's death, Bohemond not only witnessed charters issued by Borsa, but was also acknowledged as the duke's brother in these official documents, a fact that demonstrates the non-bellicose relationship between the two for the period between 1085 and 1087.[7] Nevertheless, if we are to make anything of Orderic Vitalis' short account about Bohemond's 'rebellion' in the first year after his father's death, it would be more appropriate to consider the events that unfolded as some sort of 'negotiating strategy' on the part of Guiscard's eldest son, rather than an all-out war.

Immediately after Roger Borsa and Sigelgaita landed in Italy, Bohemond reportedly fled from Salerno to the court of Jordan I (after 1046–1091), count of Aversa and prince of Capua, the eldest son and successor of Prince Richard I of Capua and the nephew of Robert Guiscard. We do not know the deeper reason behind Jordan's decision to throw his support behind his cousin Bohemond over Borsa, the eldest son by Sigelgaita, who was his own sister-in-law, but it could well have been the old spirit of resistance against the Dukes of Apulia, manifested in the Apulian rebellion of 1078–79, that fanned the flames of Jordan's desire to get involved in the political strife in his neighbouring principality. The result was that for the next three years the prince of Capua was supplying Bohemond with Capuan troops and money for the otherwise landless noble to use as a 'bargaining chip'.[8] Needless to say, Bohemond's contingent would have grown bigger depending on the scale of his successes, and these came almost immediately. The town of Oria was the first to open its gates (Malaterra talks about treason from within) to Bohemond's army of adventurers, who had flocked to his banner in the hope of looting and ravaging the fertile lands of southern Apulia, while the lands about Taranto and Otranto came next.[9]

Malaterra implies that, with the intervention of Roger of Sicily, a kind of compromise was reached between the two brothers in March 1086, to allocate a substantial piece of territory to Bohemond, specifically the towns and surrounding regions of Oria, Taranto, Otranto and Gallipoli, in the heel of the Italian Peninsula in southern Apulia, including any lands Geoffrey, count of Conversano, held directly from the duke of Apulia in Brindisi, Nardò, Montepeloso, Polignano, Monopoli, Lecce, Castellana, Casaboli and Sissignano; to this list we have to add Bohemond's patrimonial rights over parts of the capital city of Bari.[10] This reconciliation, in the shape of the dominion of Taranto, would undoubtedly have propelled Bohemond to the landed elite of the principality.

It seems that this compromise brought only a temporary halt to Bohemond's ambitions, for in September or October 1087 his men engaged Borsa's garrison troops at Fragneto, some 10km to the north of Benevento in Campania, in a small skirmish that resulted – according to Romuald of Salerno – in only one man killed in action and several dozen of Bohemond's men taken prisoner.[11] But one might ask what, exactly, Bohemond was doing so far to the north of his allotted lands in southern Apulia, some 200km from Bari and almost 300km from Taranto? This was, probably, just another step in Bohemond's 'negotiating strategy' with his brother, as we see him back in Taranto in October of the same year confirming a grant to the monastery of St Peter Imperialis, in a famous and controversial *sigillum* – a type of legal document publicly affirmed with a lead seal – in which he is named *Boamundus Tarenti Princeps* ['Bohemond prince of Taranto'] in the heading, followed by *Boamundo filio illustrissimi Ducis* ['Bohemond son of the illustrious Duke'] in the introductory paragraph of the document where we find the ruler's intitulation and the name of the recipient of the grant.[12]

Sometime in the same year (1087), Malaterra reports an important new ally who rallied to Bohemond's camp. Mihera Falluca, lord of Catanzaro in central Calabria, and one of the most rebellious Calabrian vassals of

Roger Borsa, had seized the city of Maida, some 40km to the west of Catanzaro. Then, according to our source:

> wishing to secure assistance to augment his own forces, he [Mihera] became the vassal [*homo*] of Bohemond ... He renounced his obedience to the duke [Roger Borsa], made a sworn alliance with Bohemond, and received from him Maida, which he had seized, and all the land which he had inherited from his father and held from the duke.[13]

This move was not only beneficial to the count of Taranto, in the sense that it gave him a foothold in Calabria, but it was becoming ever clearer that Bohemond's camp was transforming into a destabilising factor in southern Italian politics, by attracting disgruntled Norman leaders like Mihera. But the count's ambitions in Calabria did not end there, and Malaterra notes his eagerness to seize more lands from his brother, starting with the town of Cosenza in central Calabria, some 40km south of St Marco Argentano, where he was born. Our chronicler reports that Bohemond gained access to the lower city through negotiations with the citizens of Cosenza, which then enabled him to enforce a blockade of Borsa's garrison troops in the citadel.[14]

When news of Bohemond's campaign was brought to Borsa in Apulia, he immediately sent for his uncle, Roger of Sicily, but before either of them could march to the relief of Cosenza, the count of Taranto had seized and destroyed the citadel, although Malaterra is silent on the fate of the garrison. Then Borsa and Roger of Sicily launched a retaliatory campaign against Rossano, a town around 90km northeast of Cosenza, 'putting everything there to the flames' because the people had assisted Bohemond's troops, before heading south to Maida, apparently expecting to find Bohemond there. However, the count was able to elude them by retreating to Rocca Falluca, one of the two *castra* (the other was Catanzaro) that Mihera Falluca held as his vassal. This game of hide-and-seek ended when Borsa and Roger of Sicily dispatched messengers to Bohemond and Mihera with overtures of peace and the suggestion that a meeting take place at the Benedictine abbey of St Euphemia, in the valley of Nicastro in central Calabria.

Mihera eventually reconciled with Borsa, and he even surrendered Maida to 'the duke to whom it rightfully belonged'. Bohemond, however, chose to retire to Taranto, thus bringing the conflict with his brother and uncle to a stalemate for the next two years. The two sides reached a final settlement in the summer of 1089, when it was agreed that Borsa would concede to Bohemond the cities of Cosenza and Maida; at the end of

August the two brothers decided to exchange Bari for Cosenza, because Bohemond had made promises to the people of Cosenza that he would not erect any fortifications in their city, and Roger had made similar promises to the people of Bari.[15] Without doubt, Bohemond emerged as the winner of this prolonged conflict with Roger Borsa and Roger Hauteville. Bari was the richest and most important city in southern Italy, and its position in the Apulian littoral guaranteed Bohemond control of the southern Adriatic trade with Byzantium and the ports of the Middle East and Egypt. To put it in a nutshell, control of Bari and his possessions in Calabria bestowed on Bohemond almost as much power as Roger himself possessed, although technically he was still the duke's vassal.

Less than a year before the reconciliation of the two brothers, on 12 March 1088 Eudes (Odo), cardinal-bishop of Ostia since 1080, was elected by acclamation as Pope Urban II (papacy, 1088–99) at Terracina, on the outskirts of Rome. He was one of the most prominent and active supporters of the Gregorian reforms that dealt with the moral integrity and independence of the clergy,[16] and he immediately declared his intention of following the policy of his great predecessor Gregory VII (papacy, 1073–85). He travelled to Sicily for a meeting with Roger Hauteville shortly after his acclamation, sometime in the spring of 1088, although Malaterra is silent about the true purpose of this trip.[17] Yet because Urban's first entry into Rome in November 1088 was only made possible by Norman troops,[18] we may assume that the reason for the Pope's journey to Roger's court in Sicily, at a time when the conflict between Roger Borsa and Bohemond was still ongoing, would have been to secure Norman (military) help.

Urban turned his steps southwards again in the late summer of 1089. He visited Capua in August, where he received an invitation from Bohemond to come to Bari to consecrate the shrine of St Nicolas, after the saint's relics were carried off to Bari from the original shrine in Myra, in southwestern Asia Minor, on 22 May 1087. Between 10 and 15 September 1089 Urban also met with seventy bishops in an ecclesiastical synod at the Apulian town of Melfi, where they promulgated decrees against simony and clerical marriage.[19] But what was more important for Norman politics in southern Italy, and clearly demonstrates Urban's plan to reconcile the warring Hauteville factions (i.e. Borsa and Bohemond), was Roger Borsa's investiture with his lands in Apulia and Calabria as a papal vassal, as his father had been before him at Melfi in 1059, during the course of the synod and in the presence of Bohemond, before receiving a papal banner in token of his investiture.[20] After ordaining Elias, the new archbishop of

Bari, on 30 September, Urban then consecrated the shrine of St Nicholas the following day. Probably in response to a demand by Bohemond, the Pope consecrated another church at Brindisi sometime in the late autumn; on 25 December 1089 Urban was back in Rome.

Nonetheless, the political stability achieved in Apulia and Calabria following the reconciliation between the two brothers in the summer of 1089 was not to last for long. Precipitated by the deaths of Sigkelgaita in April 1090 and Jordan of Capua in November 1090, numerous conflicts broke out between senior Apulian nobles that Roger Borsa proved incapable of putting down on his own. In 1091 the duke of Apulia was forced to ask for military assistance from his uncle Roger and, surprisingly, from Bohemond. In May 1091 Borsa led a siege of the long-rebellious city of Cosenza that lasted for almost two months, until June or July of that year. Malaterra's detailed description of the siege of Cosenza refers to Roger of Sicily answering his nephew's call to arms by bringing with him a strong force of knights that included 'many thousand Saracens from every part of Sicily'.[21] The employment of Muslim troops had been a common, although controversial, Norman strategy since the earlier years of the Norman expansion into Sicily in the 1060s–70s.[22] By the early 1090s Malaterra acknowledges that the Muslim soldiers in the Norman army in Sicily – both stipendiary and owing service – were reckoned in their thousands and that they constituted the majority.[23] Following the conquest of the island in 1091, many Muslims carried on fighting under the Hautevilles, both as personal bodyguards and as infantrymen and archers.[24] Yet unsurprisingly, their presence is only attested in the sources when they were fighting outside Sicily, as, for example, during the sieges of Salerno in 1076, of Cosenza in 1091, of Castrovillari in 1094 and of Amalfi in 1096.

Following two months of relentless blockade of their city from all sides, the citizens of Cosenza threw open their gates to Borsa after 'they were genuinely reconciled to the duke's grace'. But Malaterra leaves no doubt as to the key role played by Roger of Sicily in the course of the siege: '[Roger Borsa] having acquired the city through the advice and valour [*strenuitas*] of his uncle.' Roger of Sicily also received half of the city of Cosenza as a reward for his services to the duke of Apulia. In the same year the Apulian town of Oria – between Taranto and Brindisi – revolted against Bohemond, and its citizens routed the besieging army led by the count, even managing to capture its standards and baggage.[25]

The political turmoil in southern Italy prompted, once again, Pope Urban's involvement in the affairs of the duchy of Apulia. We find him in the presence of Bohemond at Anglona, some 90km southwest of Taranto, on 20 November 1092, before heading to Taranto for the Christmas celebrations. He was in Salerno in January 1093 and then in the Apulian town of Troia (to the south of Lucera) in March.[26] In August 1093 Roger Borsa and Bohemond were with Urban at Monte Cassino, where they had asked him to consecrate the monastery of St Mary of St Banzi.[27] Sadly, Urban's attempts to mediate between the different warring parties were in vain; the troubles went on unabated.

The instability in southern Italian politics was once again manifested at the end of 1093, when, following a serious sickness that his doctors were unable to diagnose or treat, rumours of Roger Borsa's death spread like wildfire throughout the duchy. At this point, Malaterra accuses Bohemond of crude opportunism, following his brother's fight for life at Melfi, in Apulia:

> When he [Bohemond] heard, and all too easily believed, the rumour that his brother [Borsa] had just died, he seized the *castra* [in Calabria] which were under his brother's rule, and persuaded them to join in sworn alliance with him. He realised that if his brother was really dead, something he professed himself reluctant to accept, they would remain faithful subjects to him, saving their fealty to his brother's legal heirs, and until the latter came of age they would acknowledge him as the land's legitimate ruler as the 'faithful' uncle of these heirs.[28]

In addition, a number of Roger's vassals also revolted at the news of their lord's death, among them William of Grandmesnil, his brother-in-law, who swiftly occupied Rossano. Malaterra's bitter criticism towards the rebels is palpable: 'So because of the powerlessness of his [Borsa's] heirs, everybody showed how great their loyalty was to those heirs by taking away and usurping for themselves what was rightfully the property of the duke.'[29] I should point out that Roger Borsa had married Adela, the daughter of Robert I, count of Flanders, just the year before (1092), and they eventually had three sons: Louis, who died young in August 1094; William, who succeeded Borsa as William II in 1097; and Robert Guiscard, who died young in 1109.

Informed about his brother's medical condition, and feeling threatened by Roger of Sicily's aggressive attitude – Malaterra reports he had marched to Calabria to defend his nephew's interests – Bohemond reneged on his hostile behaviour and hastened to Melfi, where Borsa was lying ill, to restore the lands he had seized and reconcile once again with his younger brother. We know nothing of Bohemond's activities in 1095, although it would seem that he remained on non-bellicose terms with Borsa, being very well aware that he was unable to undermine him because of the protection he enjoyed from his powerful uncle, Roger of Sicily. Fate, however, had different plans for this ambitious young knight, as the closing months of 1095 witnessed the meeting of the Council of Clermont and the preaching of the First Crusade.

Chapter 5

The Crusader – From Italy to the City

For in that same year, on the instructions of Pope Urban, an expedition to Jerusalem was recruited on a massive scale from every land. Bohemond had previously, along with his father Guiscard, invaded Romania, and had always wanted to conquer it for himself. Seeing a great multitude of people travelling through Apulia but lacking a leader, he hastened there, and wishing to be the army's leader and to make them his followers, he placed the badge of this expedition, namely the cross, on his garments. The warlike young men of the whole army, both from the duke's part and the count's, were keen on anything new as is the custom nowadays, and when they saw Bohemond's cross and were summoned by him to follow his example, they eagerly flocked to do so.

[Geoffrey Malaterra, IV. 24.]

A Crusading Model or an Opportunist?

The protection that Roger Borsa derived from his uncle Roger Hauteville in mainland Italy against the ambitions and expansionary activity of his half-brother could explain to a large extent the untenable situation in which Bohemond had found himself in Apulia around the mid-1090s: 'for, as we have said, he [Borsa] used him [Roger Hauteville] like a whip to terrify all those who opposed him'.[1] As we saw in the previous chapter, Bohemond's own authority in Apulia and Calabria was being steadily eroded by the combined forces of Borsa and Roger of Sicily; in 1091 the citizens of Cosenza threw open their gates to Borsa, and in the same year the Apulian town of Oria, between Taranto and Brindisi, revolted against Bohemond. As Shepard aptly put it: 'exposed to both "a whip" in the form of his formidable uncle and to irrepressible dissidence on the part of his own subjects, Bohemond's ambition was likely to be restless and to seize upon an opportunity for advancement elsewhere'.[2] Therefore, the count's eyes would turn to the East once more, in the hope of reaping richer pickings than Apulia or Calabria could ever yield.

Bohemond seems to have paid little heed to the preaching of the First Crusade at Clermont in November 1095. In the summer of the following year he was taking part in the siege of the Campanian city of Amalfi, as the citizens of the city had revolted against Roger Borsa's authority and elected a duke of their own. This was but one in a series of rebellions that had frayed the power of Roger Borsa since his second reconciliation with Bohemond the year before. For that reason, we see the duke leading a grand army of Normans, Lombards and, probably, Arabs from Sicily against the rebels in July and August 1096, accompanied by his uncle and his half-brother Bohemond.[3] Malaterra refers to the siege of Amalfi as a highly organised military operation, which had every potential to lead to the surrender of the city to Borsa and his allies:

> [they besieged the city] on every side, blockading it from the sea with their ships, and carefully arranging the cavalry and infantry along the steep mountains which surrounded it ... The city was so closely pressed that they would, so we think, have certainly captured it had there not occurred an unfortunate event.[4]

The 'unfortunate event' that Malaterra refers to was none other than the coming of the armies of the First Crusade. Pope Urban had planned the departure of the crusade for 15 August 1096, the Feast of the Assumption, but already in the spring of that year a number of armies of peasants and petty nobles had set off for Jerusalem on their own, led by a fiery priest from Picardy called Peter the Hermit. Behind Peter's expeditionary forces followed six large armies from northern France, Lorraine, Flanders, Normandy and Provence; these armies were commanded by some of the leading aristocrats of the time from France or its borders: Godfrey of Bouillon, duke of Lower Lotharingia; Count Hugh of Vermandois, brother of the king of France; Duke Robert of Normandy; Count Robert II of Flanders; Count Stephen of Blois; and Raymond of Saint Gilles, count of Toulouse. Although the Provençal leader, Count Raymond IV of Toulouse, had been consulted by Urban II in 1095–96 and travelled with the Pope's representative, or legate, Adhemar, bishop of Le Puy, there was no overall leader.[5]

Preparations for the expedition were marked by a burst of solar activity and the first good harvest for years – a favourable blessing. This had been preceded by a particular shower of falling stars that was visible in several places in western Europe and throughout Apulia and Calabria on a Tuesday night in April 1095, an astronomical event that acted as a catalyst for the launch of the First Crusade, because 'from that time on, the people of Gaul, and, indeed, of all of Italy too, began to proceed with their arms to the Holy Sepulchre of the Lord, bearing on their right shoulders the sign of the cross'.[6] As the crusader armies set off for the first major stop in their quest to reach Jerusalem, the imperial capital of Constantinople, some of them proceeded via southern Italy and the Italian ports of Bari and Brindisi, and we are told that it was the coming of these armies that disrupted Borsa's siege operation against Amalfi:

> Seeing a great multitude of people [crusaders] travelling through Apulia but lacking a leader, Bohemondhastened there, and wishing to be the army's leader and to make them his followers, he placed the badge of this expedition, namely the cross, on his garments. The warlike young men of the whole army, both from the duke's [Borsa] part and the count's [Roger of Sicily], were keen on anything new as is the custom nowadays, and when they saw Bohemond's cross and were summoned by him to follow his example, they eagerly flocked to do so. Hence they assumed the cross, and immediately bound themselves by a vow to make no further attack on any Christian land until they had reached the land of the pagans. Seeing the greater part of their army desert them in this way, the duke and the count sadly disbanded the expedition; and so the city which had been so weakened as to be close to surrender was saved by this unfortunate occurrence.[7]

Contemporary and later chroniclers, including Malaterra (with his aforementioned comments), Lupus Protospatharius, Romuald of Salerno and Ralph of Caen, make it clear that Bohemond's action in taking the cross and setting off with the rest of the crusaders for Jerusalem was a spontaneous decision explained by his deep religious zeal and his desire for pilgrimage to the Holy Sepulchre.[8] Whether Bohemond was actually planning to follow the crusade long before the summer of 1096, and simply grabbed his chance when the crusaders were passing by from Apulia, we cannot be sure. Nevertheless, there must have been some sort of information about Urban's preaching at Clermont that would have travelled south to Italy in the spring of 1096 for, as Yewdale believes, it is unthinkable that the Pope should have neglected to inform Roger and Bohemond, his own vassals, with whom he had enjoyed rather close personal relations in the last few years.[9] Then, there is the opinion of Anna Komnena about Bohemond's deeper motives in joining the First Crusade, which – unsurprisingly – paints him in the darkest colours possible, as a greedy, cunning and treacherous man, who simply bears an old grudge against Alexios Komnenos:

> ... the simpler-minded [crusaders] were urged on by the real desire of worshipping at our Lord's Sepulchre, and visiting the sacred places;

but the more astute, especially men like Bohemond and those of like mind, had another secret reason, namely, the hope that while on their travels they might by some means be able to seize the capital itself, looking upon this as a kind of corollary. And Bohemond disturbed the minds of many nobler men by thus cherishing his old grudge against the Emperor.[10]

Finally, it is worth quoting William of Malmesbury's view on Bohemond's motives in taking the cross, one that casts a more pragmatic light into the Norman's ambitions in the late summer of 1096:

His [Urban II's] more secret intention was not so well known; this was, by Bohemond's advice, to excite almost the whole of Europe to undertake an expedition into Asia; that in such a general commotion of all countries, auxiliaries might easily be engaged, by whose means both Urban might obtain Rome, and Bohemond, Illyria and Macedonia. For Guiscard, his father, had conquered those countries from Alexios, and also all the territory extending from Dyrrachium to Thessaloniki; wherefore Bohemond claimed them as his due, since he obtained not the inheritance of Apulia, which his father had given to his younger son, Roger.[11]

Assessing the exact number of Bohemond's followers for the First Crusade can be very problematic for modern historians;[12] Albert of Aachen, who was a contemporary of the First Crusade and wrote his account in Germany on the basis of eye-witness reports, recounts about ten thousand cavalry and 'very many troops of infantry', which is surely a greatly exaggerated figure.[13] Lupus Protospatharius' 'more than 500 knights' reads more realistically, and this number confirms that the Italo-Norman contingent was, indeed, one of the smallest in the crusading army.[14] Additionally, we have a list of the counts who followed Bohemond on his expedition, namely his nephew Tancred, Richard of Principate and his brother Rainulf, Humphrey of Montescaglioso, and nine others.[15] What is very important in this case is the presence of Richard and Humphrey, the two most powerful and influential Apulian magnates after Roger Borsa himself, even if it is almost impossible to estimate the size of their contingents. Finally, another key point about the Italo-Norman knights and lords who took the Cross that late summer of 1096 was the almost complete absence of names related to the courts of Roger Borsa and Roger of Sicily; Russo's research has discovered that 'Italian' recruitment seems to have taken place partly within the extended Hauteville family network, with particular reference to the 'second-rate' members of families established in Campania and the Basilicata region of Apulia, areas that were outside Bohemond's territorial possessions.[16]

Sadly, we know next to nothing of Bohemond's preparations before setting off for the Holy Land. Yewdale has indicated the existence of a document dated August 1096 in which Bohemond extended to Guidelmus Flammengus, governor of Bari, full right to sell or otherwise dispose 'de cuncta hereditate que michi in eadem civitate mea Baro pertinet [of all my inheritance present in the same city of Bari]', apparently in preparation for embarking on the crusade.[17] Bohemond would probably have installed trusted governors in all the major cities and towns of his Italian principality, although we have no evidence of a regent being appointed before his departure.

Modelling Bohemond's March to Constantinople

The plan of every Latin army on the First Crusade was to meet at Constantinople, no matter when they departed or where they started from or how closely they were connected to Pope Urban. Each aimed for Constantinople as the major rallying point to recuperate, receive instructions and 'refuel' before entering hostile territory in western Anatolia. The diverse armies which made up the First Crusade took two distinct routes to Constantinople;[18] the northeastern French army of Godfrey of Bouillon took the overland route through the Balkans, advancing via Strasburg and Vienna, before crossing into Byzantine territory south of the Danube at Singidunum (modern Belgrade), and then down the valley of the Morava to Naissus (modern Niš), Sardica (modern Sofia), Philippopolis (modern Plovdiv), and Adrianople (modern Edirne); this was one of the four main arterial military roads that linked Constantinople with the northern Balkans, and it was complemented by a number of spurs to east and west, giving access to the south Danube plain, the Haimos mountains and the Black Sea coastal plain. Nevertheless, the vast majority of the Latin armies chose the sea crossing of the Adriatic from the Italian ports of Bari and Brindisi, disembarking at the Illyrian port of Dyrrachium before following the Via Egnatia; I explained the strategic importance of the Egnatia for the Norman invasion of the Greek mainland in 1082, hence it will suffice here to simply remind readers that the aforementioned military road was the main artery connecting the imperial capital with Thessaloniki, the empire's second largest city, and Dyrrachium, the biggest imperial port in the southern Adriatic Sea.

In view of the Norman invasions of the Balkan territories of the Byzantine Empire in 1081 and 1084, Bohemond must have anticipated that his contingent would not receive a warm welcome from the imperial units stationed at Dyrrachium and in Greece. Yewdale assumed that the Norman leader would have dispatched legates to Alexios, informing him of his plans and assuring him of their friendly character, long before he embarked on the campaign, a course of action that I find perfectly plausible, although there is no shred of evidence to confirm it.[19] Indeed, how else can Bohemond's unhindered landing on the Illyrian coast, without any resistance offered by the imperial forces in the region, be explained?: 'All of these [Norman counts] crossed over in the service of Bohemond and landed at Bulgaria [Byzantine Illyria] where they found an abundance of grain and wine and all kinds of food for the body.'[20] At the same time Anna Komnena reports that the emperor tried to protect his own subjects by sending orders to the local commanders of the ground and naval forces to be vigilant of the actions of the crusaders, to establish strong garrisons at key points along their route, and to dispatch mobile forces to observe and follow their line of march.[21]

Still, the Norman leader took some precautions to ensure the unopposed landing of his contingent on the opposite coast of the Adriatic, thus arranging for his army to disembark at different points along the Gulf of Avlona, before meeting up on All Saints' Day, 1 November, at the port city of Avlona.[22] Almost certainly he would have dispatched a reconnaissance unit to Avlona with orders to await the arrival of the main contingent, as his father had done fifteen years earlier. Then their route took them to 'Andrinopolis' (Greek: *Dryinoupolis*),[23] modern Gjirokastër (Greek: *Αργυρόκαστρο*) in southern Albania, a city situated in a valley between the Gjerë mountain range and the river Drino (Albanian: *Drino*, Greek: *Δρίνος*), the western tributary of the river Vjosë (Aoös) and one of the main invasion routes that cut through the Illyrian mountain ranges and led to Lake Ohrid and the Via Egnatia.

Because Bohemond had been campaigning in the Balkans for three years under his father between 1081 and 1083, he knew very well the topography and geography of the southern Balkans, including the main arterial roads that led eastwards towards Thessaloniki and the capital, Constantinople. In 1082 he had fought through the country between the western Macedonian city of Kastoria and the Epirotic city of Ioannina, and he would have been familiar with all the invasion routes that could funnel his army from the Illyrian coast to the interior of Greece. Therefore, he chose to march his army southeastwards through the valley of the rivers Drino and Vjosë, which would have been extremely fertile around that period of the year as November came at the end of harvest. Indeed, the author of the *Gesta Francorum* attests to the fertility of the region between Lake Ohrid and the Normans' first major stop in Greece, the city of Kastoria on the Egnatia, which they reached just in time to celebrate Christmas.[24] This source is adamant about Bohemond's desire to march on friendly terms with the local authorities and the people, hence avoiding any ravaging of the land and looting of foodstuffs; rather, he encouraged his troops 'to be good and to be humble and not to ravage this land which belonged to Christians and to take only that which they needed to nourish themselves'.

From Kastoria in western Macedonia the Norman army would have marched north towards the town of Florina to pick up the Via Egnatia and proceed to Edessa and Thessaloniki. However, the author of the *Gesta Francorum* reports that after their departure from Kastoria there were some scuffles with the local population regarding the provisioning of the Norman army, allegedly after the locals refused to sell provisions to Bohemond's men because 'they were very frightened of us, for they refused to see us as pilgrims but as men come to devastate their land and to kill them'. Regardless of whether this allegation is true or not, there would undoubtedly have been mounting suspicion among the locals about the true intentions of the Normans, fanned by grim memories of Bohemond's campaign in Greece fifteen years before. The Normans grabbed what they wanted anyway, and they went on to sack a town of heretics, probably Manichaeans, in the area around modern Bitola, to the north of Florina in northern Macedonia; the author of the *Gesta Francorum* describes the ferocity and sheer brutality of the siege of the town: 'We attacked it from all sides and very soon it came under our control, and lighting a fire we burned the town along with its inhabitants.'[25]

Before reaching Thessaloniki, Bohemond's army had to overcome another obstacle: crossing the river Vardar (Greek: Αξιός), the longest river in north Macedonia. Attempting to cross one of the biggest rivers in the southern Balkans would have been a difficult task for a medieval army in mid-summer, when the river's water level drops significantly, let alone in the middle of February, which is when the Norman army reached the banks of the Vardar. And there was an additional danger lurking on the opposite bank:

> The flooding river blocked their advance and the opposite bank, filled with threatening enemies, frightened many [of the Latins]. There

seemed to be a fear that those who crossed first would have the Turkopoles in front of them and those who delayed would have the Turkopoles behind them.[26]

Eventually, it was Bohemond's nephew Tancred who emerged as the hero of the day – or at least, this is how he has been portrayed by the author of the *Gesta Francorum* and by Ralph of Caen, the author of the *Gesta Tancredi* ['The Deeds of Tancred'], whose primary interest is – as the title implies – Tancred's career. The latter source provides the best description we have about the first clash between the Norman crusaders and troops in the service of the Byzantine emperor, which took place on Ash Wednesday, 18 February 1097; the author clearly describes the showers of arrows released from a distance by the Turkopole and Patzinak horse-archers and, crucially, Tancred's battlefield reaction to this extraordinary tactic, which is why it is worth quoting in full:

> The Greeks [Turkopoles and Patzinaks] therefore came out from their hiding places and shot a terrible flight of arrows. While the arrows flew they had the appearance of a cloud, when they fell it seemed like hail, and where they stood, they seemed like a field of grain. But the Greeks, despite having launched many attacks, did not reach the Franks. Tancred, who was familiar with every manner of fighting, did not resist them quickly, rapidly, or all at once, but rather step by step. When an arrow struck about a spear's throw away he headed towards it so that the others might fall behind his back. Tancred was well versed in this type of battle from many contests and therefore recognised how to gain victory. So, he held back the unbridled spirits of his men through his prudence.[27]

When the Norman soldiers managed to capture some of the attacking Turkopoles and Patzinaks and brought them to Bohemond, to his furious and resentful questions as to why they had attacked his army they could only answer that they were simply obeying orders from the emperor.[28] It seems more likely that this attack was provoked by Norman plundering of the region, rather than a change in the emperor's attitude towards Bohemond and his men. Finally, Alexios dispatched an imperial *kouropalates*, a high-ranking title conferred on members of the imperial family and – since the eleventh century – to high-ranking generals outside the imperial family, to safely escort Bohemond and his army to Constantinople.[29]

Meeting the Emperor in the City

Bohemond entered Constantinople on 10 April 1097, but he was not the first of the crusade leaders to arrive at the lavish 'gathering' that Alexios had set up in his magnificent capital. Hugh of Vermandois had been one of the first to arrive in Constantinople, sometime at the end of October 1096, but not before having been shipwrecked on the Epirotic coast after his fleet was caught up in a great storm during the crossing of the Adriatic. Godfrey of Bouillon, along with his brother Baldwin, was reported to have arrived around the same time in the early winter of 1096. Robert of Flanders had set off from the Apulian ports in December, while Stephen of Blois and Robert of Normandy, who were travelling together, must have set out later than the others, for they were only ready to cross from Italy in early April 1097. Raymond of Toulouse's army column was not far behind Bohemond's, probably around a few days away.

The armies themselves were excluded from the city, which made sense for its protection, and they were amply provisioned outside the walls; the troops were allowed inside only in small groups. Yet Emperor Alexios had two main concerns regarding the influx of so numerous and diverse armies to his capital; although he was certainly deeply worried that the arrival of the crusaders would put a huge strain on his provisioning arrangements, his cardinal consideration was to avoid the more pertinent danger of an attack on his capital – but not in the form of a potential conquest of the capital by the Latin armies. Alexios was much more fearful of the social turmoil that might be stirred up within the city by political factions hostile to the Komnenoi regime; he was acutely aware that there were old contenders to worry about because as recently as 1094 he had survived major plots by the sons of Romanus IV Diogenes. For that reason he dispatched personal messages that underlined the lavish reception the crusade leaders were to receive in the capital, emphasising his friendship, his generosity, and even his fatherly solicitude for the participants on the First Crusade in general, before throwing everything into bedazzling them with his hospitality and lavish gifts.[30]

On the other hand, the emperor was cautious enough to monitor the activity of the Latin leaders in great detail while they were marching through the Balkans, to prevent contingents linking up before they reached Constantinople.[31] He also sought to invite the various leaders to march ahead of their armies and to meet with him and discuss 'with them privately about his wishes, and made use of the more reasonable ones as intermediaries with the more recalcitrant'. Hugh of Vermandois and

Bohemond were brought swiftly to the capital, while others such as Raymond of Toulouse and Godfrey of Bouillon appeared more reluctant to march ahead of their armies – they were fully aware that it was the size of their contingents that gave them negotiating power with the Byzantine emperor and with the rest of the crusade leaders.

Nevertheless, things did not go as planned for Alexios in his dealings with some of the Latins. Because Godfrey's army was by far the largest of the lot, it presented grave problems for the Byzantine authorities. The duke had been refusing to obey the emperor's summonses to his palace, probably because he had been warned against trusting Alexios; in fact, Anna asserts that 'a false rumour reached the others that the Counts had been thrown into prison by the Emperor', which could very well have been circulated by the political factions hostile to the Komnenoi within the capital. As a combination of charm and cajolery on the part of Alexios had failed to convince the duke of their aligned interests, the emperor became increasingly hostile. A few days after Christmas 1096, Godfrey did agree to move his troops to a less threatening position further from the city and along the shores of the Bosphorus, but not before the emperor had to dispatch an armed contingent with orders to use force to move Godfrey and his men, while restricting supplies flowing to their camp and limiting their access to markets. Eventually, it was Alexios' promise to offer his son and heir John as a hostage in a gesture of good-will that pacified Godfrey and his men, thus agreeing to be transported across the Bosphorus to join up with the other knights at the designated holding camp near Kibotos.

Finally, just like every other crusade leader before and after him, Godfrey had to swear an oath of fealty to Alexios Komnenos. Although the exact terms of it remain unclear, Anna is explicit that 'the oath which was required of him [Godfrey], namely, that whatever towns, countries or forts he managed to take which had formerly belonged to the Roman Empire, he would deliver up to the Governor expressly sent by the Emperor for this purpose'.[32] The lands that Godfrey and the rest of the crusaders had to return to the empire included all of Anatolia as far as Antioch and perhaps the lands beyond, although it did make clear that this was a reciprocal agreement under which Alexios had to fulfil his obligation to protect and provision the Latin armies, as a good lord ought to do. This particular ceremony of 'adoption' was well understood on both sides; the Byzantine emperors often established a spiritual and paternal relationship with foreign magnates, while the oath of fealty was a key element in the lord-vassal social structure that was well established in western Europe by the time of the First Crusade.[33]

Meanwhile, Bohemond's arrival in the imperial capital again stirred up Anna's virulent attacks against the Norman on account of his motives for joining the crusade:

> ... the rest of the Counts, and especially Bohemond, who cherished an old grudge against the Emperor, were seeking an opportunity of taking their vengeance on him ... The other Counts agreed to Bohemond's plan, and in their dreams of capturing the capital had come to the same decision (which I have often mentioned already) that while in appearance making the journey to Jerusalem, in reality their object was to dethrone the Emperor and to capture the capital.[34]

Yet despite Anna's vitriolic comments about the Norman, it is likely that Alexios would have found in Bohemond someone he could work with. This was probably because the count knew and spoke Greek,[35] although with a distinct 'barbarian accent', and was used to the customs, manners and machinations characteristic of the East. First of all, however, both had to overcome the mutual suspicions and mistrust imbued in them since their previous encounter in the Balkans fifteen years before. And what better way to break the ice than a lavish reception and ceremonial dinner at the imperial palace!

A good sense of humour is always necessary in this kind of situation, as we read in the *Alexiad*:[36] 'So when Bohemond entered, he [Alexios] smiled at him cheerfully and asked him about his journey and where he had left the Counts. All these things Bohemond explained clearly as he thought best, and then the Emperor joked and reminded him of his former daring deeds at Dyrrachium and his former enmity,' only to receive the Norman's firm reply that 'though I was certainly your adversary and enemy at that time, yet now I come of my own free will as a friend of your Majesty'. Afterwards, when dinner was served, Alexios offered Bohemond two plates of food, one prepared by his cooks in a typical Byzantine style, and one left uncooked so that Bohemond's own cook could prepare it for him. The emperor was not 'wrong in his surmise. For that dreadful Bohemond not only refrained from tasting the viands at all, or even touching them with the tips of his fingers, but pushed them all away at once.' Finally, after Alexios asked Bohemond to take the customary oath of fealty like the rest of the Latin leaders, and the Norman 'readily accepted', the emperor – in a typical Byzantine fashion that had been tried and tested for centuries –

showered Bohemond with gifts and gold, in a scene that is more emblematical than historical:

> Then the Emperor selected a room in the palace and had the floor strewn with every kind of riches, and so filled the chamber with garments and stamped gold and silver, and other materials of lesser value, that one could not even walk because of their quantity ... Bohemond was amazed at the sight and exclaimed 'If all these treasures were mine, I should have made myself master of many countries!' and the attendant replied, 'the Emperor makes you a present of all these riches to-day'. Bohemond was overjoyed ... but when these treasures were brought to him, he who had admired them before had changed his mind and said 'Never did I imagine that the Emperor would inflict such dishonour on me. Take them away and give them back to him who sent them.' But the Emperor, knowing the Latins' characteristic fickleness, quoted the popular proverb, 'Let bad things return to their own master.' When Bohemond heard of this and saw the porters carefully packing the presents up again, he changed his mind ... For by nature the man was a rogue and ready for any eventualities; in roguery and courage he was far superior to all the Latins who came through then, as he was inferior to them in forces and money ... For he was sad in mind as he had left his country a landless man, ostensibly to worship at the Holy Sepulchre, but in reality with the intent of gaining a kingdom for himself.

After Bohemond had accepted the imperial gifts, he got down to the serious business of negotiating with the emperor. Sadly, exactly what the Norman requested, or what Alexios offered, remains unclear, because no account survives by a person who attended the negotiations. Nevertheless, we have two accounts, one Greek and one Latin, of what may have happened behind closed doors. The two matters both accounts seem to agree on is that the negotiations were secretive and that the two men struck some sort of deal about the future regime of Anatolia.[37] According to Anna: 'Bohemond demanded the office of Great Domestic of the East, for he was trying to "out-Cretan a Cretan". For the Emperor feared that if he gained power he would make the other Counts his captives and bring them round afterwards to doing whatever he wished.' The Norman must have aimed high in his negotiations, perhaps because he knew that the highest office of the land armies of the empire presumably still lay vacant following the disgrace of Adrian Komnenos, the military's previous Domestic.[38] Yet he was soon brought down to earth by Alexios who

Archangel Michael and Joshua, Church of St George Diasorites, Naxos island, southern Aegean Sea. This is a rare surviving example of a cross-in-square type of Byzantine church built and decorated in the second half of the eleventh century (probably in the early Komnenian period).

(**Left**) St George and St Demetrius, Church of St Anargyroi, Kastoria, western Macedonia, *c*.1160–80, depicted as typical mid-twelfth-century Byzantine cavalry officers. (**Right**) Joshua, monastery of St Lucas in Veotea, central Greece, twelfth century, depicted as a Byzantine infantry soldier.

Battle scene between units of Byzantine and Arab cavalry. Image from an illuminated manuscript, the 'Madrid Skylitzes', twelfth century.

Bohemond and Patriarch Daimbert of Pisa on their way to the Holy Land. Image from the thirteenth-century edition of *Histoire de l'Outremer*.

Two battle scenes depicting Norman soldiers, Church of St Nicolas in Bari, eleventh century.
(© Raffaele D'Amato)

Mount Demirkazik (3,756m) in the Aladaglar mountains, Niğde Province, Turkey, part of the formidable Taurus mountains separating Anatolia from Upper Mesopotamia and Syria.

Aerial view of the castle of St George in Kephalonia, Ionian Sea, which was built by the Byzantines in the eleventh century.

The Via Egnatia in the river valley of the Skhumbi, resurfaced by the Italian military in 1940.
(© *Walter Wilmot*)

The medieval walls of Dyrrachium (modern Durrës).

The river Vjosë upstream from Tepelenë, Albania.

(**Below**) The tower of Bohemond in the castle of Ioannina. (© *Michael Vakaros*)

(**Above left**)
The mausoleum of Bohemond in Canosa di Puglia.

(**Above right**)
Castle of St Marco Argentano.

(**Left**) Roman caltrops.

The liberation of Bohemond from his captivity by the Danishmendits. Image from the illuminated manuscript, Maître du Roman de Fauvel, 'Libération de Bohémond', 'Li rommans de Godefroy de Buillon et de Salehadin et de tous lez autres roys qui ont esté outre mer jusques a saint Loys qui darrenierem' (BnF 22495).

The Lefke Gate of Nicaea's city walls.

refused to grant his demand, apparently suspecting Bohemond's intentions, although he tried to allay his fears and flattered him by saying that 'the time for that has not come yet; but by your energy and reputation and above all by your fidelity it will come ere long'.[39]

In contrast, the author of the *Gesta Francorum* argued that Alexios made a very specific proposal to Bohemond: 'he said to him that if he freely swore loyalty to him, he would give him land beyond Antioch, the breadth of which would take fifteen days to cover and the width of which would take eight days to cover'.[40] Whatever the case, there is no doubt that the emperor offered land and money to Bohemond and probably a high office in the armies that marched through Anatolia, an offer that the Norman deemed too good to dismiss, hence he decided to become – perhaps – the most loyal 'adopted son' of Alexios in the Latin armies of the First Crusade.

Unsurprisingly, the agreement between Alexios and Bohemond found many critics. Bohemond's nephew Tancred had already tried to slip away from the capital in an attempt to avoid taking the oath of fealty to the emperor. According to Tancred's biographer, Ralph of Caen: 'Bohemond, who was captivated by the superficial sweetness of these words, did not sense the poison hidden below the surface. Furthermore, the promise of the riches of Constantinople, for which he had long shed blood on land and sea, led him astray.'[41] Later on, he added:

> What could he [Tancred] work out? Should he fight? But the enemy was stronger. Should he seek an accommodation? But the enemy was inexorable. Should he retreat? But the sea blocked his path. Seeing that the leaders of the Franks had been corrupted by gifts and that Bohemond similarly had been ensnared, he struggled with himself and turned these matters over in his heart.[42]

At about the same time Raymond of Saint Gilles, count of Toulouse, finally arrived at Constantinople. He was also dismayed by the oath that the rest of the crusade leaders were forced to take, and concerned about Bohemond's role in this process. When Alexios demanded an oath from him, piling on the pressure through Bohemond as well as his palace officials, Raymond replied that 'he had not taken the Cross to pay allegiance to another lord or to be in the service of any other than the One for whom he had abandoned his native land and his paternal goods. He would, however, entrust himself, his followers, and his effects to the Emperor if he would journey to Jerusalem with the army.'[43] Hence, we see the count throwing the ball back into the emperor's court, only to receive a firm response from

Alexios that emphasised the dangers lurking on the empire's borders from other neighbouring peoples: 'the Germans, Hungarians, Kumans, and other fierce people would plunder his empire if he undertook the march with the pilgrims'.

Eventually, Anna describes Alexios as effectively making Raymond his right-hand man in the crusade, telling him to be ever vigilant in the case of Bohemond:

> he [Alexios] often sent for Isangeles [Raymond of Saint Gilles] and explained to him more clearly what he suspected would happen to the Latins on their journey, and he also laid bare to him the suspicions he had of the Franks' intention. He often repeated these things to Isangeles and opened, so to say, the doors of his soul to him and, after stating everything clearly, he enjoined him to be ever on the watch against Bohemond's wickedness and if the latter tried to break his oath to check him and by all possible means frustrate his plans. Isangeles replied to the Emperor, 'Bohemond has acquired perjury and treachery as a species of ancestral heritage, and it would be a miracle if he kept his oath. However, I will endeavour as far as in me lies always to carry out your orders.'[44]

In her *Alexiad*, Anna wished to portray her father as a master diplomat, a brilliant negotiator and tactician who was fully aware of Bohemond's every trick, and therefore he 'enlisted' Raymond to act as his 'watch-dog' over the Norman leader during the course of the First Crusade. Whether this is true or not, or whether Bohemond did manage to deceive Alexios into thinking that he had actually been bribed into becoming 'his man' in the crusade, it is impossible to know with certainty. Some decades ago Shepard suggested an appealing approach to the issue of Alexios' relationship with Bohemond.[45] He contended that Anna paints a rather misleading picture of their relationship, to the point where Alexios was, in fact, led to suppose that he had bought Bohemond, at least for the duration of the crusade, arguing that Alexios' treatment of the Latin leaders bears the hallmark of the 'divide-and-rule' tactics which he had successfully applied to the Patzinaks and Kumans for the past decade or so.

There is little doubt that, during the crusaders' stay in the imperial capital, the emperor benefited from treating Bohemond as 'an effective collaborator and apologist', as Shepard puts it, for he had reason to feel apprehensive about the Normans from southern Italy 'paying a visit' to his capital. On the other hand, he explains that Bohemond sought close ties with Alexios in order to gain greater prominence and influence among the crusade leaders and, crucially, to ensure for himself a position in the East. This arrangement worked well for both parties so long as the crusading host was in the vicinity of Constantinople, and they both needed each other. But the arrangement faltered once the crusaders marched into Anatolia and provisioning the army from Constantinople became all the more difficult. Shepard saw that Bohemond's 'special relationship' with the emperor's representative in the crusade, Tatikios, was becoming irrelevant the further east the Latins marched, to the point where Bohemond began to unravel it in the opening days of February 1098. We will see that he eventually came out against the Byzantine emperor in May 1098, when he suggested that the crusaders should disregard Alexios' territorial rights in the region of Antioch.

Chapter 6

The Crusader – Conquering Antioch

Then the Turks, enemies of God and of holy Christianity, who were inside guarding the city of Antioch, heard that lord Bohemond and the count of Flanders were not among the besiegers, and so they came out of the city and boldly began to battle with our men, choosing to attack that part of the siege which was the weakest. Knowing well that the most valiant warriors were gone, they decided to come against us on a Tuesday and injure us.

[*The deeds of the Franks*, p. 55]

From Constantinople to Nicaea

The Latin armies of the First Crusade had to overcome a number of enemies on their way to the Holy Sepulchre, the first of which were the armies of the Seljukid Sultanate of Rum that had been established in northwest Asia Minor at the end of the 1070s, following the internecine wars in the Byzantine Empire between 1077 and 1081. Certainly by the time of Alexios Komnenos' coup d'état in April 1081, Suleiman ibn Qutlumush had occupied Nicaea and Nicomedia and proclaimed himself sultan. Meanwhile other parts of Asia Minor had become subject to new Turkic lords: the Danishmends in Sebasteia (Sivas), Kaisarea (Kayseri) and Amaseia (Amasya); the Mengucheks in Keltzene, Kamacha and Tephrike (Divrigi) on the upper Euphrates; and the Saltuqs in Theodosioupolis (Erzurum). Of these, the emirate of the Danishmends was the strongest, and interchanging rivalry and unity between the Seljuk sultans of Rum and the Danishmends characterised the internal politics of Turkish-dominated Asia Minor from the 1080s until the 1170s.[1]

By the closing decade of the century the Byzantines still held the Mediterranean coastline of Asia Minor, from the Propontis to the river Maeander (modern Büyük Menderes river) that flows to the Aegean Sea close to Miletus. Undoubtedly, Alexios' foreign policy in the East was dominated by the issue of the expanding Seljuk state in Bithynia, and the main strategic goal for the first fifteen years of his reign was to push back the borders between the two states that had been set on the river Drakon by a treaty on 17 June 1081. Following Suleiman ibn Qutlumush's death in battle against the Great Seljuk Sultan Malik Shah's brother Tutush near Aleppo in May/June 1086, Malik Shah proposed an alliance with Alexios, to be cemented by a marriage between the emperor's daughter and Malik Shah's son Barkyaruq; the marriage, however, was never concluded.

In 1092, and with the alliance between Alexios and Malik Shah still in force, the emperor launched an attack against Nicaea to help the army of Malik Shah's *amir* Buzan then besieging the city, while the Byzantine general Manuel Boutoumites destroyed the Nicaean fleet near Kios on the Bithynian coast. By the end of 1092 Suleiman ibn Qutlumush's successor, the former governor of Nicaea Abu al-Qasim, was forced to sign a peace treaty in Constantinople. Yet following Malik Shah's sudden death on 19 November 1092, and the internecine struggle that raged between the new sultan, Barkyaruq, and his uncle Tutush, Suleiman's son Kilij Arslan I (ruled 1092–1107) grabbed power in Nicaea.[2] Hence, on the eve of the coming of the First Crusade, the most the Byzantines had achieved in Asia Minor between 1081 and 1096 was the temporary halting of Turkish incursions into northwest Anatolia.

The first target of the Latin armies after their departure from Constantinople would have been the city of Nicaea, which lay on the path of a major Roman military route that cut through Asia Minor.[3] That route left from Chrysoupolis or Skoutàrion (modern Üsküdar), a district on the Anatolian shore of the Bosphorus right opposite Constantinople, and it went south via Nicomedia (modern İzmit) and Nicaea (modern İznik) to the major imperial military base at Malagina (Greek: Μαλάγινα) in the valley of the Sangarius river in northern Bithynia, and thence to the key junction city of Doryleum (Greek: Δορύλαιον), some 10km southwest of modern Eskişehir. Here the road split: the southwesterly branch went via Kotyaion (modern Kütahya), and the southeasterly branch via Amorion (Greek: Ἀμόριον), down to Akroinon (modern Afyonkarahisar), and from there southeast to Ikonion (modern Konya). A second military route diverged to the east at Doryleum, heading along the valley of the Tembris river (modern Porsuk Çayı) and on to the north of Charsianon Kastron and across to Bathys Ryax and Sebasteia, and from there it split, leading to Kaisarea in a southwesterly direction, and to Melitene (modern Malatya) in a southeasterly one.

As the crusaders had been arriving outside the city of Nicaea in a piecemeal fashion since 6 May, the defenders of the city were able to dispatch urgent letters to Kilij Arslan pleading for help. Since the beginning of the year, the latter had been preoccupied in the East countering the competing interests of the Great Seljuk Sultan Barkyaruq and the Danishmends in and around the area of Melitene, as he believed he had thwarted the threat from the Christians after massacring the armies of Peter the Hermit in Bithynia (at Xerigordos) in October 1096. As Kilij Arslan hastened westwards to deal with this new threat to his dominions, the Latins were struggling to impose an effective blockade of the city; Bohemond and the Normans took up a position along the north wall of the city, with Robert of Flanders and Godfrey to the east, while the south gate was left for Raymond of Toulouse, who was the last to arrive from Constantinople.[4]

Another force dispatched to take part in the siege was a unit of Byzantine troops under the command of Tatikios, a highly skilled and experienced army officer of Turkic origin, who had become one of the emperor's most trusted generals and a member of his personal entourage.[5] He first appears in the sources as a scout during Alexios' campaign against the rebel general Nicephorus Basilakes around 1078 and, following the Komnenian military coup, he earned the important title of *grand primikerius*. During the campaign against the Normans that culminated at the Battle of Dyrrachium, Tatikios commanded the unit of two thousand Turkopoles that was dispatched to reconnoitre Robert Guiscard's camp upon the arrival of the Byzantine army in the vicinity of the city, and was defeated by a contingent of Norman troops. Between 1086 and 1095 he appears repeatedly, fighting the Patzinaks in the Balkans and the Turks who were expanding around Nicaea. Therefore, Tatikios was not only Alexios' representative with the armies of the First Crusade, but he and his soldiers were also familiar both with the fighting tactics of the Turks of Anatolia, and with the topography and military routes that led to the interior of Asia Minor.

The siege of Nicaea began on 14 May 1097 and lasted for about five weeks, both because of the crusaders' difficulty in organising an efficient blockade of the city and of the challenge its fortifications presented. Nicaea's walls were probably a little over 30ft (9m) high, and the towers (of which there were more than one hundred) were about twice that height, while a moat also ran around the perimeter of the city.[6] On top of that, almost the entire western side of the city's fortifications – some 40km long – was adjacent to the Ascanian Lake, thus making the need for a naval contingent almost inevitable. Yet even at this early stage of the Latin march into Anatolia, the problem of supplying the armies was already becoming acute, and we can see for the first time the significant role played by Bohemond in the campaign, since he was the leader who managed to negotiate sufficient supplies to be sent to Nicomedia, just 20km northeast of Nicaea.

Kilij Arslan's swift return to his capital on 14 May, the day the siege proper began, precipitated the first major pitched battle of the First Crusade between the Latin armies and the Turks of Anatolia. According to the account by Raymond of Aguilers, the Turkish attack on the crusaders was two-pronged, with one body of troops directing its assault against the armies of Robert of Flanders and Godfrey of Bouillon camped outside the eastern gate of the city, while the other body would manoeuvre and try to enter the city through the south gate, which had been left unguarded as Raymond of Saint Gilles and his men had yet to pitch their camp after arriving from Constantinople. Unsurprisingly, this account, which was written by a chronicler who was a chaplain with Raymond's army, hands over to the Provençals the key tactical role of defeating the Turks, as they are reported to have fought off the southern attack, thereby enabling the Germans to fight off the other force.[7]

Albert of Aachen, a German canon living in or around the city of Aachen on the Rhineland, who wrote a history of the First Crusade sometime in the second quarter of the twelfth century on the basis of accounts from returned crusaders, gives a much more plausible version of events. He points out that Kilij Arslan was aware of the fact that the south gate of the city was left unguarded because the Provençals were still a few days' march away, while the Latins reacted to the sultan's arrival by dispatching riders to find Raymond and urge him to speed up his march and come to their aid. Hence, Albert's account confirms Raymond of Aguiler's story that the Provencals had just arrived to take part in the siege of Nicaea when the body of Turks attacked them:

> About ten thousand of them, all archers, led the way in the first line down into the valley of Nicaea, carrying in their hands bows of horn and bone fully drawn for shooting, and all of them were mounted on horses which were very swift of movement and very skilled in warfare. Thus Suleyman and his men descended, striving to burst in with the charge through the gate of the town, which was guarded by Count Raymond blockading it. But they were repulsed strongly and overcome by this same count and by Baldwin the count's brother.[8]

According to Albert's account, while the Provencals were receiving the full brunt of the enemy attack, the rest of the Latin leaders rushed to their aid, with Godfrey's Lotharingians and Bohemond's Italo-Normans delivering the crushing blow that forced the Turks to retreat back to the mountains around Nicaea. The account significantly enhances the chivalric prowess of both leaders:

> Duke Godfrey and Bohemond did not curb their horses but let them have their heads and flew through the midst of the enemy, piercing some with lances, unsaddling others, and all the while urging on their allies, encouraging them with exhortations to slaughter the enemy. There was no small clash of spears here, no small ringing of swords and helmets heard in the conflict of war, no small destruction of Turks was wrought by these outstanding young knights and their allies.[9]

As Kilij Arslan's plan of brushing aside the crusader armies to reinforce the defenders of Nicaea failed pitifully because of the stiff resistance put up by the Provençals, the crusaders were now free to besiege the city as the sultan fell back to rally more troops. However, every Latin leader would have been fully aware that, in order to establish an effective blockade of the city, they needed a naval squadron that would block access to the city via the Ascanian Lake. For that reason, a unit of soldiers with small skiffs was dispatched from the capital under Butumites, another of the emperor's trusted officers. On top of that, the crusaders tried to dash the morale of the defenders and spread terror among their ranks by hurling the heads of the dead into the city.

Sadly, most of the accounts we have of the siege of Nicaea are quite brief. Raymond of Aguilers and the anonymous author of the *Gesta Francorum* describe the construction of 'wooden siege engines and wooden towers, by means of which we could knock down the towers on the walls', but this process was interrupted by the Turkish attack.[10] As the siege resumed, following the outcome of the battle, the Provençals managed to undermine a wall-tower by digging and setting fire to its foundations, although the Turks were able to repair the damage during the night. This is also pretty much the same story told by Anna Komnena, although she is quick to praise her father for providing the Latins with the designs for the siege-machines and the boats on the lake.[11]

Albert of Aachen's history of the siege, although chronologically confused, includes many anecdotal stories from the siege of the city, including brief descriptions of attacks against the walls of Nicaea by soldiers from the armies of Godfrey of Bouillon, and then by Raymond's troops, while he also mentions the incident of the attempted flight of Kilij Arslan's wife from the city after she was terrified by the burning of the wooden roof of a wall-tower that caused it to collapse.[12] Finally, once the defenders realised they had no hope of being rescued, they decided to surrender to the imperial unit that was besieging them from the direction of the lake, and most of the sources agree that either Tatikios or Butumites (the sources are not clear as to who exactly brokered the deal) had secretly negotiated the surrender of Nicaea with the leaders of the defenders.[13] According to the knight Anselm of Ribemont, on 19 June (1097) the citizens of the city, making a circuit of the walls and carrying crosses and imperial banners, 'reconciled the city to the Lord, as Greeks and Latins inside and outside the walls shouted together, "Glory to you, Lord!"'.

During the siege Alexios had observed events from a safe distance at the nearby Pelecanum, an encampment at a location between Chalcedon (modern Kadıköy, southeast of Scutarion, on the Marmara Sea) and Nicomedia. The primary reason for his decision to stay put was his plan to equip and monitor a force that would try to recover lost imperial lands south of Smyrna throughout the summer of 1097, before moving inland in an effort to recover a substantial swathe of territory in western Asia Minor.[14] Therefore, it was at Pelecanum that the emperor met most of the Turkish notables after the fall of the city, offering many gifts and titles to those who were willing to serve him as their lord, while also honouring the rest who were sent on their way laden with gifts. The emperor also met most of the crusade leaders, presumably to discuss strategy, although we hear nothing about the details of their discussions. What we do hear about, however, is Alexios' attempt to draw concessions from the remaining group of crusaders who had refused to take the oath of fealty back in Constantinople – namely Bohemond's nephew Tancred who, fuming and raging like a caged lion, addressed the emperor in the following manner, in an obvious effort to preserve his dignity:

> ... after having been freed by my own efforts, your violence brought me back here unwillingly ... Behold, it has come to this that I break the oath of alliance sworn by my relative [Bohemond] ... Let it never happen that I am bound by an oath to anyone who breaks his own word to others. Therefore, if you wish to rule, strive to serve and you can be certain of Tancred's service when you have made clear that the army of Christ is your own. If you are the common leader, in the interest of everyone I will not refuse to serve you.[15]

Into Enemy Country

Unable to plunder Nicaea, or to exact any retribution for the armies of Peter the Hermit that had been massacred by the Seljuks and left to rot on the outskirts of Nicomedia, the vast crusader army that had gathered outside Nicaea began to march south towards Doryleum between 26 and

28 June. It quickly split in two groups, obviously in order to keep up with the supply and baggage trains and for better defence against possible enemy attacks. Unsurprisingly, Bohemond appears at the head of the first group of armies – the vanguard – heading towards central Anatolia, with Robert of Normandy and Stephen of Blois making up the rest.[16] Then came the second group, which was probably a larger force, comprising the rest of the army under Robert of Flanders, Hugh of Vermandois, Godfrey of Bouillon and Raymond of Toulouse. Trying to assess the size of each group of armies that marched south from Nicaea in June 1097 is an exercise in futility, yet John France estimated the numbers for Bohemond's group to be fewer than twenty thousand in all, while the second would have totalled some thirty thousand.[17]

After leaving the Bithynian mountains behind and coming into central Anatolia, the crusaders found themselves in broken country with no easily defensible positions. On top of that, it proved that Kilij Arslan's plan was to ambush the advancing crusaders during the next phase of their march near the strategic road junction at Doryleum that commands the obvious point of entry to the Anatolian plateau via a broad valley. The exact location of what would become known as the Battle of Doryleum has been a subject of intense debate for many decades, but John France speculated that it took place on a plain some 3–5km northwest of the modern town of Bozüyük, around 50km northwest of modern Eskişehir.[18] What is clear, however, is that the battle took place at a point where two river valleys met, one from the north and one from the west, both converging in a southeasterly direction towards Doryleum, for Albert of Aachen and William of Tyre say that Bohemond's force was well to the right of the main force, as well as around 3km ahead of it.[19]

We have no credible account of the numbers under Kilij Arslan, and the *Gesta Francorum*'s report of some 360,000 Seljuk troops and William of Tyre's account of 200,000 are both, surely, exaggerated figures. France has suggested, based on Cahen's conclusions about the Turkish settlement in Anatolia in the previous decades, that the Seljuk army would have been many times smaller than the crusader force, or roughly equal to the total mounted host of the Latins.[20] Therefore, a battle of movement on the part of the Turks could have nullified the numeric advantage of the Latins simply by ambushing and winning the field from their vanguard, in a less confined space in comparison to the attack against the Provençals at Nicaea a few weeks before.

Making use of intelligence gleaned by his scouting parties, Kilij Arslan chose to lay his ambush at the point where the crusader vanguard would have approached along the river valley from the west before turning south towards Doryleum. Scarcely had Bohemond's group of armies approached from the west at the point where the two river valleys met, late in the evening of 30 June, than they became aware of the presence of a substantial Turkish force on the southern 'exit' of the river valley. After the crusaders had pitched their camp by a marsh, which gave them some protection from the enemy, Ralph of Caen reports:

> both sides deployed their forces in such a manner that the river which flowed between the forces obligated the faster to bend back towards the slower. Afternoon began to merge into twilight as the battle lines of the Latins and barbarians began their mutual attack. The approaching night was spent half in rest and half in labour. The faithful were more prompt and around the first hour of the morning preceded the infidels to the banks of the aforementioned river where the Turks' less than zealous leader had established their first camp.[21]

Early in the morning of 1 July, and before the crusaders had a chance to fully deploy in their battle formations, the Seljuks marched *en masse* against the westerners. The anonymous author of the *Gesta Francorum*, who was with the knights in vanguard during the Turkish attack, claims that the battle raged from the third to the ninth hour (i.e. from 8am to 2pm). Contemporary historians have identified two distinct stages of the battle; the first includes the desperate resistance by the first group of the crusader armies against Turkish attempts to encircle and overrun them. Most of the Latin sources describe the ferocity of the Turkish attack, but the *Gesta Francorum* is the only one that provides a more detailed account of the fighting tactics of Kilij Arslan's men:

> By the time all this was done, the Turks had already encircled us and came at us from all sides, brandishing their weapons and hurling them, and shooting arrows from an incredible distance. And as for us, we knew we could not withstand them or hold the weight of so many enemies, but we went forward to meet them united as one.[22]

The Turks applied their usual steppe tactics of releasing constant showers of arrows from a distance and falling back when their enemies charged forward to neutralise them. Then, pretending to retreat, they would make a sudden turn and come back to harass them. Their horses were quicker, more agile and more manoeuvrable than the Frankish cavalry, mostly because their equipment was significantly lighter, although the horses themselves did not differ much.[23] Their principal weapon was the bow, but they also carried a small round wooden shield, a lance and a sword. Yet the influence from the Byzantines was becoming stronger and from the time of the crusade the chroniclers mention heavily armed knights with hauberks.[24] The main tactical aim of the Turks was, in general, to confuse and demoralise the enemy, and isolate and break up their formations before charging in with their swords and lances. As most of our Latin sources agree, these steppe tactics were, with the exception of Bohemond and the several Latin mercenaries who had served the Byzantine emperors since the mid-eleventh century, completely unknown to the crusaders, who would not have fought against any large Seljuk forces before.[25] Nonetheless, we should bear in mind that the emperor had not only sent Tatikios to accompany the crusaders with a force of about two thousand light cavalry, but also instructed the crusader leaders during their stay in the capital 'in the methods normally used by the Turks in battle; told how they should draw up their battle-line, how to lay ambushes; advised not to pursue too far when the enemy ran away in flight'.[26]

The first stage of the battle would have found the Franco-Norman cavalry driven back against the perimeter of their camp, and forming the outer shell of resistance against the enveloping tactics of the Turkish horsemen; the camp was partially protected by a marsh on its northwest side. An attempt made by the Frankish cavalry to counter-attack was probably a spontaneous reaction to the frustration created by the deluge of arrows fired by the enemy horse-archers, 'but the Turks ... purposely opened their ranks to avoid the clash, and the Christians, finding no one to oppose them, had to fall back deceived'.[27]

The second stage of the battle began around noon, after Bohemond had sent an urgent message to Godfrey and the mounted armies of the second group urging them to speed up their march through the western river valley and come to the relief of their comrades. And it seems that they arrived in the nick of time, as Godfrey and the Provençals forced the Turkish left flank to break their attacks on the crusaders' right flank, while the rest of the arrivals deployed their units on the right of Bohemond's battle-group. Whether the battle developed into an orderly Latin attack against the main Turkish army, or whether it broke down into a pell-mell fight in which skirmishes were the rule, we cannot say with certainty. What we can be sure about, however, is that the bulk of the newly arrived crusader group did not waste any time in charging at the surprised and frustrated Seljuks, mainly focusing instead on their left flank and centre, thus forcing them to flee to the south.

Against the advice Alexios had given them, the crusaders pursued the defeated foe for many hours, thus preventing them from regrouping and taking large amounts of booty from their camp. Yet despite its outcome, the Battle of Doryleum was a victory of chance for the crusaders and it proved a very close shave indeed. Although this was one of the rare cases in the history of the crusades to the Holy Land where the Latins enjoyed numerical superiority over their enemies, their victory was in no way due to the superior battle-tactics applied by them or to the mistakes made by the Seljuks. If the messengers sent by Bohemond to Godfrey had not made it through the Turkish lines, or if the Latin reinforcements had not arrived on time, the armies of Bohemond and Robert of Normandy would have been cut to pieces or forced into a disorderly retreat, the outcome Kilij Arslan was hoping for. But still, this first battle experience against a relatively unknown enemy taught the Latins some very valuable lessons about steppe warfare.

The Road to Antioch

The Latin victory at Doryleum dealt a severe blow to the prestige and political authority of Kilij Arslan, especially since it came shortly after the loss of his capital, Nicaea. North-western Asia Minor was steadily slipping away from Turkish control; although the Turks were far from being driven out of the region, Doryleum not only paved the way for the gradual Byzantine reconquest of western Asia Minor under the Komnenoi, but also reaffirmed God's will to the crusaders by taking them one step closer to their ultimate target – Jerusalem.

The sources confirm that the passage of the crusader armies through Anatolia faced very little effective resistance, with the Turks melting away instead of engaging the Latins in pitched battle; undoubtedly, the Christian triumphs at Nicaea and Doryleum would have had a devastating effect on the morale of their enemies, as we read in the 'Damascus Chronicle' of Ibn al-Qalanisi (c. 1071–1160), a twelfth-century Arab politician and chronicler in Damascus: 'When the news was received of this shameful calamity to the cause of Islam, the anxiety of the people became acute and their fear and alarm increased.'[28] Rather, it was hunger, thirst, disease and the intolerable mid-summer heat that proved to be the biggest enemies of the crusaders and, crucially, of their horses during their march, as the anonymous author of the *Gesta Francorum* bitterly complains:

> And so we pursued them through deserts and a land which was waterless and uninhabitable, from which we only just escaped and came out

alive. Hunger and thirst harassed us, and we had nothing to eat other than spiky plants which we plucked and crushed in our hands. Such was the food on which we miserably survived. A great number of our horses died there, and as a result many of our mounted warriors became foot soldiers. For want of horses, our oxen became our riding animals, and because of such necessity our goats and sheep and dogs became our pack animals.[29]

Although the sources are quite vague about the route the Latin armies followed after their departure from Doryleum, France suggested that the most likely one would have taken them south via Amorion (Greek: Ἀμόριον), then to Nacolia (modern Seyitgazi), down to Akroinon (modern Afyonkarahisar) and Philomelium (modern Akşehir), and from there southeast to Ikonion (modern Konya).[30] This being so, the *Gesta Francorum*'s tale of hardship and suffering endured by the western European armies reflects the very realistic problems that a medieval army would have faced while marching in a hostile land like central Anatolia, which has a semi-arid continental climate with hot, dry summers, when the average temperature can easily reach 30°C, while most of the region usually has low precipitation throughout the year; this is, beyond doubt, a scenic though rather frightening landscape, and a harsh arid environment for a large force to traverse at any time of the year, let alone in the peak of summer, since the *Gesta Francorum* puts the crusaders' arrival at Ikonium on the Feast of the Assumption (15 August).

From Ikonion, the armies proceeded southeast to Heraclea Cybistra (Greek: Ἡράκλεια Κύβιστρα), a town in southern Cappadocia, near modern Ereğli, which owed its importance to its position near the point where the road to the Cilician Gates – the gateway to Syria – enters the Taurus mountains. The local Turkish garrison had planned an ambush on the vanguard units of the crusader armies, but they were quickly routed by the Frankish knights who swiftly occupied the town on 10 September, thus providing a crucial resting place for the campaigning armies, who decided to spend four days there to recuperate. There followed the crusaders' extraordinary strategic decision to diverge from the more direct 'pilgrim route' to Antioch via the Cilician coast and the cities of Tarsus, Adana and Alexandretta (modern Iskenderun), and march instead northeastwards via Kaisarea-in-Cappadocia (modern Kayseri) across the Taurus, and then south via Goxon (modern Göksün) and Maraş (modern Kahramanmaraş).

Modern historians have been puzzled by the crusaders' strategic decision to deviate north via Kaisarea, which would have added another

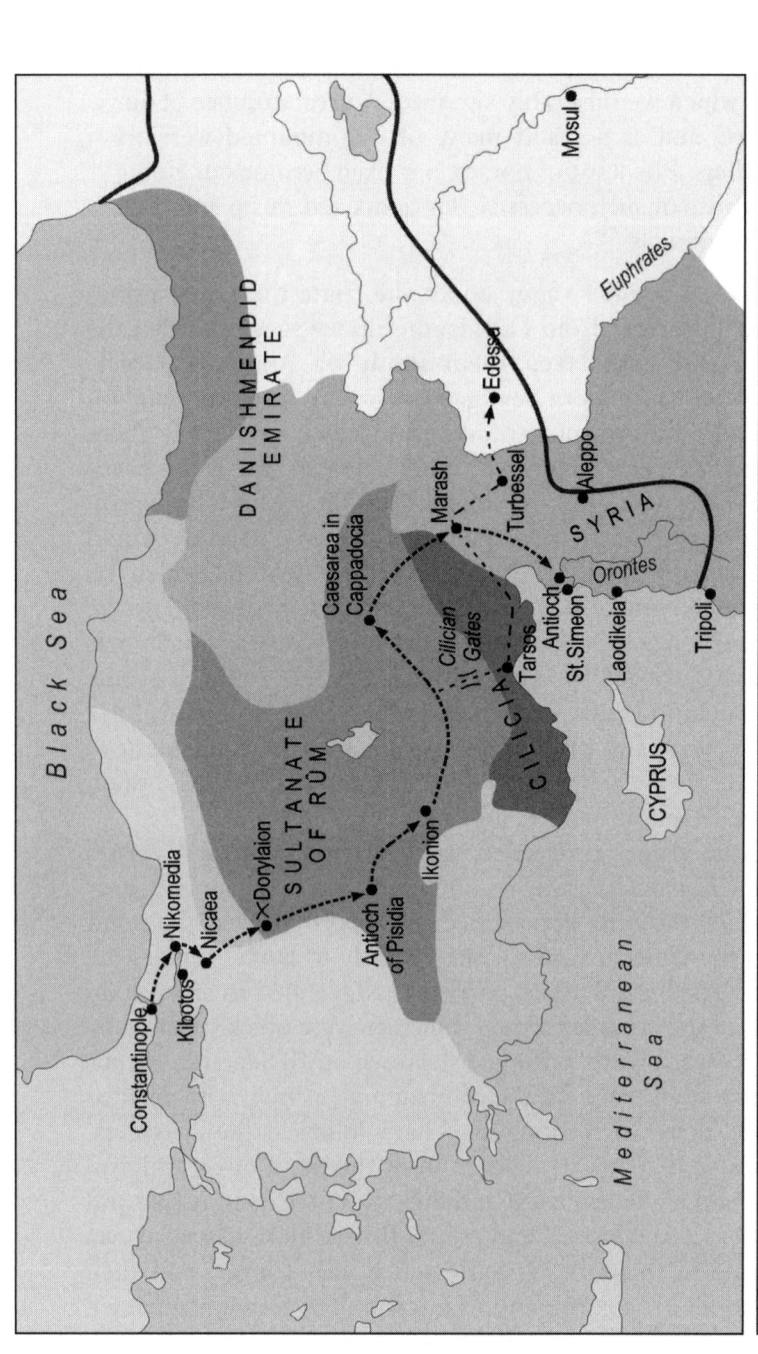

The route of the First Crusade.

300km to their long journey. The most likely explanation, however, is that they had credible intelligence about a favourable political and diplomatic climate in the Armenian principalities of the region. Around the Taurus mountains in Cilicia and the Upper Euphrates valley there were a number of Armenian lords who had gradually been transforming their domains and castles into centres of dynastic identity for about two decades before the coming of the First Crusade, mainly benefiting from the power vacuum resulting from the Byzantine civil conflicts of the 1070s and the overall instability in the neighbouring Muslim regions after the death of the Seljuk Sultan Malik Shah in 1092.[31] The most important of them was the Armenian Thoros of Edessa (d. 1098), also known as Theodore son of Hetum, who is called a 'Greek' – i.e., an Armenian of Chalcedonian denomination. A former Byzantine officer (*kouropalates*), he had been employed as governor of Edessa (modern Şanlıurfa) in Upper Mesopotamia by the Seljuk emir of Damascus, Tutush, after the latter conquered the city in 1094, although Thoros quickly rebelled against his new lord and established a more or less independent rule until the arrival of the crusaders in 1097. Another was Oschin, the lord of the castle of Lampron (near modern Çamlıyayla in Mersin Province) in the Taurus mountains, which guarded the passes to Tarsus and the Cilician Gates. Then there was Gabriel of Melitene (d. 1102/3), another *kouropalates*, who was married to Thoros' daughter and became an independent ruler of Melitene (modern Malatya) after 1086 until the conquest of the city by the Turkish Danishmends in 1101.

The examples of Thoros, Oschin, Gabriel and other less powerful Byzantine-Armenian lords residing in the wider region of Cilicia and Upper Mesopotamia at the time of the arrival of the First Crusade point to the preservation of a strong sense of cohesion among them that relied, first, on a common religious identity that was Orthodox/Chalcedonian, in contrast to the overwhelming majority of the local populace who adhered to the Armenian dogma, and secondly, on close inter-familial relations. The persistence of such elements related to the Byzantine administrative system and court hierarchy points to a common political ideology rooted in Constantinopolitan imperial concepts, and these Armenian lords would come to thrive in the complex politics of the area during the closing decades of the eleventh century by playing off the Turkish emirs of neighbouring cities.

On the advice of the emperor, who would certainly have wanted to control subsequent events, the leaders of the First Crusade established communications with at least some of the aforementioned Armenian lords, as we read in the *Chronicle* of the twelfth-century Armenian historian Matthew of Edessa (d. 1144): 'the army of the Westerners moved forth [from Constantinople] with a formidable number of about five hundred thousand men. T'oros, the ruler of Edessa, and the great Armenian Prince Constantine, the son of Ruben, were informed [of their coming] by letter.'[32] Moreover, as the Latin armies advanced eastwards, many of the cities in their path ejected their Turkish garrisons and threw open their gates to the Latins, as the Turkish control over the region was greatly resented by the local Christian population.[33] In what modern historians have coined the crusaders' 'Armenian strategy', Bohemond was always in the forefront of (military) events; he was in the vanguard that entered Kaisarea unopposed, around 27 September 1097, and his force pursued the Turkish besiegers of another town to the northeast of Kaisarea, before arriving at Coxon on 4 October, which the local Christians promptly surrendered to him.

At the same time, two smaller groups, led by Bohemond's nephew Tancred and Godfrey's brother Baldwin, took the shorter route through Cilicia. The latter has, generally, been treated as a private enterprise affair, to the point where the leaders rapidly abandoned the ethos of holy war in favour of straightforward conquest, thus gradually revealing the fundamental divisions between the different contingents that would later threaten to undermine the entire crusade; we read in a passage by Albert of Aachen about the quarrel between Tancred and Baldwin over the key city of Mopsuestia, an ancient city in Cilicia, located some 20km east of Antioch-in-Cilicia (modern Adana) on the Pyramus river (now the Ceyhan river), where Tancred ordered an attack on Baldwin's forces that were encamped on the outskirts of the city, in an incident where the ardour and greed of two young men, both claiming to be acting in the name of their superiors (Bohemond and Godfrey), simply got out of hand.[34] The attack outside Mopsuestia followed another episode between the two after the conquest of Tarsus when, in the morning following the take-over of the city's citadel by Tancred's troops, Baldwin – who had arrived later –demanded that Tancred share the spoils of Tarsus with him or else turn the entire city over to him. With tensions running high, and to avoid bloodshed, both leaders agreed to allow the citizens of Tarsus to decide whom they wished to be their prince, Baldwin or Tancred. In the dialogues reported by Albert of Aachen, both Tancred and Baldwin presented their cases on behalf of their leaders, in what can only be read as a model of competing masculinities and chivalric prowess (or 'my lord is more powerful than yours' kind of attitude).[35] Take the following extract from Baldwin's speech as an example:

> You [Tarsiots] should not believe that Bohemond and this Tancred whom you so respect and fear are in any way the greatest and most powerful chiefs of the Christian army, nor that they bear comparison with my brother Godfrey, duke and leader of the soldiers from all of Gaul, or any of his kin ... Know in fact that you and all your things, your city also, are to be consumed and destroyed by the sword and fire of this same duke [Godfrey], and neither Bohemond nor this Tancred will stand as your champions and defenders.

Eventually, Baldwin's arguments carried the day with the citizens of Tarsus and, to quote Ralph of Caen: 'Losses and gains ended up just as they had begun, unchanged, so that it is with merit that the common complaint could be raised that "he who had, had, and he who lost, lost".' Frankopan has argued that Baldwin's behaviour in Cilicia indicates he was acting under the instruction and auspices of the Byzantine emperor, which could help explain his determination to drive off Tancred in the first place, and his act of handing Tarsus and Mopsuestia over to Tatikios who, less than six months later, would himself hand them over to Bohemond's control when he left the crusader camp in search of supplies and reinforcements.[36]

As Baldwin became embroiled in the complex politics of the Armenian princes of the region, in February 1098 he was invited to Edessa by the Armenian Thoros to form an alliance. Baldwin gradually convinced Thoros to adopt him as his son and heir, only to attack him soon after his request was granted, besieging him in his own citadel. On 9 March Thoros would be assassinated by the Armenian inhabitants of the city, probably at Baldwin's command, thus leaving him as the sole ruler of Edessa and the first head of a new Latin principality in the Middle East. Again, Frankopan sees the conquest of the key city of Edessa as part of a wider strategic plan, hatched by the emperor and Baldwin, to take control of the approaches to Antioch; some clues include the fact that the count started to wear Byzantine clothes and to grow his beard in the local fashion, but – most importantly –Alexios granted him the official title of *doux* (governor), a title that he did not hold before.[37]

After Tancred had separated from Baldwin's army at Mopsuestia in early October 1097, he chose to carry on with his march along the Cilician coast, apparently, according to Albert of Aachen, to subdue a number of smaller castles that controlled key passes on the southern side of the

Taurus mountains, before entering Alexandretta (modern İskenderun), just 60km north of Antioch:

> Now that the enemy, who had scattered through the mountain regions after encountering the Christians, and had occupied the Christians' fortresses and places unjustly, heard of his [Tancred's] warlike strength, some took flight, others sent mules and horses and precious gifts of gold and silver, and were joined in friendship with him, so that they might find him peaceable in all the lands they possessed.[38]

Was Tancred acting on behalf of his uncle, Bohemond? Can we say that Tancred's conquests along the Cilician coast were the first definite evidence of Bohemond's designs upon Antioch? The primary sources cannot support any definitive answer to these questions, hence modern historians can only speculate about the true motives of Tancred's side-expedition in the region. Meanwhile, sometime in early October 1097 the main crusader army was marching south to Maraş (Ancient Greek: Γερμανίκεια; modern Kahramanmaraş), where they were received on friendly terms by the inhabitants of the city. The final obstacle before the approaches to the city of Antioch was the well-fortified city of Artah (modern Reyhanlı), which was located 40km east-northeast of Antioch, to the east of the Iron Bridge on the Roman road from Antioch to Aleppo.

Albert of Aachen describes how the citizens of Artah rose up against their Turkish lords, who had locked themselves up in the citadel, and massacred them before opening the city gates to the Latin vanguard units. An attempt by the Turks in Antioch to dispatch reinforcements to Artah, after learning of the citizens' uprising against the garrison of the city, was thwarted by the quick reaction of the Latin vanguard that went out to confront them, and was also supported by the main units of the armies of Robert of Flanders.[39] The road to Antioch was now open.

The Siege of Antioch

Antioch, one of the most heavily defended cities of the empire, was built in a strong natural position on the eastern bank of the Orontes river, although the city walls touched the river only at the Bridge Gate. Its eastern part was covered by Mount Silpius, rising to an average height of 512m, while north of its highest point stood the citadel at around 700m. The city was enclosed on its most exposed sides by double walls, which allegedly were wide enough for a chariot to ride on the battlements; three gates penetrated the walls on the city's western side (the Dog Gate, the

Gate of the Duke and the Bridge Gate), with another two on the northern and southern sides (St Paul's Gate and St George's Gate respectively). The eleventh-century Arab Nestorian physician Ibn Butlān wrote in the mid-eleventh century that the city had a double circuit wall with five gates and, allegedly, 360 towers; although archaeology has been unable to confirm the total number of towers, we know that these were refortified in 971, two years after the city was retaken from the Arabs, when Emperor John I Tzimiskes sent twelve thousand workers to reconstruct the city's walls (along with its towers), which had been damaged by an earthquake.[40]

As the crusaders were to find out soon enough, there were three ways to subdue the city: starvation, treachery or trickery. During the siege of the city by the Byzantines in 969 a daring party scaled the walls of Antioch using ladders while the Muslim guards were asleep, and there is every reason to believe that Tatikios may have advised the Latins to follow the same course of action.[41] As the arrival of the Christian army before Antioch on 21 October triggered a debate on strategy, it quickly became blindingly obvious that the exhausted crusaders were too few to mount a full-scale blockade of the city. Yet at the council of leaders described by Raymond of Aguilers, we learn that a number of Latin leaders favoured a winter lull in the hostilities in anticipation of reinforcements from Europe, proposing instead a distant blockade of Antioch with the erection of crusader outposts to harass the besieged garrison and thwart any relief mission.[42] This seems like a reasonable idea, but it was overruled by Raymond of Toulouse's passionate appeal to press on with the siege as soon as possible. As France rightly pointed out, the great virtue of the close siege was that it kept the army together under the control of its leaders; a distant blockade could have had a very adverse effect on the sense of purpose of the Christian army.[43]

Meanwhile, the deaths of the Seljuk sultan Malik Shah in 1092 and of his brother (and *emir* of Damascus) Tutush two years later had thrown Seljuk Syria into political turmoil. By early 1095 the greatest part of the Seljuk military elite in Syria had been eliminated and while the new sultan Barkyaruq – Malik Shah's son – was practically unable to intervene in the internal matters of the western fringes of his empire, the power vacuum in Syria was filled by Tutush's sons, Ridwan (in Aleppo) and Duqaq (in Damascus).[44] By the time the Latin armies were setting up their siege camp outside Antioch, the Seljuk governor of the city, Yaghi-Siyan, had begun making diplomatic overtures to each brother, hoping one or the other might come to his aid. It would be over two months before one of them did.

Ominously, the two major problems for the crusaders during the winter months were the provision of food and other supplies for the army and the prevention of desertion among their ranks. Logistics were crucial at this point in the campaign, and the task of bringing supplies to the Latin army by land was taken over by Bohemond, who would organise foraging expeditions in the region of Antioch during the winter (1097/98) while attempting to neutralise several smaller garrisons in the area that were harassing the Christian armies. With regard to providing supplies by sea between Cyprus and the port of Saint Symeon (modern Samandağ), the medieval port of Antioch located at the mouth of the Orontes river, there are references in the sources to fleets from the three major Italian maritime cities, Venice, Genoa and Pisa, operating throughout the eastern Mediterranean, and it can be assumed, in general, that all of the non-Byzantine ships operating in support of the crusader armies had to obtain their supplies in ports under the control of the imperial government. Finally, the crucial role of the Byzantine navy in the aforementioned operations has been undervalued by the Latin sources of the period, and Bachrach has emphasised that the Christian success at Antioch in 1098, and the strategic decision of the crusaders to take the coastal route southward towards Jerusalem, rather than the inland Damascus road, was directly conditioned by the support that the Byzantine government had promised.[45]

Bohemond led numerous foraging expeditions between the city of Antioch and the port of Saint Symeon, and he was involved in numerous skirmishes with the Turkish garrisons that were harassing the supply lines of the crusaders. In November 1097 one of these skirmishes developed into a small-scale battle with a Turkish force from the castle of Harem, an important stronghold built by the Byzantines shortly after 969 some 30km east of Antioch. We read in the *Gesta Francorum* that the crusade leaders (with Bohemond the most vocal among them) agreed on an aggressive strategy towards the Turkish garrison at Harem, and on 18 November:

> they sent some of their warriors to diligently search for that place where the Turks were. When our men had found the place where they were hiding, our warriors, who were searching for them, went forth to meet them. But little by little our men fell back to where they knew Bohemond waited with his army. Very quickly two of our men were killed then. When Bohemond heard this he hurled forward with his men, like the boldest athlete of Christ. The barbarians burst upon our men, for our men were few, who nevertheless joined battle.

Indeed, many of our enemies were killed, and the captives were led before the city gate where they were beheaded in order to increase the suffering of those inside the city.[46]

This is the first time that the Latin sources attest to an ambush laid against a Turkish army, when the vanguard of the Norman contingent led by Bohemond fell back upon the main body immediately after coming into contact with a Turkish force from Harem. Bohemond's leadership skills during this clash give a clear indication of his growing experience and adaptability to the tactical environment of the Middle East, where he was facing an enemy whom he got to know better and better with every passing month. Therefore, it is small wonder that the Norman already stood out as the most important figure in the First Crusade.

Bohemond's next initiative to tighten the noose around the city of Antioch as much as possible was the erection of a wooden siege tower on a hill on the northern side of the city, which they called, appropriately, 'Malregard' (or 'Evil Eye'). Yet both Bohemond and the rest of the crusade leaders would have been fully aware that none of these constructions would have been able to prevent a relief army from breaking their siege of Antioch. Hence, a few days after Christmas 1097 the crusaders had to face the first major challenge to their operation to take Antioch, when Duqaq of Damascus was spotted leading a small expeditionary army to an area where Bohemond and Robert of Flanders were foraging for provisions for the main Christian army. The intention of the Turkish force was, clearly, to ambush and encircle the foraging armies before marching to the relief of Antioch. Although vastly outnumbered, Bohemond and Robert decided to engage the enemy, and eventually managed to break their formation by mounting coordinated cavalry charges against the Turkish centre. This move had a surprising effect on Turkish morale, forcing Duqaq to retreat to Damascus.[47] It needs to be emphasised here that there is a difference between these Moslem troops and the Turks who had engaged the crusaders at Doryleum. The forces that Duqaq (and later Ridwan of Aleppo and the governor of Mosul, Kerbogha) put in the field were composite armies of Arabs, Seljuks and probably other nationalities like the Iranian Daylami, Kurds and other Bedouin tribes, but in which the Seljuks were the dominant party. In contrast, Kilij Arslan's army was almost entirely Turkish.[48]

The Christian armies were challenged again on 9 February 1098, when news of the mobilisation of troops from Aleppo under Ridwan reached the crusade's leaders. The Latin reaction was to dispatch Bohemond, who by this time was effectively the leader, and a force of every available knight to face the Aleppans. By now the horses that had survived the march through Anatolia would not have been more than a thousand in number and therefore this would also have been the number of the mobilised Frankish knights.[49] Although heavily outnumbered by the enemy, Bohemond took the bold decision to ambush the Seljuks on a narrow neck of land between Lake Bengras and the river Orontes, some 11km east of Antioch.

The outcome of this battle is significant because once again we see Bohemond pursuing an aggressive strategy and setting an ambush against a larger Seljuk force.[50] He had seen first-hand at Doryleum how difficult it was for the Frankish cavalry to resist the encircling manoeuvres and the showers of arrows of the Turkish cavalry, and so he decided to take the initiative himself. He used the topography of the region to his advantage, probably influenced by the outcome of the battle at Nicaea into choosing narrow ground where his enemies did not have the space to perform their usual encircling tactics; thus, he was able to trap them more easily with the few hundred horsemen he had brought with him. Once he managed to get his cavalry into close quarters with their enemies, the Turks were no match for their superior Frankish counterparts. On top of that, we also see Bohemond keeping a division in reserve, in case the main body of the army became encircled by the Turks, a tactic that he would follow again a few months later against the main relief force of the *emir* of Mosul, Kerbogha. Finally, the battle against Ridwan was the first time that the crusaders fought under a single leader who had overall command of the dispatched force. Bohemond's remarkable adaptability to any battle situation, and his pursuit of a battle-seeking strategy to make optimum use of limited forces, explains why he was viewed by his allies and his enemies alike as the true military leader of the First Crusade.

Bohemond's success at the lake battle heralded a decisive phase of the siege operation, during which the Latin leaders were able to gradually tighten their blockade on Antioch and its defenders. To support Bohemond's construction of the 'Malregard' tower on the north side of the city opposite St Paul's Gate, the Christian leaders agreed to build a counterfort on a hill (and a Muslim cemetery) outside the Bridge Gate, to the southeast of the city, which eventually came to be known as Mahommerie's Tower, and Bohemond and Raymond of Toulouse were dispatched to ensure the smooth flow of men and materiel from the Syrian coast. Thus, with the Bridge Gate blocked, the Latins were then able to complete the siege by establishing Tancred at a tower outside the St George Gate to the south of the city, on 5 April 1098.

Meanwhile, the departure from the camp of the emperor's representative with the crusade, Tatikios, around the end of January 1098 came as a huge shock to the demoralised besiegers of Antioch, sparking a smear campaign in the Latin sources against Alexios Komnenos and his man. According to Raymond of Aguiler's account:

> While these affairs were conducted in camp, an unconfirmed story spread that the army of the Emperor was approaching, an army composed, it was said, of many races, Slavs, Patzinaks, Kumans, and Turkopoles ... Actually Tatikios, that disfigured one, anxious for an excuse to run away, not only fabricated the above lie but added to his sins with perjury and betrayal of friends by hastening away in flight after ceding to Bohemond two or three cities, Tursol [Tarsus], Mamistra and Adana. Therefore, under the pretence of joining the army of Alexios, Tatikios broke camp, abandoned his followers, – and left with God's curse; by this dastardly act, he brought eternal shame to himself and his men.[51]

The anonymous author of the *Gesta Francorum* adds:

> In the meantime, Tetigus [Tatikios], our enemy, hearing that the army of the Turks was marching against us, claimed to be filled with fear for our sake, thinking that we had all been killed or had fallen into the hands of our enemies; and making up all kinds of lies, he said: 'High lords and valiant men, you see the dire hardship that we are in, and no help can come to us from any direction. So, allow me to return to Romania, my homeland, and do not be doubtful, I will make sure that ships are sent here by sea filled with grain, wine, barley, meat, flour, cheese, and all good things that are needed.'[52]

Albert of Aachen also notes: 'Tatikios with the cut-off nose who, terror-stricken as they were, had withdrawn in false faith from the allies to that same emperor [Alexios], to carry a message about the promised relief, which he had not done faithfully at all, since he did not return to Antioch again.'[53]

Tatikios' notorious departure was portrayed as a traitorous act, and soon afterwards was used to show that he – and, accordingly, the emperor Alexios – had betrayed the crusaders, abandoning them to their fate at Antioch. Yet modern historians have pointed out that these judgements were unjustified.[54] In fact, less than two months after Tatikios' departure, on 4 March an 'English' fleet – presumably having sailed from the English outpost at Laodicea, in Cilicia, rather than being English in origin –

arrived at the port of Saint Symeon, bringing emergency supplies to the Christian armies at Antioch.[55] The timing of the fleet's appearance in Syria should not be considered a coincidence, as no ship would have been able to sail from a port under Byzantine control without imperial permission. Therefore it is safe to assume that Tatikios had delivered what he had promised. Why, then, all the bad press about him and the emperor?

Shepard suggested that it was simply a clever ploy by Bohemond to further his own interests in Syria over those of the emperor. Bohemond must have felt that the further he marched away from Constantinople, the less dependent he became on the power, influence and money of Alexios Komnenos to support him over the other crusade leaders. By the spring of 1098, therefore, and with the military situation outside Antioch deteriorating by the day, Bohemond's association with the emperor as one of his 'trusted men' would have looked – to say the least – disappointing to the ambitious Norman. Yet the latter was bound to work in close cooperation with Tatikios throughout the campaign, and if the Norman had any aspiration to change his allegiance, he would have had to find a way to get rid of Alexios' man on the crusade.

Anna Komnena, whose narrative can help us reconstruct the chain of events in that winter of 1097/98, talks about Tatikios being tipped off by the emperor's 'right-hand man' Bohemond about a secret plan on the part of the other leaders to kill him and also, presumably, his men; Anna reports that a number of Latin leaders had heard a rumour that Alexios had reached some secret agreement with 'the Sultan' to attack the crusaders.[56] The ploy seems to have worked marvellously well for the Norman, as Tatikios departed to arrange for the provisions to be despatched to the Latin camp, but – crucially – not before 'ceding to Bohemond two or three cities, Tursol [Tarsus], Mamistra, and Adana'; for such a grant to have been made, we may safely assume that Tatikios would have taken Bohemond at his word!

Nevertheless, it was the late spring before Bohemond took the next step in his plan to supplant the emperor in his rights to Syria and the city of Antioch, apparently once he was sure that Tatikios had no intention of returning to Antioch. Sometime in May he proposed to the other commanders on the crusade that the city should belong to whoever managed to take it, provided that the emperor failed to keep his promise to arrive at the head of an army to take possession of it.[57] Therefore, by the late spring of 1098, following the departure of Tatikios and in the absence of any Byzantine authority, it is apparent that Bohemond had seen a golden opportunity. The situation in the Latin camp had not improved, despite

Byzantine promises for reinforcements, and while rumours of a large Seljuk relief army approaching from Mosul were circulating, Bohemond found a more receptive audience for his alternative plan for Antioch. Therefore it is around this time that we see the Norman publicly coming out against the emperor as a willing adversary, especially if we consider – according to Shepard – that our earliest extant outright condemnation of Alexios' 'traitorous' behaviour against the crusaders comes in a postscript added by Bohemond to a letter addressed to Pope Urban II, which is dated 11 September 1098.[58]

By the end of May 1098 Bohemond had been conducting negotiations of some sort with a commander of a tower of the walls of Antioch named Firuz, a Turkish convert to Christianity according to some sources, to allow his men – and the rest of the crusaders – into the city.[59] It is quite likely that both men could communicate in Greek, since we know that Bohemond knew the language quite well, despite his 'barbarous accent', while Firuz would have spoken Greek as a result of living in the Greek-speaking city of Antioch for many years. It seems the other crusade leaders had misgivings about handing over such a rich and flourishing city to Bohemond, especially Raymond of Toulouse, who saw these developments as a betrayal of his oath to the emperor, and the *Gesta Francorum* records that they all wished to share control, but on a conditional and temporary basis; the city was ultimately to be ceded to Byzantium. Yet as news of 'so many thousands and Kerbogha's incomparable weaponry and the splendour of his possessions'[60] began to trickle back to the crusader camp, a hastily assembled meeting was called to discuss, once again, the future of the city. We read in the *Gesta Francorum* that on 29 May:

> all our leaders came together and took counsel, and said: 'If Bohemond can get the city by himself, or through others, we shall happily give it to him, with the stipulation that if the emperor comes to our aid and fulfils all the conditions that he promised and swore to give us, by right we shall let him have the city; otherwise, Bohemond shall take possession of it.'[61]

The attack on the city of Antioch was launched on 2 June, four days after the last council of the Christian leaders, and it began with a feigned pull-out of the army from the environs of the city, signalling to the defenders that their enemies were retreating because of the imminent arrival of a relief army.[62] However, the Christian armies led by Robert of Flanders and Godfrey of Bouillon swiftly reassembled under the city walls after sunset and made ready for battle, while Bohemond's men, ready to follow their leader's plan, were on the southeastern side of the city's defences, for it is clear that Firuz's tower was on that side of the city. When the order was given by the Norman, the first group of his men made their way up a ladder to the top of the battlements that were controlled by Firuz. The latter was waiting for them, but he failed to spot Bohemond with the first group of about sixty knights scaling the walls; apparently thinking that he was betrayed, he exclaimed 'Micro Francos echomé!' ['We have few Franks!']. Perhaps because he wished to be sure that Firuz would keep his side of the deal, Bohemond decided not to follow the first group of knights up the walls. But once one of his trusted men came down and gave him an overview of the situation – 'O brave man, why are you just standing there? What did you come here to get? Look, we have already taken three towers' – he ordered an all-out attack. Gathering at the top, Bohemond's men made their way along the walls, killing those they met, until they were in position to signal to Godfrey and Robert of Flanders, who were waiting below one of the city's gates. Once the gates were flung open and the Christian soldiers began pouring into the streets of Antioch, Bohemond had but one thing in mind: '[he] wasted no time with this and ordered that his glorious banner be planted on a hill opposite the citadel'.[63] Even in the heat of battle, he was already thinking about its aftermath. The following morning Bohemond was injured in the leg during the failed attack to take the citadel.

The Besiegers Become the Besieged

Following the capitulation of the lower city of Antioch on 3 June 1098, and with the citadel still in enemy hands, Bohemond's role as *the* military leader of the crusade was to emerge once more when a large relief force from Mosul under *emir* Kerbogha appeared outside Antioch the following day (4 June), to find the Latins trapped inside their newly acquired trophy. An initial attack by Kerbogha's troops failed to break into the city, with the *emir* soon settling for a blockade of Antioch since he was fully aware that, after eight long, painful months, the crusader army would have been exhausted, depleted and apprehensive.

It is not difficult to imagine that Kerbogha's blockade of Antioch soon had the desired effect on the Latins, since there were practically no more supplies within the city; we read in Albert of Aachen's history:

> With the city thus blockaded on all sides, and the gentiles' forces increasing from day to day and barring their way out all round, famine grew so great among the Christians that in the absence of

bread they did not shrink from eating camels, donkeys, horses, and mules, but even chewed pieces of leather found in the homes which had hardened and putrefied for three to six years ...[64]

For one of the chroniclers and participants of the crusade, Fulcher of Chartres, and for many others who found themselves besieged within the Antiochean walls that summer, there was an obvious explanation for their suffering: God was punishing them for the sins committed by some of their comrades who slept with local women, both before and after taking the city.[65] With morale in the crusader army having reached its nadir, the expedition needed a miracle more than ever: and they got one. One day a random man of no distinction named Peter Bartholomew informed Raymond of Toulouse and the bishop of Le Puy, Pope Urban II's legate in the crusade, that he had seen multiple visions of St Andrew in which the saint revealed to him the location of the Holy Lance. After a lance was 'miraculously' discovered under the Church of St Peter in Antioch, the Christian resolve was significantly strengthened at a critical moment.[66] Yet for the leaders, there was only one way out of this desperate situation they had found themselves in: they must take the fight to the enemy.

During this crucial stage of the siege of the Christian army around the end of June, Raymond of Aguilers reports that 'all of the crusaders [leaders] promised to follow the commands of Bohemond for a period of fifteen days after the fight so that he could arrange for the protection of Antioch and make battle plans'.[67] This, certainly, was an extraordinary concession, made to an extraordinary man, in an extraordinary set of circumstances. What is important to emphasise here is Bohemond's suggested battle plan, which was, in essence, similar to the one implemented/executed against the relief force under Ridwan of Aleppo back in February. Once again, Bohemond would make use of the topography of the battlefield to his advantage and would keep a number of units in reserve in case the enemy should attempt to encircle them.

Kerbogha had pitched his camp on the north side of the Orontes. Hence, the only way for the crusaders to reach the camp was to leave the city through the Bridge Gate, on the southwestern side of the defences, which was the only one that connected the two banks of the river. On 28 June the Latins sallied out of the city in battle order in four major divisions:[68] Hugh of Vermandois, Robert of Flanders and Robert of Normandy were deployed on the right wing; the Lorrainers, Burgundians and other French troops under the command of Godfrey of Bouillon formed the centre, and Provençal and Aquitanian troops were posted on the left wing under Bishop Adhemar of Le Puy. Tancred and Bohemond's units formed the reserve divisions of the army to prevent any encircling manoeuvres from the enemy, while the flanks of the Latin armies were covered by the Orontes on the right and the high mountains on the left. The infantry and the archers were placed in front to hold back the enemy's attacks, while the cavalry was kept behind in order to break out and win the battle with its heavy charge when the opportunity arose. This tactic of deploying the heavy cavalry behind the foot soldiers had been seen before, both at Hastings (1066) and at Dyrrhachium (1081), and indeed embodies the whole idea of the infantry serving as a shield for the cavalry.

The crossing of a river, or a river bridge, by an army while enemy units hold the opposite bank has always been one of the most dangerous undertakings in war, so Bohemond had every right to be afraid that Kerbogha would let one or two divisions cross the river and then fall upon them while the rest of the army was still on the bridge; this is exactly what the Scots did to the English army at the Battle of Stirling Bridge[69] in September 1297. But despite Bohemond's fear, the Latins were left free to deploy as they wished, perhaps because Kerbogha intended to use encircling tactics to outflank the entire army. There is a debate, however, on the deployment of the crusaders on the battlefield immediately after they had marched over the Orontes river, and whether the divisions changed their formation from column into line.[70]

Kerbogha would have seen that the left wing of the Latins was the last to cross the Orontes bridge, and thus he ordered his right-wing units to attack them before they were fully deployed on the battlefield alongside the other divisions. Eventually, some fifteen thousand[71] horsemen from the sultanate of Rum succeeded in bypassing Adhemar's division to arrive at the rear of the left wing of the Latin army. Bohemond's precaution of keeping his Norman troops in reserve proved a wise decision, since the Seljuks were now completely cut off from the main army, but they were also prevented from attacking the Latin centre from the rear. Even after the rest of Kerbogha's army had been overpowered by the frontal cavalry attacks made by Godfrey's and Hugh's divisions, the Anatolian Turks kept up an immense pressure on the Normans; abandoning their usual encircling tactics, they charged against them with their swords and lances, before they were eventually beaten off by the Norman infantry units who formed a protective 'ring' around the cavalry.

France offers a different version of events, based on his examination of the topography of the battlefield terrain between the Bridge Gate and the mountains, while taking into consideration the likely dispersal of

Kerbogha's units during the siege of Antioch.[72] He believes that because the plain between the Orontes and the mountains opposite the Bridge Gate was too wide – about 4–5 kilometres – for the small crusader force to cover its full extent, it would have been impossible for the Latin army to have its flanks covered by the river and the mountains respectively. Rather, the Latins would have taken full advantage of the dispersal of the Turkish forces on the perimeter of Antioch's fortifications, thus choosing to exit the city from the Bridge Gate, on the southwestern side of the city's defences, a point that was quite distant from where Kerbogha had pitched his camp and headquarters, some 5km to the northwest of the city. The crusaders hoped to deploy their units fast enough to catch the enemy unawares, and defeat any units blockading the Bridge Gate before the main army had time to organise and march against them. France believes that the short fight and retreat that developed following the crusaders' fighting exit from the city must have been a result of their being attacked piecemeal and in no order by Turkish detachments that were gradually leaving their besieging posts and pressing forward with the attack without waiting for orders from Kerbogha's headquarters. And while Adhemar's long march westwards towards the plain would have served to cover the flanks of the army, the force that arrived at their rear could have been a Turkish force that was besieging St George's Gate to the south of the city.

Finally, Rubenstein has raised the possibility of a number of Turkish commanders deserting Kerbogha during the initial stages of the battle. Although neither the Muslim nor the Latin sources corroborate this allegation, Rubenstein picks on comments about the Turkish commander's arrogance, as reported by the influential Arab historian Ibn al-Athīr (1160–1233): 'thinking that the present crisis would force the Muslims to remain loyal to him [Kerbogha], he alienated them [the Turkish troops] by his pride and ill-treatment of them. They plotted in secret anger to betray him and desert him in the heat of battle.'[73] Rubenstein also alleges collusion between Tancred and Kerbogha's own man, Ahmad ibn-Marwan, whom he had appointed commander of the Antiochean citadel immediately after the Turkish army's arrival outside the city, and he makes up a scenario in which the grass fire that was reported by the author of the *Gesta Francorum* to have broken out in the Turkish camp was a signal to retreat by other dissatisfied leaders in the Turkish army, whom ibn-Marwan had identified and contacted earlier.[74] Yet this scenario seems to me to be far-fetched, and a simpler explanation could be that the grass fire was intended as a sort of smokescreen, which, as France underlines in his account of the battle, was 'a well-known device of Islamic armies to confuse and choke the enemy',[75] or it could well have been started accidentally in the heat of battle.

As soon as the battle started to turn in favour of the crusaders, ibn-Marwan sent word down from the citadel that he wanted to surrender, probably in accordance with the terms of an earlier verbal agreement – implied by Raymond of Aguilers[76] – with Bohemond that he would give up the citadel to him if Kerbogha was defeated in battle. Raymond of Toulouse had been posted to blockade the citadel and protect the Christian flanks from a potential attack from the rear:

> he ordered that his own banner be given to him [ibn-Marwan]. He took that and quickly put it up on the tower. But the Longobards [Italo-Normans] who were positioned there at once said, 'This is not Bohemond's banner.' He then asked them and said, 'Whose is it?' And they replied, 'The count of Saint-Gilles'.' Then he took the banner and returned it to the count [Raymond of Toulouse]. And just at that time, that wise man Bohemond arrived, and he gave him his own banner. The emir accepted it with great joy and made a pact with lord Bohemond that those pagans who wished to become Christians would remain with him, while the others he would allow to leave safe and sound and without harm. He agreed to all the demands of the emir, and then quickly placed his men inside the citadel.[77]

There are two things to take away from the Battle of Antioch concerning the strategy and battle tactics of the crusaders; first, even if the Latins did not actually use natural obstacles to cover their flanks, we have to admire Bohemond's strategic initiative in keeping a reserve division that seemed to offer great protection for the Latins' flanks. Secondly, outside Antioch the Latin East experienced for the first time the mixed unit formations of infantry and cavalry, where the foot-soldiers acquired the fundamental role in Middle Eastern warfare as a sort of a 'protective shield' for the heavy cavalry, which by this stage of the crusade had evolved into a formidable fighting unit, with better armour protection as well, which was most needed in the East.

Chapter 7

Lord of Antioch

On the other hand if we [crusaders] abandon Antioch and the Turks recover it, the result will be more disastrous than the last occupation. So let us give it to Bohemond, a wise man, respected by the pagans, a man who will protect it well.
[Raymond of Aguilers, p. 74]

The Contest for Control of Antioch

The defeat of Kerbogha's army on 28 June 1098 marks an important milestone in the progress of the crusade towards its objective: the liberation of the Holy City of Jerusalem. Nonetheless, many would have expected the Latin armies to take advantage of the momentum of their victory over the *emir* of Mosul and to march south because, as Raymond of Aguilers explains, 'not one city between Antioch and Jerusalem would have thrown one rock at them, so terrified and weakened at this time were the Saracen cities following the defeat of Kerbogha'. However, the same chronicler also decries the Latin leaders' actions: 'luxuriating in idleness and riches, the crusaders, contrary to God's commands, postponed the journey until the Kalends of November'.[1] In a sour atmosphere of division after a great triumph, every Latin leader would find himself squabbling about the future of this strategic Syrian city for many months after its conquest, thus setting the tone for a period of intense rivalry within the crusader contingents.

Although he failed to capture the citadel of Antioch, Raymond of Toulouse was still in possession of the governor's palace, the Bridge Gate and its tower, the fortified bridge across the Orontes and *La Mahommerie*. This gave him a strong bargaining card against Bohemond's claim for complete control of city, as the count of Toulouse could potentially cut off the supply roads to and from the port of St Symeon. In spite of Raymond's foothold in the western approaches to the city, by the end of August Bohemond had managed to wrest control of most of the lower city and, crucially, of the entire citadel.[2] Bohemond was acting as if he were the legal authority in Antioch, as shown by a charter in which he donated the Church of Saint John to the Genoese.[3] Yet, while Bohemond and Raymond were bickering for control of Antioch and seeking out allies

118 *Bohemond of Taranto*

among the other lords, the leaders of the crusade had already dispatched Hugh of Vermandois and Baldwin of Hainault to Constantinople, sometime in early July, presumably to inform the emperor of the outcome of the siege and impress upon him their desperate situation.

The sources contradict each other as to whether the Latin leaders wanted to offer Alexios the city, according to the terms of their oath sworn in Constantinople earlier in the campaign (see *The deeds of Franks*, p. 89), or if they simply wished to denounce the emperor as a traitor to God's Will because he had failed to support the crusade at its most critical stage (see Albert of Aachen, V. 3, p. 341). If we believe – and I think we should – the account of the anonymous author of the *Gesta Francorum*, then it would have been sensible for the Latin leaders to postpone the march against Jerusalem and to give their armies some respite while awaiting for the arrival of the imperial armies. Yet, as we saw in Raymond of Aguiler's account, there were many in the crusader camp who regarded this delay as a strategic disaster, not least because it seemed to contradict the spirit and purpose of their whole undertaking: the liberation of Jerusalem. The whole issue about who would assume command (and possession) of Antioch was clearly tied to the wider question of the alliance with the emperor, hence the mission of Hugh of Vermandois to the imperial court in early July 1098.

But where does the role of Alexios Komnenos fit into the wider picture of the crusade's progress in Syria? We know that the emperor had been informed of the plight of the crusader leaders during the siege of Antioch from one of their own, Stephen of Blois, who had fled the siege on 14 June 1098, when Kerbogha's army was approaching. Stephen found Alexios at Philomelium (modern Akşehir, some 100km northwest of Ikonion), a strategic town in central Anatolia from where the emperor could maintain contact with the westerners but also supervise the reconquest of western Anatolia from the Turks. Stephen had a private meeting with the emperor, sometime at the end of June, and his account of the situation at Antioch could not have been more bleak: 'You should know that Antioch really has been taken, but the citadel has not fallen. Our men are badly besieged and most likely have already been killed by the Turks. Go back, therefore, as fast as you can, so that they might not find you and these men that you lead.'[4] The source of this report, the *Gesta Francorum*, is also keen to portray Alexios as an untrustworthy leader and, frankly, a coward:

> Then the emperor, shaking with terror, secretly summoned Guy [Bohemond's half-brother Guy of Hauteville (*c.* 1061–1108)] the

brother of Bohemond, and some others, and said to them, 'High lords, what should we do? Behold, all our men are shut in and badly besieged, and maybe at this very hour they have been killed by the hands of the Turks or led off into captivity, as this miserable count, who shamefully fled, has just described. If you want, we can quickly turn back and beat a hasty retreat, so that we will not die a sudden death, as the others have died.'

But before we rush to condemn Alexios Komnenos for abandoning the crusaders to their fate, I believe that any leader would have taken the decision to pull out of a campaign that, according to the eye-witness report of one of its leaders, may already have reached a bloody finale. Furthermore, we should bear in mind that, by the time Alexios met with Stephen, he had already enjoyed a series of military victories over the Anatolian Turks during the Byzantine campaigns in the spring of 1098.[5] Indeed, at a strategic level, the passage of the crusade through central Anatolia and the conquest of Nicaea had brought about the ensuing collapse of the Turkish command and control of the regions of Phrygia and Pisidia, in western Asia Minor. This, then, led to the Byzantine reconquest campaigns of spring 1098, under the emperor's brother-in-law John Doukas, which within a short time brought about the imperial recovery of a considerable number of towns and territories between the Gulf of Smyrna in the Aegean Sea and the valleys of the Hermos and Meander rivers. It was these repeated victories over the local Turkish commanders that enabled Alexios Komnenos to advance his army from their camp at Pelekanos on the coast of the Marmara Sea (where he was based before the conquest of Nicaea) as far south as the Phrygian town of Philomelium – the easternmost advance of imperial troops in central Anatolia since the rebellion of Botaneiates in 1077. Under these circumstances, then, we should give more credit to Anna's account of her father's pondering over the overall situation in Asia Minor in the early summer of 1098, which reveals a more cautious attitude towards the Turks in Anatolia, since the Byzantine high command had come to realise that – at least for this campaigning season – no further territorial gains were possible. We read in the *Alexiad*:

> For these reasons, as his [Alexios'] forces were insufficient against such numbers [of Turks], and he could not change the Franks' [crusaders] decision, nor by better advice convert them to their advantage, he considered he had better not proceed any further, lest by hastening to the assistance of Antioch he might cause the destruction of Constantinople.

Therefore, it is reasonable to assume that, with the crusaders being unaware of the emperor's decision to withdraw his troops back to the capital, rumours would have circulated for several months following the victory over Kerbogha's army that the emperor's arrival in the region was imminent. To learn more about the emperor's whereabouts, and to try to break the deadlock in the negotiations over the control of Antioch, an embassy was dispatched to Alexios in early July, as I mentioned earlier, led by Hugh of Vermandois and Baldwin of Hainault. Although we have no details of the exchanges between the emperor and the Latin delegation, the meeting had no effect and the crusaders received no help from Constantinople.[6] As news of the imperial departure reached Antioch around the end of the summer, it prompted a furious reaction against the Byzantines, as we read in the famous letter of the Princes to the Pope dated 11 September 1098, which was written partly, or even entirely, by Bohemond.[7] Undoubtedly, this was a key moment in the crusade, as relations between Alexios and the crusade leaders had become poisonous. In turning their backs on the emperor, and berating him for not having done enough to help the expedition, the Latins found themselves looking for another leader to break the deadlock: Urban II:

> Although we have triumphed over the Turks and the pagans we cannot do the same with the Greek, Armenian, Syrian and Jacobite heretics. We ask you [Urban] again and again, our dearest father, as father and leader to come to the place of your fatherhood, and as vicar of St Peter to sit on his throne and have us as your obedient sons in all legitimate actions, eradicating and destroying all types of heresy with your authority and our valour.

Then, in the closing section of the aforementioned letter, we read: 'We, your sons, who obey you in everything, most pious father, you should separate from the unjust emperor [Alexios Komnenos] who has never fulfilled the many promises he has made us. In fact, he has hindered and harmed us in every way at his disposal.'

Some of our primary sources give us bits and pieces of information about the raiding activities to the southeast of Antioch by members of Raymond of Toulouse's retinue, dating back to 5 June 1098. More specifically, we read in the *Gesta Francorum* of the 'adventures' of a much-celebrated hero of the crusade, Raymond Pilet (or Pelet; 1075–1143), who was reported to have expanded his raiding activities into the Ruj valley (between the Orontes river and the modern Syrian city of Idlib, southeast of Antioch). Whether acting under the auspices of his lord, Count Raymond, or out of personal ambition, Pilet managed to gain control of the town of Tell Manus on 5 June, only to be defeated by a Muslim force a couple of months later, on 27 July, outside the city of Maarrat al-Nu'man (in modern northwestern Syria, 33km south of Idlib).[8] Then, in the early autumn of 1098, Count Raymond's foraging raids into the southern approaches of the Ruj valley also began with an expedition against the town of Al-Bara, approximately 15km west of Maarrat al-Nu'man, which capitulated on 25 September.[9] Even though historians are not entirely sure about the strategic plan behind Raymond's activities so far south of Antioch, Asbridge has suggested that the count of Toulouse's operations between September 1098 and the following January may have been an attempt to establish a new powerbase in the fertile Ruj valley, to act as a counterweight to Bohemond's increasing power in (and hold over) the Syrian metropolis.[10]

Meanwhile, Bohemond's growing power in Antioch can be seen once again in the account of the dispute about the course of the crusade between the Latin leaders, and Bohemond and Raymond in particular, that took place during the council meeting on the feast of All Saints (1 November):

> Now Bohemond had been asking every day about the agreement that all the chief lords had made with him about giving him the city [of Antioch]. But the count of Saint-Gilles did not want to soften to any agreement with Bohemond, because he was afraid to perjure himself against the emperor ... Bohemond recited his agreement and showed his costs. And the count of Saint-Gilles also disclosed the words and the oath which he had made with the emperor on the counsel of Bohemond. The bishops and Duke Godfrey, the count of Flanders and the count of Normandy, and the other chief lords went apart from the rest and went to where the chair of Saint Peter is, so that they might come up with a judgement between the two. But then afterwards, fearing that the path to the Holy Sepulchre might become jeopardised, they would not say what their judgement was. Then the count of Saint-Gilles said, 'Before the way to the Holy Sepulchre is abandoned, if Bohemond agrees to come with us, all that has been judged by our peers, namely Duke Godfrey and the count of Flanders and Robert the Norman, and all the other chief lords, I faithfully agree to, except that which concerns my faithfulness to the emperor.'[11]

Raymond's second phase of expansion in the Ruj began just a few weeks after the council of the crusade leaders in November. Marching south from Al-Bara towards Maarrat al-Nu'man, the armies of Raymond of

Toulouse and Robert of Flanders reached the town on 28 November and set up a siege, while Bohemond's contingent arrived shortly after to join the operation.[12] Both of our sources for the siege portray the Provençal count as the overseer of the entire operation, and especially as the leader who supervised the construction of the wooden towers that were required to break into Maarrat al-Nu'man. In contrast, Bohemond and his men are dismissed as 'only half-hearted in pressing the siege, [although they] acquired the greater number of towers, horses, and captives, and thereby led to hard feelings between the Normans and the Provençals'.[13]

The besiegers managed to get a foothold into Maarrat al-Nu'man on 11/12 December 1098, with Bohemond reportedly seizing control of a great number of towers and a significant part of the town which, again as Asbridge points out, would have been intended to be used as a bargaining card by the Norman against his rival, Raymond of Toulouse: 'Raymond wanted to give the city to the bishop of Al-Bara, and Bohemond held to some of his captured towers and warned, "I shall agree to nothing with Raymond unless he cedes the Antiochean towers to me."'[14] Eventually, Bohemond left Maarrat al-Nu'man after it had become clear that no agreement could be reached between the leaders over the fate of the town, and the Provençal count managed to gain full control of the town sometime before 13 January 1099, and to install Peter of Al-Bara as commander there. Yet by this stage of the expedition, it seemed obvious that Raymond could not resist Bohemond's claims over the city of Antioch and in the middle of January 1099 the former prepared to set off for Jerusalem without the latter.

A vivid indication of the rough times which the crusaders had endured after the conquest of Antioch, and the further difficulties they were about to face during the journey to Jerusalem, is offered by the terrible scene of deprivation witnessed during the winter of 1098/99 when starved and weakened Christian soldiers were driven to such desperate measures as to '[tear] apart the bodies of the dead since one could discover bezants in their stomachs. But others, in fact, cut their flesh as morsels which they cooked and ate.'[15] Bearing this in mind, therefore, it is easier to understand the decision taken by key leaders including Godfrey of Bouillon, Robert of Normandy, Robert of Flanders and Tancred, to request – according to Raymond of Aguilers – a significant sum of money each from the wealthy count of Toulouse in return for continuing on their journey.[16] Rather than 'learning from the bad example of Bohemond', as Frankopan has suggested,[17] the rest of the crusade leaders were – in my view – simply looking for a way to support their starving and rapidly diminishing contingents for the final push to the Holy Sepulchre; they were pragmatists rather than materialistic or greedy. For Raymond, however, his operations in the Ruj valley could be seen to have been launched as a coordinated effort to establish a powerbase in the region to work as a counterweight to Bohemond's increasing power in the city of Antioch.

In the spring of 1099 imperial representatives arrived in the Levant to catch up with the Latin armies which were, by that time, far south of Antioch at Arqah in Syria. As was to be expected, Alexios' representatives protested vigorously about Bohemond's occupation of Antioch in contravention of their previous oath and agreement, and it is enlightening to follow Raymond of Aguilers' report of the arguments exchanged between the crusade leaders (and Raymond of Toulouse in particular) regarding Alexios' role in the campaign:

> Emissaries from the Emperor Alexios arrived in camp at this time protesting Bohemond's possession of Antioch in contradiction of oaths made to the Basileus ... The Byzantine envoy further stated that Alexios would give large sums of gold and silver, and that crusaders should await him until the Feast of Saint John [24 June] so that he could journey with them to Jerusalem. It is well to mention that it was now near Easter [early April].
>
> Many, among whom was the count of Saint-Gilles, argued: 'Let us delay our march for the arrival of Alexios. We shall have his gifts. His presence will assure trade by land and sea, and we shall be united under his leadership. All cities will lay down their arms, and Alexios may possess or destroy them as he wishes ...'
>
> In contradiction others argued: 'The Emperor has always harmed, deceived, and connived against us. Now that he realizes he is weak and we are strong through God's grace, he seeks to turn us from the Holy Sepulchre in fear that word of our success will cause others to follow in our footsteps. Let those he has often offended by words and acts beware of vain trust in him ...'[18]

Whether or not Alexios' representatives had been to Antioch before coming to Arqah cannot be corroborated by our sources. Nevertheless, they received little sympathy from the Latin leaders, who viewed the Byzantine emperor as a deceiver and certainly not a leader to be trusted. As the emissaries had to depart empty-handed, the crusade was rapidly moving to its climax as the army drew near to its ultimate goal, Jerusalem, where the host found itself outside the city's walls on 7 June 1099.

The Birth of the Principality of Antioch

Count Raymond's departure for Jerusalem in mid-January 1099 inevitably left a power vacuum that Bohemond was able to fill; the Latin sources report that the Norman directed his soldiers to evict the Provençal troops from the remaining sections of the city, hence 'in this way he gained sole lordship over Antioch'.[19] Sadly, however, the sources are silent about the way in which Bohemond managed to expand his nascent principality throughout 1099, as the march of the crusade to Jerusalem inevitably became the focus of every chronicler writing about this period. Yet it is easy to imagine that several of Antioch's neighbouring towns would have either been abandoned by their Latin garrisons, or their troops would have looked to Bohemond for some sort of political and (mainly) military cooperation (or, better, protection).

During the summer of 1099 Bohemond turned his attention to the southwest of his principality, specifically to the Byzantine-controlled Syrian port of Latakia (Ancient Greek: Λαοδίκεια; Arabic: *al-Lādhiqīyah*), one of the two main ports (along with St Symeon) in northern Syria that provided direct links to the bases in Cyprus and Cilicia: 'Bohemond, his greed for aggrandizement and acquisition unsatisfied, after a long siege had seized Latakia, a city inhabited by Greek Christians, with support and a naval attack from the Pisans and Genoese.'[20] What is more interesting is the way in which the Norman tried to gain access to the city, according to Albert of Aachen's account, by capturing two of the port's towers.

Despite the fact that none of our sources provides any description of the siege operation against Latakia, it could very well have involved the scaling of the coastal towers and/or walls with long ladders by troops on board the Italian ships. For at least two centuries before the crusades, warfleets operating in the Mediterranean included certain superstructures in the form of wooden towers, or 'castles', at the ship's stern and sometimes prow, and from the early tenth century the use of these forecastles on the ships had become the main characteristic of both Byzantine and Muslim warships.[21] These wooden superstructures could also be used against coastal defences, but they rarely had any success;[22] in fact, they may have been used by the Norman navy besieging Corfu in the spring of 1081, although this assumption cannot be corroborated by our contemporary sources. What can be confirmed, however, is the use of 'extremely large ladders from the ships' during the Byzantine operation to retake Corfu from the Sicilian Normans in 1149.[23] Therefore, I find it very likely that Bohemond would have had some knowledge of this form of siege technique during his operations in Syria.

What could explain Bohemond's campaign against Latakia is his decision to rid himself of a potentially threatening Byzantine outpost on the southwest fringes of his nascent principality, although it is less clear what may have prompted him to act at that particular moment. Nevertheless, Bohemond was soon pressured by the rest of the crusade leaders to abandon his operation, because of the fear that they (and their armies) would suffer harassment and/or open hostility from the imperial forces on their way back to Europe, after they had liberated Jerusalem on 15 July 1099. Even Archbishop Daimbert of Pisa, who had been dispatched by the Pope to the Levant to take the place of Adhemar of Le Puy, who had died of fever on 1 August 1098, and was travelling on board the Pisan fleet that assisted Bohemond in his attempt to capture Latakia, tried to disassociate himself from the latter's strategic decision to capture the Syrian port by claiming that he had been fooled into believing that 'the citizens of Latakia were false Christians, and always opposed the Christian brothers, and he [Bohemond] reported that they had been in an extreme degree traitors to the pilgrims among the Turks and Saracens'.[24]

Following Daimbert's decision to withdraw the Pisan ships from the waters off Latakia, Albert of Aachen reports that 'seeing he was destitute of help and his forces were greatly weakened ... Bohemond withdrew far from the siege of the walls with all his company, and, I know not whether from love or fear, he was forced to comply with the will of his brothers, whether he liked it or not.' Political association with the Norman leader had begun to look embarrassing for many Latin leaders of the crusade, yet they showed the necessary determination to restrain his ambitions when it was needed. Eventually, it was Raymond of Toulouse who foiled Bohemond's plans to capture Latakia, staying there until sometime between September 1099 and the summer of 1100, when he received a letter from Emperor Alexios 'demanding' that he hand over the city to the imperial officers, a request he complied with.[25]

Therefore, the boundaries of Bohemond's expanding principality around the end of 1099 – although not yet clearly defined – can be outlined here; in Syria, they extended from mid-way between St Symeon and Latakia to the south, to the port of Alexandretta (modern İskenderun) on the northern coast of Syria and the Gulf of Alexandretta. Inland, the new Norman principality stretched as far as Al-Bara and Maarrat al-Nu'man in the southeast, forming a sort of bulge deep into Aleppan territory. A Norman zone of control would also have encompassed the Ruj valley, between the Orontes river and modern Idlib, and the northern Syrian towns of Harem and Artah, before curving westwards towards the sea to the north of Alexandretta.

Bohemond's claim over the Cilician cities of Tarsus, Mamistra and Adana, with their friendly Armenian populations, would also prove crucial in establishing a sort of buffer-zone to shield his Syrian possessions from Alexios' twofold goal of undermining the Norman base in Antioch and wielding power over the coastline between Lycia and Cilicia.[26] The aforementioned cities may have been occupied by Latin armies during the approach of the crusade to Antioch, but their status by the end of 1099 was rather obscure. Baldwin of Boulogne had eventually established himself at Tarsus, following the fierce row that had erupted between him and Tancred in the autumn of 1097 over exerting control over the city, installing a garrison there before he departed for Edessa in February 1098. However, Asbridge has underlined that, following Baldwin's establishment of the first Latin principality in Edessa, in March 1098 the latter renounced his rights over Tarsus, apparently recognising that the distance between the two cities would make the effort to hold both of them unsustainable, thus leaving the way open to Bohemond to pursue a closer diplomatic relationship with the city's Armenian population over the next couple of years.[27]

During the same period in the autumn of 1097 Ralph of Caen reported that a certain Ursinus – probably Oschin, the Armenian lord of the castle of Lampron in the Taurus mountains, who had recently captured the city of Adana after massacring the Turkish garrison there – had:

> sent messengers to summon the son of the marquis [Tancred]. Upon the arrival of this important guest [at Adana], he [Oschin] went out personally and sweetened the path, offering his right hand and his faith, and promising not only the forces of those allied to him but also his own personal forces. He offered up the spoils of Mamistra [Mopsuestia], which was situated nearby and could be captured easily.[28]

Ralph's description of the events shows that Tancred was welcomed into Adana as an ally and, more likely, as a client ruler, because the same source reports that the Norman dealt with the Turkish leader of the garrison at Adana, and 'gave laws to the people of Mamistra, laws which were more paternal than princely in nature'.[29] Oschin's political manoeuvre to invite Tancred into his city, while providing the crusader armies with provisions, was no doubt intended to divert the Latins away from his lands and into Syria. Therefore, although there is nothing to suggest that Tancred took personal control of Adana in 1097/8, he did establish himself as a ruler of

Mamistra, even beating off an attempt by Baldwin of Boulogne to claim the city for his lord Godfrey, as we saw in the previous chapter. Before his departure from the city, Tancred left a garrison of some fifty men, although Ralph of Caen does not report who was left in charge of the town.[30] Consequently, of the three main Cilician cities mentioned here, Mamistra (Mopsuestia) is the most likely to have been closely connected to the Principality of Antioch before 1100.

Around mid-November 1099 Bohemond and Baldwin of Edessa travelled to Jerusalem to fulfil their crusader vows and celebrate Christmas. In a diplomatic masterstroke, the Norman then helped to elevate Daimbert of Pisa to the patriarchal throne of Jerusalem,[31] before 'escorting' the newly ordained bishops Roger of Tarsus, Bartholomew of Mamistra and Bernard of Artah to their respective episcopal sees; sometime after his return north, his army clashed with a Turkish mounted contingent from Damascus somewhere in the western vicinities of his principality. Bohemond's campaign to Jerusalem and subsequent return to Cilicia should be understood as a diplomatic manoeuvre by the Norman, not only to take advantage of the patriarchal vacancy created after the election of the first Latin Patriarch of Jerusalem, Arnulf of Chocques (supported by Godfrey of Bouillon), was pronounced uncanonical in the autumn of 1099, by pushing for the election of the likeliest candidate, Daimbert, but also, and more importantly, to consolidate his political influence in the northern borders of his principality over the claims of the Byzantine emperor.[32]

From Expansion to Captivity

Our sources record remarkably little about Bohemond's activities in 1100, although sporadic evidence of clashes with Turkish forces have led modern historians to assume that he was probably conducting a series of campaigns/raids against the emirate of Aleppo to the east of his principality. The Arab biographer and historian of the city of Aleppo, Kamal al-Din 'Umar ibn Aḥmad Ibn al-Adim (1192–1262), records an important victory for the 'Franks from Antioch' over the Turkish army of the *emir* of Aleppo in June. That battle was won with reinforcements received from the Latin garrisons of the towns of Zardana, al-Atharib and Sarmada – three key border-towns that dominated the flat plain between the principalities of Antioch and Aleppo, some 30km to the west of the latter Syrian city. This is clearly an indication of the territorial advance that Bohemond's troops had achieved by around 1100 over the Turkish garrisons in the region.[33]

Building upon his successful operations against the Turks in the early summer of 1100, Kamal al-Din reports that Bohemond was still in the vicinity of Aleppo with a strong military force, probably preparing for a campaign against Ridwan's capital, while the Armenian Matthew of Edessa notes that he was besieging the Cilician city of Maraş (Ancient Greek: Γερμανίκεια; modern Kahramanmaraş);[34] the latter had been conquered by the Latin armies in October 1097 after a short period of Turkish rule under a certain Chawuldur, and they promptly handed it over to the Byzantine emperor.[35] It was in the early summer of the same year when Bohemond received a plea for aid from Gabriel (d. 1102/3), the Armenian ruler of Melitene (modern Malatya) some 380km northeast of Antioch, against the expanding strategy of the neighbouring Danishmendid Turks from the north, who were based in central-northeastern Anatolia around Amasya (Greek: Ἀμάσεια) and Sebasteia (modern Sivas) and to the north of the river Halys. Perhaps considering the Norman a less dangerous ally than Baldwin of Edessa, the latter's principality being closer at some 220km to his south, Gabriel agreed on a closer link with the Norman Principality of Antioch, which would probably have meant that he was granted the city back as a fief from Bohemond.[36]

At all events, Bohemond set out for the besieged city of Melitene around July 1100 with a relief force of a few hundred knights. Just before their arrival in the vicinity of the city, and after receiving advance warning and – most likely– an estimate of his army's numbers, the leader of the Danishmendid besieging army, Gümüştekin Danishmend Ahmed Gazi, 'took five hundred knights from his own army and met him [Bohemond] on the plain of that region'.[37] Although Albert of Aachen's laconic report suggests that the *emir* deployed an elite force from his own personal guard to do battle with the Normans, it is better to follow Ralph of Caen's description of the events that unfolded between the two armies.[38] Ralph describes Gümüştekin's military manoeuvring as the typical Turkish (steppe) battle-tactic of feigned flight – withdrawing the bulk of the army from the field and making it look like they were routed in order to entice the enemy into giving chase, thus luring them into a pre-arranged location where an ambush was ready. Our chronicler notes that Bohemond was advised not to chase after the retreating Turks but rather to enter the city of Melitene so that his men could recuperate and resupply after an exhausting 'ten or more days journey from Antioch'. Bohemond was too experienced in the fighting tactics of the Turks to have dismissed this sound advice, yet:

> acting on his own stupid audacity, he said, 'far be it that Bohemond now do something that he never remembers having done. They [the

Turks] have acted like foxes who seek the shadows as soon as they hear the dogs barking.' Therefore, he set out against the Turks, and soon joined in a battle against them that he never should have entered.

It would be very interesting to have the chance to read how Bohemond's troops reacted in the event of an ambush by steppe horse-archers like the Danishmendid troops but sadly the primary sources do not go into the details of the battle that unfolded that day. What we do know, however, is that both Bohemond and his second-in-command, Richard of Principate, were captured by the Turks in what turned out to be a disastrous outcome for the Norman's adventurous campaign that summer; those who were not killed or executed in battle were taken in chains to the Danishmendid city of NeoKaisarea (modern Niksar). We read Matthew of Edessa's dramatic comments about the impact of Bohemond's defeat and capture on the crusaders: 'Hearing the news of this defeat, all the Christian peoples shook and trembled with fear, while the whole Persian nation [Turks] rejoiced and was happy; for the infidels had regarded Bohemond as the veritable king of the Franks, and all the people of Khurasan had trembled at his name.'[39]

Nevertheless, instead of suffering extended territorial losses to the neighbouring Turks [to the east] and to the Byzantines [to the north], the principality of Antioch seems to have enjoyed a period of expansion thanks – to a great extent – to the brilliant strategic thinking, martial skills and determination of Tancred, who acted as Bohemond's regent in Antioch until 1103. Tancred's first strategic masterstroke was his campaign that reclaimed the coastal Cilician towns of Tarsus, Adana and Mopsuestia from the Byzantines, sometime in April 1101.[40] On top of that, Anna describes that the imperial officers Butumites and Monastras, who had been dispatched by Alexios to Cilicia with enough forces to contain Tancred's activities, 'reached Cilicia and found that the Armenians had already concluded a truce with Tancred'.[41]

However, Tancred's greatest military achievement in his two years as regent was the siege and conquest of the key port of Latakia, a feat that had eluded Bohemond in 1099. Ralph of Caen writes that Tancred launched his operation in the summer of 1101, and it lasted for almost one-and-a-half years.[42] In his account, Ralph highlights the formidable defences of the port-city, which posed a serious tactical challenge to the modest besieging army, especially bearing in mind Tancred's lack of the necessary siege engines and fleet to impose an effective blockade by cutting off its communications with the Byzantine bases in Cyprus. It was Raymond of Toulouse's failed attempt to relieve Latakia sometime in the spring of 1102, probably acting under orders from Alexios, followed by a fateful tactical decision by a considerable number of defenders who fell for a simple but brilliant trick set up by Tancred, that eventually sealed the fate of the city.

The Norman had ordered his army to collect large quantities of grain and store it without adequate guard-protection in plain sight of the defenders of Latakia, no doubt aiming to entice them into launching a quick sortie in order to capture the collected grain and perhaps even to try to loot the Norman camp. According to Ralph of Caen, the defenders quickly took the bait and dispatched a large raiding party against the besiegers' camp! But while the Latakians were busy collecting their booty, they were oblivious to the fact that a party of Tancred's soldiers was lying in wait for them to return to the city laden with the spoils of war, in order to ambush them at the most critical moment, when they were about to 'queue' to enter the city through its main gate. This stratagem allowed Tancred to inflict high casualties on the defenders of Latakia, who, following this critical setback, 'had no trust in the walls or in themselves'; the city opened its gates soon after.

Bohemond's Release and the Battle of Harran

During his regency between 1101 and 1103 Tancred did nothing much to bring about his uncle's release from Turkish captivity because 'it seemed that Bohemond's return would be a hindrance to his [Tancred's] continued prosperity'. However, Gümüştekin seems to have allowed Bohemond to communicate with the outside world in order to raise the amount of money needed to secure his release; we know, for example, that Bernard of Valence, who had been Adhemar of Le Puy's chaplain, was appointed by Bohemond while in captivity to serve as the Latin patriarch of Antioch in 1100, holding this office until 1135.[43] Eventually, Bohemond's release was due to the generosity of important figures like Patriarch Bernard, Kogh Vasil (d. 12 October 1112), the Armenian ruler of Raban and Kaysun (modern Keysun Kalesi, in Adıyaman Province, southeastern Turkey), and Baldwin of Bourcq, who had succeeded his cousin Baldwin of Boulogne as the second count of Edessa, after the latter left for Jerusalem to replace his brother Godfrey (d. 18 July 1100) as king of Jerusalem (he was crowned on 25 December 1100), with Ralph of Caen implying that 'he [Baldwin of Bourcq] was a particular enemy of Tancred'.

Kogh Vasil's involvement in Bohemond's release, by paying some 10,000 *dahekans* to free the Norman, is critical to understanding the delicate balance of power between the local Latin, Armenian and Turkish potentates in northern Syria and Cilicia, because, according to Matthew of Edessa's account of the events, 'after a number of days [following his release] Bohemond went to his city of Antioch and by a solemn oath became an adopted son of the Armenian Prince Kogh Vasil'.[44] The disastrous campaign in Melitene in 1100, coupled with Baldwin of Bourcq's adverse attitude towards Tancred, would have made it abundantly clear to Bohemond that he needed whatever allies he could find in order to shield the northern borders of his principality – the alliance with Kogh Vasil proved fruitful, albeit short-lived, considering Bohemond's departure for western Europe in 1104/5. But for the time being, the Norman immediately claimed back from Tancred all of the towns and fortresses that his nephew had conquered within the last two years, including 'Latakia, Mamistra, Adana and Tarsus, which he [Tancred] gained by dint of his own effort … he [Tancred] had to beg for two small towns'. Surely Bohemond's move reflects his frustration at his nephew's failure to aid in his release.

By the end of 1103 the northern borders of Bohemond's principality would have extended to the city of Tarsus and the river Cydnus (Greek: Κύδνος; also Baradān or Baradā, in modern Mersin Province) in the northwest, and to the city of Sarvandikar (Sarvanda k'ar; Turkish: Savranda) at the southern end of the Amanus Pass (or 'Syrian Gates') in the northeast, where Raymond of Toulouse was briefly captured and held by Tancred's men in 1101.[45] During the first half of 1104 Muslim sources report that Bohemond planned to tighten the noose around Ridwan's capital by either raiding or demanding tribute from several towns on the western approaches to Aleppo, including Al-Muslimiyah (16km northwest of Aleppo) and Qinnasrin (25km southwest of Aleppo, on the west bank of the Queiq river). This aggressive strategy resulted in Ridwan's request for a truce with Bohemond, which involved a payment of 7,000 *dinars* and ten horses in return for the release of the Muslim prisoners the Latins held as prisoners.[46]

Baldwin II of Edessa also pursued an aggressive strategy during this period by organising frequent raids against the fertile plains around Harran, a strongly fortified town just 45km southeast of Edessa and 60km due east from the Edessan stronghold (since 1101) of Suruç, possession of which would not only have significantly increased Baldwin's resources, but also would have made Edessa itself safer from attack from Mesopo-

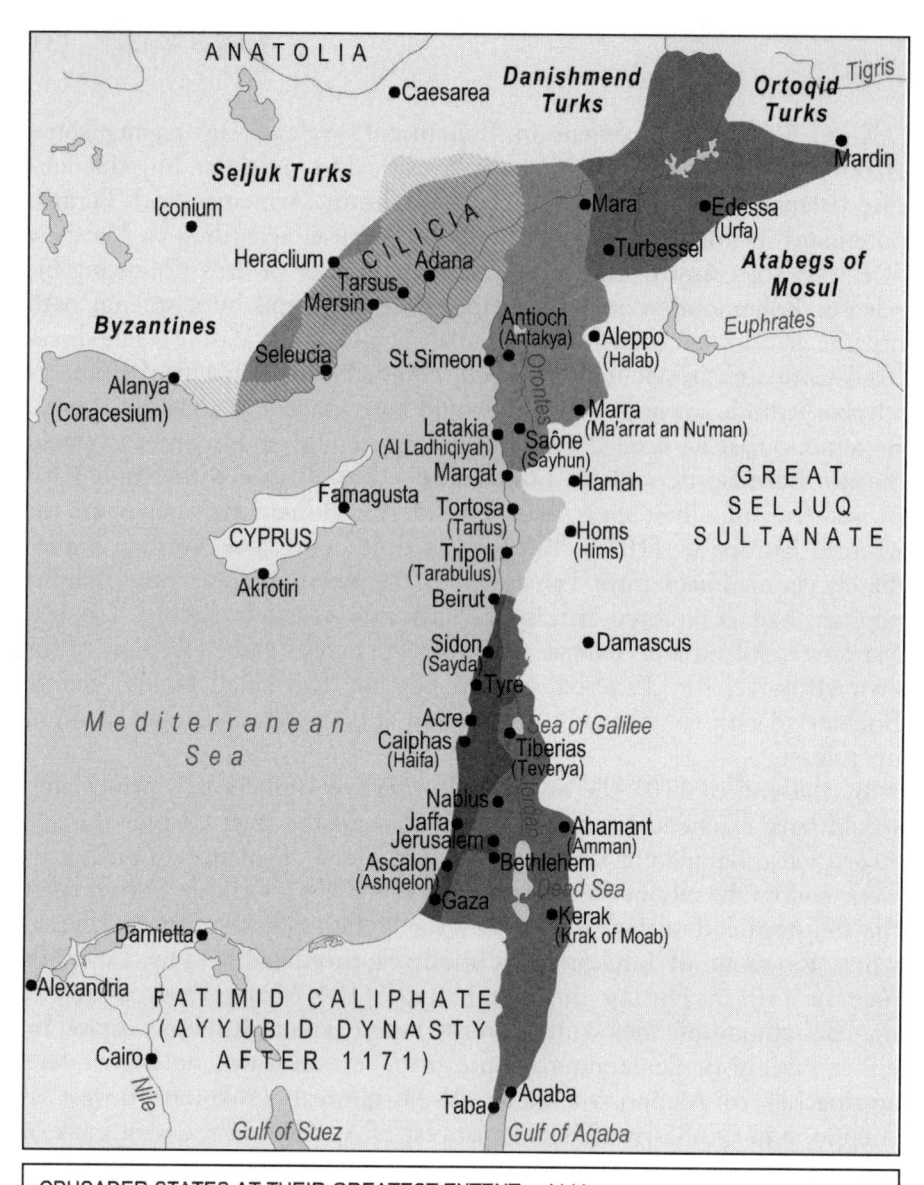

CRUSADER STATES AT THEIR GREATEST EXTENT, c.1144
- Principality of Antioch, 1098-1268
  (after 1198, the western region was lost to Lesser Armenia)
- County of Edessa, 1098-1144
- County of Tripoli, 1109-1289
- Kingdom of Jerusalem, 1099-1187
- Kingdom of Jerusalem after the Treaty of Jaffa, 1229
- Kingdom of Lesser Armenia (Cilicia), 1198-1375

The Middle East.

tamia.[47] Baldwin also wanted to strengthen his position among his Armenian allies in the north and west of his principality by granting villages to important Armenian prelates such as Barsegh Pahlavuni, the Armenian *Catholicos* of Cilicia from 1105 to 1113, and Kogh Vasil of Raban and Kaysun.[48]

Eventually, it was Baldwin's expansionist strategy in the region of Harran that sucked Bohemond into Edessa's conflict with the neighbouring Turkish principality of Mardin. In the spring of 1104 the historian Ibn al-Qalanisi reports that Jikirmish (or Chökürmish, d. 1108), *atabeg* (governor) of Mosul, and Sökmen (or Soqman ibn Ortoq, d. 1104), the Artuqid lord of Mardin and Hasankeyf (in modern Batman Province of eastern Turkey), some 200km east of Edessa, 'had joined forces and made a solemn agreement with one another to prosecute the Holy war against the Franks, the enemies of God, and to devote their entire strength and means to active warfare with them'.[49] Therefore, the first major battle of the newfound crusader states in the aftermath of the First Crusade was prompted by a plea for military assistance from Baldwin II to Bohemond, when the former's capital was threatened by the combined armies of Jikirmish and Sökmen.[50]

According to al-Qalanisi, 'at the beginning of Sha'bān [29 April] they [Jikirmish and Sökmen] encamped at Ra's al-'Ain', a town some 100km east of Harran, exactly on the modern Turkey-Syria border, before marching against Edessa. Albert of Aachen's account of the events, however, differs somewhat from the version given by Ralph of Caen and al-Qalanisi. The latter pair maintain that Edessa was besieged for some days by the Turkish army before the arrival of Bohemond and his retinue in the area of Harran on the eve of the battle. Albert, on the other hand, reports that Baldwin sent his plea for help upon learning of the approach of the Turkish army, probably through his intelligence, and that Bohemond's arrival at Harran came before Jikirmish and Sökmen were able to begin the siege of Edessa.

I find Ralph's and al-Qalanisi's version of events more plausible, and I believe that Baldwin's plea for reinforcements would have been dispatched to Antioch based on early intelligence about the imminent invasion of Edessan territory by a formidable Turkish force, thus giving Bohemond enough time to muster all the forces available to him for the march to Harran. And the lord of Antioch would have needed plenty of time to do that, as we learn from our Latin sources that he was accompanied by Tancred, Bernard of Valence the Patriarch of Antioch, Daimbert of Pisa the Patriarch of Jerusalem, and Benedict, the archbishop of Edessa.

Furthermore, for Bohemond to have managed to muster some three thousand cavalry and seven thousand foot-soldiers, according to Albert of Aachen, before marching the 350km from Antioch to Harran in a northeasterly direction (bypassing the enemy territory west of Aleppo), and all that in just eight days (the Turkish army encamped at Ra's al-'Ain on 29 April, and the battle took place on 7 May) sounds implausible. What we can be sure about, however, is that the Christian forces that were to face the combined Turkish army at Harran lacked cohesion from the outset, as the multitude of their leaders would suggest, namely Bohemond of Antioch, Tancred, Baldwin II of Edessa and his cousin Joscelin of Courtenay (d. 1131) lord of Turbessel (Arabic: Tell Bāshir, Turkish: Tilbeşar, in modern Gaziantep province). On top of that, William of Tyre reports that Bohemond and Baldwin II were wrangling over the control of Harran, surely not the best situation for an army in desperate need of unified command against a formidable foe.

All our sources identify Edessa as the target of Jikirmish's and Sökmen's forces. Albert of Aachen's report also suggests that Baldwin II made the necessary arrangements for the defence of his capital before leaving Edessa for the city of Harran to await the arrival of reinforcements under Bohemond and Tancred. A critical question that emerges at this point is: Where was the Edessan army? Albert writes further down in his account that 'three thousand cavalry and seven thousand infantry [from Antioch] ... marched to the appointed place, that is to say, onto the plains of the city of Aran, or Caran [Harran], where Baldwin was only just awaiting their arrival with all the army he had collected'.[51] If the Edessan army had been operating in the vicinity of Harran before the arrival of the Turkish combined army, then Jikirmish and Sökmen may have wanted to distract it away from Harran or even to take Edessa while the crusaders were engaged elsewhere. The other scenario would have involved Baldwin leaving Edessa for Harran to assemble an army against the Turkish invasion, apparently considering the option of a pitched battle more preferable than a prolonged siege of his capital.

Sadly, the accounts given by our primary sources for the battle are so contradictory that it is difficult for modern historians to put together a detailed picture of the series of clashes between the Latin and Turkish armies that we have come to identify as the Battle of Harran. What we can be sure about, however, is that once the Turkish leaders learned of the arrival of the Latin reinforcements under Bohemond, they dispatched a large force – probably under Sökmen – to draw the crusaders away from

Harran before they could manage to establish a full-scale siege of the city, and perhaps also to allow for Jikirmish to enter Harran with supplies and reinforcements. The Turks were reported to have made extensive use of their typical feigned flight tactic to entice the crusaders into giving chase, with Matthew of Edessa reporting a pursuit of two days and Ralph of Caen writing about a three-day chase.

A long-drawn-out pursuit of an enemy who used the feigned flight tactic was not uncommon and was reported for the first time as early as 512 BC, when the Persian King Darius I mustered a large expedition to invade the land of the Scythians north of the Danube. As the latter were probably caught unawares by this massive Persian invasion, they chose not to face Darius's slow and heavily armoured army in open battle, choosing rather to send their families to the north, while the main body of Scythian warriors drew the Persians away along the north coast of the Black Sea by a prolonged feigned flight that lasted for twenty days.[52] Hence, we read Herodotus' question about the outcome of the Persian invasion of 512 BC: 'How can such a people [the Scythians] fail to defeat the attempt of an invader not only to subdue them, but even to make contact with them?'

Therefore, bearing in mind Bohemond's significant experience in the steppe tactics of the Turks, and especially considering his recent defeat and capture by Gümüştekin in 1100, when the Norman let himself be duped by the Turkish feigned flight tactics, do we have any well-grounded explanation of the two or three day chase of the Turkish army at Harran in 1104? Was Bohemond overruled by Baldwin II? Was Baldwin II less experienced in the Turkish steppe tactics and not able to recognise the danger his army faced? Sadly, modern historians have no definite answer to these questions.

According to Albert of Aachen, the battle took place 'on the plain before the town of Raqqa', which is situated about two days' march south from Harran on the northeast bank of the Euphrates river. When they reached Raqqa, Albert and Ralph of Caen report that the Turks crossed to the southern bank of the Balikh river, which flows due south from a spring on the modern Turkish-Syrian border and joins the Euphrates at Raqqa. The crusaders were then deployed for battle on the northern bank of the Balikh, according to their marching formation: Baldwin and Joscelin commanded the Edessan left wing, while Bohemond and Tancred commanded the Antiochean right. Ralph of Caen notes that the crusaders were caught unawares when the Turks turned to fight, so much so that Baldwin and Bohemond fought without armour.

Albert of Aachen reports that it was Sökmen, with about thirty thousand men, who opened the battle by charging against the right flank of the Latin army under Bohemond and Tancred, only to be met with fierce resistance by the outnumbered Christians. Whether because he realised he could not break the Antiochean army wing, or because he was applying a pre-arranged battle manoeuvre, Sökmen eventually fell back on the southern bank of the Balikh, with Baldwin's forces following in disorder. Based on what happened next, however, it is safer to assume that this was another Turkish feigned flight manoeuvre, since Sökmen was able to draw Baldwin's forces into an ambush on the opposite river bank, where some ten thousand Turks – perhaps those under Jikirmish – 'rose from ambush and attacked them fiercely head-on with bows and arrows, assaulting them severely and shooting them with arrows, until the whole army was put to flight'. Baldwin and Joscelin were taken prisoner, while Bohemond, who had not taken the bait, retreated in relatively good order, although he lost men as he fought his way back to Edessa; a sally made by the garrison of Harran would only have increased the confusion. Appointing Tancred as regent of Edessa in Baldwin's absence, Bohemond returned to his capital.

The galvanising effect of the outcome of the Battle of Harran on Muslim morale is best summarised in al-Qalanisi's comments in his *Damascus Chronicle*:

> This was a great and unexampled victory for the Muslims; it discouraged the Franks, diminished their numbers and broke their power of offence, while the hearts of the Muslims were strengthened, and their zeal for the victory of the Faith and the war against the heretics was whetted and sharpened. The people joyfully noised abroad the good news of the victory over them, and became assured of their destruction and the turning of fortune against them.[53]

This was the first significant defeat of crusader arms in battle in the Middle East, and there came the immediate realisation in the Turkish and Byzantine camps that the Latins in the Levant were not invincible, thus encouraging a series of campaigns against the Edessan and Antiochean principalities in the years to come. On top of that, however, the territorial losses suffered by the Principality of Antioch in the immediate aftermath of the Battle of Harran were serious enough to arouse great concern in Bohemond's and Tancred's minds. In particular, Bohemond lost control of the strategically important Ruj valley, between the Orontes river and Aleppo, while the forward strongholds of Ma'arat-al-Numan, Kafartab and Albara were handed over to Ridwan of Aleppo, probably because

Bohemond chose to withdraw their garrisons back to Antioch to compensate for the losses his forces sustained at Harran.[54] Albert of Aachen also reports that Ridwan ordered his troops to lead raids deep into Antiochean territory, perhaps in an effort to rouse the local Muslim populations against the Latins.[55]

Bohemond's troubles were compounded in the northern regions of his principality as well. Ralph of Caen details[56] that in the aftermath of Harran the citizens of Tarsus, Adana and Mamistra ejected the Antiochean garrisons from their cities and 'invited' the Byzantines in once again. On top of that, Ralph notes the devastating Aleppan raids inflicted on the city and surrounding region of Artah (modern Reyhanlı), located 40km east-northeast of Antioch, on the Roman road from Antioch to Aleppo. Finally, the same source notes that a sizeable Byzantine naval squadron occupied the port-city of Latakia, carrying 'craftsmen and troops, so that they could both wage war and undertake building operations'. A relief expedition that was immediately launched by Bohemond failed to eject the Byzantine troops from the city.

By the end of 1104, in a meeting in Antioch with Tancred and the rest of his officers, Bohemond is reported to have summed up the rapidly deteriorating geo-political situation of his principality in the following words:

> The Greeks and the Turks enclose us all around. We have irritated the two richest powers in the world, Constantinople and Persia. The East terrifies us by land, and the West terrifies us by land and by sea. Moreover, lest I leave it out, Artah, which had been the shield of Antioch, now stretches the bow and directs the arrows. We are few and even our small numbers are shrinking on a regular basis. Our forces were greatly reduced by the loss of the count of Edessa ... We must search for help from the men across the sea. The people of the Gauls must be roused.[57]

Perhaps Bohemond knew that he could defend his principality against the fragmented nature of Turkish politics in Syria, yet he must also have been fully aware that he could not possibly match the Byzantine Empire in resources and manpower. Therefore, with his diminishing territories 'sandwiched' between the Byzantines and the Turkish emirates, Bohemond conceived a strategy that could radically change the geo-political map of the eastern Mediterranean: an attempt to replace the Byzantine emperor with someone more sympathetic to him – a plan reminiscent of the Fourth Crusade some hundred years later.

The Principality under Tancred, 1105–13

Fulcher of Chartres summed up the effect of the defeat of the Antiochean and Edessan armies by the Muslim forces led by Jikirmish and Sökmen at the Battle of Harran on 7 May 1104: 'this engagement was far more disastrous than all previous battles, as the result showed'.[58] The scale of the territorial contraction clearly demonstrates the fragility of the Antiochean successes in the previous five years and the instability of Latin rule in the region. It is at this point that the Latin Principality of Antioch faced the most serious challenge of its existence.

In the spring of 1105 the city of Artah either expelled its garrison and allied itself with Ridwan of Aleppo, or simply opened its gates to an Aleppan army raiding the region. The authorities in Antioch could not allow this strategic city to fall into enemy hands, with Tancred '[calling] on all the Christian men who were in the area for assistance, appointing Antioch to be their meeting place ... some thousand cavalry and nine thousand infantry assembled'.[59] Following a short siege of the city, Tancred met with Ridwan's forces in the vicinity of Artah, with the Latin forces emerging victorious on 20 April 1105. Tancred proceeded to consolidate the Principality's control of its eastern frontier regions, precipitating the flight of local Muslim garrisons from the areas of al-Jazr and Loulon (a strategically important site that controlled the northern exit of the Cilician Gates). On top of that, large parts of the Ruj valley were reoccupied by the Latins, although the details of this process are unclear.

Having fended off the threat from Ridwan of Aleppo, Tancred focused his strategy on defending his principality from its three major opponents: the Byzantines, who were threatening Antiochean influence in Cilicia and along the northern coast of Syria (especially in the key port of Laodicea/Latakia); the Muslims of Aleppo; and the Banū Munqidh, an Arab family that ruled a small emirate in the Orontes valley in northern Syria from the mid-eleventh century until 1157. Tancred's strategy aimed at gaining control of strategic castles and outposts on the frontiers with these enemies, from where he could launch raids and counter-raids against them, thus expanding the Antiochean zone of influence: a sort of 'aggressive defence'.[60]

In the south, one of Tancred's most significant successes was the capture of Apamea, on the east bank of the Orontes river to the west of Kafartab. Taking advantage of internal strife in the city, he captured it following a short siege in August 1106, which enabled him to counter the threat to the principality posed by the city of Shaizar on the west bank of the Orontes. In the east, Tancred's most significant successes were against the Muslims of Aleppo, on whom he inflicted two serious blows in 1111 with the capture of the key towns of Al-Atharib and Zardana, mid-way between Antioch and Aleppo. This strategic setback forced Ridwan to negotiate a treaty with Tancred that included an annual payment of 20,000 *dinars* and significant quantities of cloth and horses.

In the operational theatre of Cilicia, Tancred faced the aggressive strategy of the Byzantine empire, coupled with the ambiguous and circumstantial policies of the local Armenian potentates. We will see in chapter 8 that in 1107 Alexios Komnenos recalled his senior officer in the region, Monastras, to the capital owing to Bohemond's imminent invasion of the Balkans. Oshin, the man who replaced Monastras at Tarsus, was a local Armenian lord who had allied himself with the crusaders back in 1097; according to Anna Komnena, he was defeated by a combined naval and land invasion by the Antiocheans, who targeted Mamistra sometime in 1107.[61]

It was only a few years later, between 1109 and 1111, that Tancred managed to expand his conquests in the region and exert authority over most of the major cities of Cilicia. Hence, in spite of the Treaty of Devol (agreed between Bohemond and Alexios Komnenos in September 1108), Tancred led a campaign that successfully captured Tarsus, while Albert of Aachen records that in 1111 a certain 'Guy Capreolus, prince of the towns of Tarsus and Mamistra' answered Tancred's military summons.[62] Bohemond's invasion of the Balkans in 1107 may also have facilitated Tancred's capture of the Syrian port of Latakia, which was definitely under Antiochean control by 1108, although it may have been captured as early as 1105 following the Battle of Artah.[63] There is little doubt, therefore, that for Bohemond's nephew the Treaty of Devol was a dead letter.

Chapter 8

Back to Europe

Bohemond was now getting alarmed by the Emperor's threats and had no means of protecting himself (for he had neither an army on land nor a fleet at sea; and danger menaced him from both sides), so he devised a plan which was exceedingly sordid, and yet exceedingly ingenious. First of all he left the town of Antioch to his nephew Tancred, the son of Marceses, and had a report spread about himself, which said that Bohemond had died, and while still alive he arranged that the world should think of him as dead. And the report spread more quickly than a bird can fly and proclaimed that Bohemond was a corpse! And when he found that the report had taken good hold, a wooden coffin was soon prepared and a bireme, in which the coffin was placed, and also he, the living corpse, sailed away from Sudei, which is the harbour of Antioch, to Rome ... And to make the corpse appear stale and odoriferous, they strangled or killed a cock and placed it with the corpse; and that villain Bohemond enjoyed this fictitious evil all the more; I for myself am astonished that he being alive could bear such a siege of his nostrils, and be carried about with a dead body ... For this man, who was not dead except in pretence, did not shrink from living with dead bodies. The device of the barbarian was unique in the world of our time, and was directed towards the downfall of the Roman hegemony ... When he reached Corfu, and was now safe, so he arose from the dead and left the corpse-bearing coffin there and basked in more sunlight and breathed purer air and wandered about the town of Corfu ... The Duke [of Corfu town] happened to be a certain Alexios of the Armenian theme. When Bohemond saw him he looked at him with haughty bearing and speaking haughtily in his barbarian language ordered him to give Alexios the Emperor the following message. 'This message I send to thee, that Bohemond the son of Robert, who has in these past years taught thee and thy Empire how strong I am in courage and perseverance, God knows that, wheresoever I may go and whatever crisis of fortune I experience, I shall never bear patiently the wrongs that have been done me. For ever since I passed through the Roman Empire, and took Antioch and enslaved the whole of Syria by my sword, I have had my fill of bitter treatment from thee and thy army, disappointed in one hope after another and involved in countless misfortunes and barbaric wars. But now let me tell thee that, though I died, I have come to life again, and have slipped through thy hands ... But I myself, who was reported to thee and thine as dead, am going to my own country as a living man to myself and mine and full of dire intentions against thee ... For as soon as I reach the continent opposite and see the men of Lombardy, and all the Latins and Germans and the Franks, our subjects and most warlike men, I shall fill thy towns and countries with many murders and much bloodshed until I plant my spear on Byzantium itself.' To such a pitch of arrogance was the barbarian carried.

[*Alexiad*, XI. xii]

Anna Komnena's account of Bohemond's long visit to western Europe between 1105 and 1107 is pretty much useless, as the princess was only aware of one important thing: the Norman's marriage to Constance, the daughter of the French King Philip I (d. 29 July 1108). Furthermore, the *Alexiad* is full of the usual tirade against Bohemond's activities that targeted, beyond any doubt to our author, her father and the empire. Yet, as Rowe argued, Anna attacked Bohemond 'in terms so vague as to tell us nothing of the time, place and circumstances under which Bohemond conducted his anti-Byzantine campaign', adding that 'her account is not factual in character but rather an interpretation, in the light of subsequent events, of the rumours and fears concerning the meaning of Bohemond's voyage to the West which circulated at that time through the imperial court and disturbed the minds of the Emperor and his advisers'.[1]

Rounding up Support in Italy and France

Bohemond's triumphal return to the Apulian capital-city of Bari in January 1105 should come as no surprise considering the Norman's anxiety to keep the public back home informed about his military achievements in the Levant. Following the victory over Kerbogha's relief army outside Antioch in 1098, the anonymous *Historia Belli Sacri* (composed sometime after 1131) described how Bohemond dispatched the *emir*'s tent to the Cathedral of St Nicolas in Bari, apparently for public display of his triumph over the Muslims seven years earlier.[2] Another source reported that he allegedly gave to the Church of St Sabinus at Canosa two thorns from Christ's Crown of Thorns that purported to bear traces of the Redeemer's blood. Little wonder, therefore, that upon his arrival in the city that had been his stronghold until the mid-1090s, Bohemond was treated as a sort of a medieval 'rock-star' with people flocking to catch a glimpse of him 'ac si ipsum Christum essent visuri' ('as if they were going to see Christ himself').[3] Therefore, his strategic decision to quit Antioch and the Levant and return to Europe, six years after the liberation of Jerusalem, provoked a completely different public reaction compared to the criticism the Norman had sustained, even from chroniclers as close to the Norman court in Sicily as Geoffrey Malaterra, following the abandonment of the joint siege operation with Roger Borsa and Roger of Sicily against Amalfi in July and August 1096; Bohemond was now a hero rather than a villain.

It was probably between the months of January and September 1105 that Bohemond busied himself with the preparations for the fleet that he planned to carry his army across the Adriatic Sea.[4] Then, sometime in September[5] of that year the Norman departed from Bari to Rome to meet with Pope Pascal, accompanied by Daimbert, the former Patriarch of Jerusalem,[6] who had travelled with Bohemond back to Italy to appeal to the Pope himself regarding his deposition from his high office. Although we lack the precise date of the encounter between the two, we do know of a papal privilege granted at Bohemond's request to the cathedral of St Nicolas of Bari on 18 November.[7] Finally, according to Orderic Vitalis, before setting out for France Bohemond had already dispatched envoys to Henry I of England (1100–1135) 'notifying him that he wished to cross the sea to visit his court'. Henry was, of course, quite suspicious about Bohemond's visit to his country to enlist men for his campaign, especially during a turbulent period when his preoccupations lay across the Channel and with Robert Curthose. Henry sent a discouraging letter back to Bohemond, suggesting that he should rather come to Normandy before Easter, and he would meet him there, although the meeting never took place.[8]

Sadly, we have very few details of the meeting between Bohemond and Pascal in Rome that autumn of 1105. But what we do know, however, proved crucial for the shifting of Bohemond's campaign into a Holy war; Pascal made him the standard-bearer of the army of Christ by giving him the banner of St Peter, before encouraging him to go to France to seek aid for his campaign.[9] On top of that, Pascal appointed Bruno, bishop of Segni, a Cluniac who had escorted Urban II during his visit to France in 1095–96, as papal legate to preach for the upcoming campaign in France, along with Bohemond himself.[10] Moreover, we have to mention a story in Orderic Vitalis, the only source that refers to the presence in Bohemond's entourage of a supposed son of the deposed Byzantine emperor Romanus IV Diogenes (1068–71).[11] This is critical in the sense that we see Bohemond using the same pattern of earning a 'blessing' for his 'restoration mission' as his father had done twenty-five years before, during the papacy of Gregory VII, when Robert Guiscard's 'fideles Sancti Petri' ('soldiers of St Peter') were given absolution from their sins to 'restore Michael VII to the Byzantine throne'.[12]

Therefore, with his prestige and morale boosted by Pascal's endorsement of his campaign, and with the right excuse in hand in the face of the supposed son of the deposed emperor, Bohemond stayed in the Eternal City at least until mid-November 1105 and then departed for France, where he hoped, first and foremost, to recruit the bulk of his followers through the launching of an unprecedented anti-Byzantine propaganda campaign, and also to secure the alliance of the French Crown. We cannot be sure if Bohemond managed to recruit any followers in Italy, simply because no primary sources mention him preaching between his leaving Rome and entering France, but it does not seem impossible that he would have taken advantage of the dissatisfaction with Alexios Komnenos of a large number of Lombards from northern Italy who had taken part in the disastrous crusade of 1101.

In March 1106 we find Bohemond in the Limousin region of southwest-central France, fulfilling a vow he had made to St Leonard, the patron saint of prisoners,[13] while a captive himself in the hands of the Danishmendid Turks, to bring his chains – allegedly made of silver[14] – to the shrine of the saint at Noblac in Limousin as a tribute to his release – and no doubt to use this event as an opportunity for another anti-Byzantine tirade against Alexios Komnenos. In fact, as Russo notes, the story of Bohemond's pilgrimage to the shrine, which happened to be recorded by Galeran of Naumburg, a German bishop, includes perhaps the most ferocious attack against Alexios in any contemporary Latin source:

> O cruellest emperor! He has oppressed many thousands of Christians with wicked treachery, some consigned to shipwreck, many to poison, more still to exile, and countless others he has handed over to pagans. This emperor is not a Christian but a mad heretic, Julian the Apostate, another Judas, friend of the Jews, pretending peace but inciting war, cut-throat to his brothers, a bloody Herod against Christ! He persecutes Christ through his limbs, he slaughters the innocent, he pours out the blood of saints like water, and he makes their remains food for the birds of the air.[15]

Another critical reason why Bohemond sought to go to France was to negotiate a marriage with Constance (d. 1125), daughter of Philip I of France, and to secure another French princess as a wife for Tancred – Cecilia, Philip's daughter from Bertha de Montfort. Bohemond's marriage to Constance in Chartres Cathedral was a well-attended event, which would have provided the Norman with another great opportunity to recruit soldiers for his campaign. Orderic Vitalis' account highlights Bohemond's immense popularity and the huge crowds that flocked to hear him speak against the Byzantine emperor:

> Then the duke [Bohemond], distinguished among the most illustrious, proceeded to the church [pulpit at Chartres Cathedral], and standing on the steps before the altar of the Virgin Mother, related to the vast assembled multitude his adventures and achievements, exhorting all who were brought up to arms to join him in his enterprise against the emperor [Alexios Komnenos], and promising cities and opulent towns to knights of approved courage. In consequence, numbers assumed the cross with ardour, and leaving all they possessed, embraced the pilgrimage to Jerusalem [Latin: 'iter in Ierusalem'] as if they were going to a feast.[16]

Following his critical political breakthrough in marrying the daughter of the French king, the climax of Bohemond's and Bruno of Segni's preaching mission in France came at the council they held at Poitiers on 26 June 1106. According to the eye-witness account by Suger, Abbot of St-Denis (d. 1151): 'The legate [Bruno] held a solemn plenary council at Poitiers ... He conducted the varied business of the synod but especially made sure that zeal for the journey to Jerusalem [should] not grow lukewarm, for both he and Bohemond aroused many of those present to make it.'[17] We can be sure that Bruno's great experience in preaching for the First Crusade with Pope Urban II at the council of Clermont in November 1095 stood him in good stead at Poitiers. Finally, one Latin chronicler attests that Bohemond went far into the southwest of France and even to Spain,[18] important centres of recruitment for a Holy war, no doubt accompanied by Bruno of Segni to add a more religious tone to his appeal, before returning to Apulia with his wife and entourage sometime in August 1106.

A Crusade Against Whom?

There are two interconnected questions about Bohemond's campaign of 1107–08 that have divided modern historians. The first is whether Pope Pascal was 'manipulated' by Bohemond into giving his blessing for a 'crusade' against the Byzantine empire. Likewise, the question that quickly follows is if we can include Bohemond's campaign against the empire into the wider movement of the crusades. To begin with the critical matter of defining the movement that was unleashed in 1096–97, although there was no single term consistently used to describe a crusade or its participants, it was invariably identified in the contemporary sources as either a pilgrimage (*iter* or *peregrinatio*), a holy war (*bellum sacrum* or *guerre sainte*), a passage or general passage (*passagium generale*), an expedition of the Cross (*expeditio crucis*) or the business of Jesus Christ (*negotium Jhesu Christi*).[19] Yet even after centuries of academic interest in the matter, defining exactly what the crusades were remains a difficult and, to a certain extent, highly controversial topic; in my view, the best definition reads as follows:

> What we today call a crusade could be described as a war answering God's command, authorized by a legitimate authority, the Pope, who, by virtue of the power seen as vested in him as Vicar of Christ, identified pilgrimage to Jerusalem as the main goal and offered to those who undertook it full remission of the penalties of confessed sins and a package of related temporal privileges.[20]

In the light of this definition, therefore, a *crusade* can be differentiated from the wider concept of a *Holy war*, which can be understood as a war against non-Christians or heretics that depended on God's will and was directed by clergy or divinely sanctioned rulers offering spiritual rewards, according to three specific criteria: first, the sole authority of the Vicar of Christ to authorise it; secondly, it was penitential; finally, it had to be preached as a 'via Sancti Sepulchri' ('road/pilgrimage to the Holy Sepulchre'), meaning that the ultimate goal for any crusade had to be Jerusalem.[21] Bearing this in mind, and with the risk of oversimplifying the issue, we could say that all crusades were holy wars, but not all holy wars qualified as crusades! However, in which category can we place Bohemond's operation? The answer to that question would depend on an inquiry into the motives behind the preaching of the 1107–08 campaign and should include not just Bohemond, arguably the brains behind it, but Pope Pascal as well.

Considering the three above-mentioned criteria that differentiate a crusade from a Holy war, our primary sources leave no doubt that the papacy supported Bohemond's campaign and gave its full backing to the recruitment of soldiers from Italy, France and, most likely, Spain. A papal legate, Bruno of Segni, accompanied the Norman during his preaching 'across the Alps into Gaul and parts of the West', offering indulgences to soldiers similar to the ones proclaimed by Urban II in 1095. The same source confirms that Pascal II also conferred on Bohemond the 'vexillium

Sancti Petri' ('banner of St Peter') during the latter's visit to Rome in the autumn of 1105. However, does this mean that Pascal gave his blessing to Bohemond to recruit troops for a crusade against the Byzantine empire?

The banner of St Peter had been conferred on other leaders before Bohemond, including William I of Normandy prior to his invasion of England in 1066 and Robert Guiscard before his campaign in the Balkans in 1080. According to Erdmann, Pope Gregory VII conferred the Petrine banner on Guiscard in an act that had both religious and legal connotations, meaning that it was both a symbol of a holy war and an indication of Roman overlordship over the Norman duke, a typical Gregorian foreign policy of the time.[22] Most modern scholars, however, would argue that these expeditions fail to qualify as crusades, and there is no reason to assume that only the handing over of the Petrine banner to Bohemond would have bestowed upon his campaign in the Balkans the same emotional and spiritual 'appeal' as a crusade to Jerusalem would have. But if we look back at the evidence I quoted in the last section regarding Bohemond's preaching in France with Bruno of Segni, both the description of the Norman's wedding to Constance by Orderic Vitalis and Suger's report of the Council of Poitiers confirm that despite Bohemond's vitriolic attacks against Alexios Komnenos, the upcoming expedition was eventually endorsed by the gathered crowds as a 'road to the Holy Sepulchre' – a crusade to Jerusalem!

If that is the case, therefore, and Bohemond and Bruno were recruiting western European soldiers who thought they were embarking on a crusade to Jerusalem rather than attacking the Byzantine empire, was the entire operation 'hijacked' by the Norman for his own ambitions? To what extent did Bruno and, most importantly, Pascal II endorse and support Bohemond's plans for a campaign against Byzantium? In 1106 the main charge levied by Latin Christians against Alexios Komnenos was that he had betrayed the armies of the First Crusade and the crusade of 1101, and that he was assaulting pilgrims bound for the Holy Land.[23] One Latin author even claimed that the emperor had actively conspired with the Fatimids of Egypt against the Franks in 1099.[24] On top of that, we have to bear in mind Rome's long-standing animosity towards the Eastern Orthodox Church, with the question of the Latin unleavened bread (the 'azymes') speaking to some of the fundamental elements in the papacy's programme of defining and delineating Christendom at this time.[25] Nevertheless, historians have been divided as to Pascal's attitude towards Constantinople.

On the one hand, Whalen has argued that there was indeed preaching for crusade for the years 1107–08, but it was *not* a crusade against the Byzantine empire *per se*, rather an expedition of 'warriors of Christ' to Jerusalem that was planned to 'deviate' and campaign against the 'tyrant' Alexios Komnenos.[26] The author does not see any blanket anti-Byzantine feeling in the writings of the contemporary Latin chroniclers that would justify a holy war against the 'schismatic' (or 'heretic') Byzantine empire but, rather, what could only be described as a pronounced 'anti-Alexian' feeling. In his view, Bruno of Segni was, in fact, 'riding on Bohemond's coat-tails' to generate support for a new expedition to the Holy Land, an expedition that both Pascal and Bruno could perfectly understand was unavoidable. And as Whalen very aptly puts it, papal manipulation of a crusade for political purposes was hardly unprecedented considering, firstly, Gregory VII's endorsement of Robert Guiscard's invasion of Byzantium in 1081 and, secondly, the former's calling upon William I of Burgundy for help against Robert Guiscard in February 1074, specifically directing the 'faithful of St Peter' towards a campaign to 'bring the Normans to peace and then cross to Constantinople to bring aid to Christians', a campaign that eventually failed to materialise.[27]

On the other hand, Rubenstein takes one step further the argument about Bohemond's and Pascal's common cause in raising an army of crusaders. For him, there is no reason to doubt that either Pascal II or Bruno of Segni opposed, or even 'went along with', Bohemond's plans for a campaign to the East. Rather, Rubenstein sees the new crusade that was promoted in western Europe as a great opportunity for Pascal to achieve two goals: first, to unite the Latin and Greek-Orthodox churches under the suzerainty of Rome,[28] and secondly, to assert clear ownership for the papacy over the historical legacy of the success of the First Crusade, which would have helped the Pope in his political struggle with the Byzantine emperor.[29] As he points out, by the early twelfth century there still did not exist a consensus as to who had initiated the First Crusade and therefore who should reap the glory of the conquest of Jerusalem. Many Lotharingian sources, especially Albert of Aachen, considered the rabble-rousing preacher Peter the Hermit of Amiens as the soul of the success of 1097–99.[30] This argument becomes all the more intelligible considering that the first king of Jerusalem was Godfrey of Bouillon, duke of Lower Lorraine, who was succeeded by his brother Baldwin, whose first action was to depose and send into exile Patriarch Daimbert of Jerusalem, Pope Pascal's hand-picked candidate for the office. For Rubenstein, the preaching for a crusade (to Jerusalem) in France in 1106 by the most brilliant leader of the First Crusade, Bohemond, accompanied by Pascal's trusted and experienced legate, Bruno of Segni, would have served to advance Rome's design in (re)shaping historical memory the way the Pope liked to. And what better way to (re)shape historical memory than to commission not one but three rewritings of the famous chronicle of the First Crusade, the *Gesta Francorum*, by three northern French monks –Baldric of Bourgueil, Guibert of Nogent and Robert of Reims – who happen to discover and rewrite it simultaneously sometime in 1106. All three came up with two central assumptions: that Urban II called the crusade and that Bohemond was its most important hero.

The Second Siege of Dyrrachium

The emperor did not remain idle over the emerging threat of another Norman campaign in the Balkans. In his effort to counter the anti-Byzantine propaganda launched in France, Alexios decided to mediate for the release of three hundred western knights of the kingdom of Jerusalem who had been captured by the Fatimids of Egypt in May 1102. He also recalled several senior officers of his army and navy to Dyrrachium: generals like Kantakouzenos and Monastras, who had many years of experience in commanding troops in Syria and Cilicia, a very important and strategic post neighbouring the newly established Latin principalities and the Seljuks. Furthermore, Anna reports that her father left the capital for Thessaloniki in September 1105, apparently to coordinate the recruitment of the army against Bohemond 'on the ground'. In fact, Alexios extended his stay in the Macedonian capital for another fourteen months due to a Serbian rebellion, which turned out to be so serious that John Komnenos, one of Alexios' nephews and a former governor of Dyrrachium, was defeated in battle by the Serbs of Raska in Dalmatia. Finally, realising that Bohemond's major hurdle in launching his operation in the Balkans would be the transportation of his army across the Adriatic, Alexios sought to win over the Italian naval powers of Pisa and Genoa, which might have been persuaded to offer their services to the Norman.[31] The emperor was deeply concerned by the possibility of Bohemond's flirting with Pisa, since it was Pisa's navy that had devastated Corfu, Kephalonia, Leukas and Zante, had clashed with a Byzantine naval squadron off Rhodes and had later joined Bohemond in the siege of Laodicea in the summer of 1099.

There is no way of knowing the exact numbers of the troops Bohemond gathered in Apulia for his planned invasion of the imperial lands in the Balkans, simply because the estimates put forward by the Latin sources vary to such an extent that I see no point in repeating them here. Nevertheless, Anna Komnena provides some details on the diversity of Bohemond's contingent, referring to 'a countless host of Franks and Celts,[32] together with the entire contingent of men from the Isle of Thule[33] who normally serve in the Roman army but had through force of circumstances then joined him; not to mention an even stronger force of Germans and Celtiberians [Spaniards]'.[34] Furthermore, the Norman navy had evolved since the time of the Norman invasion of Sicily in the 1060s, or Robert Guiscard's Illyrian campaign in 1081, and, as Pryor has argued, by the end of the eleventh century the southern Italian ports seem to have developed a technological and technical capacity to carry more horses per ship than the fifteen or so of the Byzantine navy at the time.[35] Hence, Anna Komnena reports that Bohemond had deployed a core of twelve warships but sadly she does not give a precise number for his transport vessels. Other Latin sources account for a nucleus of thirty Norman warships and some two hundred large and small ships, which may appear an excessive number that should be reduced by half for it to be credible.[36]

The sources tell us that Bohemond disembarked his invading army at Avlona and, after securing and plundering the surrounding region, he probably took over the smaller castles of Canina and Orikon to secure his flanks, as his father had done in 1081. By late October 1107, and after a failed attempt to storm the city of Dyrrachium, Bohemond began laying down his plans for a prolonged siege operation, and to prepare different types of siege machines to breach the city's defences, with his troops occupying numerous minor castles on the banks of the river Devol, in the eastern approaches to the city.

The emperor's reaction to the Norman threat was, once again, swift and decisive; he set out from Constantinople to Thessaloniki on 6 November 1107, and he would probably have reached the Macedonian capital in early December to spend the winter and raise troops for the upcoming clash. Interestingly, Anna Komnena describes how, while Alexios was on his way to Thessaloniki, he was eagerly drilling his army to march properly as a coherent unit and perform certain basic battle formations. She also reports what seems to be a new multinational unit of elite young recruits:

> These were three hundred in all, every one of them young and tall, in full physical vigour, with beards scarcely grown and very adroit in the use of the bow and very steady in throwing the spear. They had been chosen from various races and formed a kind of select army within the

general Roman army directly under the command of the Emperor as General, for he was to them not only their Emperor but General and teacher as well.[37]

On top of that, sometime in the early winter of 1107/08, a Venetian naval squadron of unknown size arrived in the waters off Dyrrachium, apparently in accordance with the treaty of alliance agreed between the Venetian *doge* and the Byzantine emperor in 1082.[38] Critically, however, Alexios had dispatched orders for the local troops in the region around Dyrrachium to strongly defend the mountain and coastal passes and to refuse access further inland to the foraging parties of the Norman army. As a result, Anna reports that the lack of supplies, and probably dysentery, severely afflicted Bohemond's troops:

> For all the food-stuffs he had originally brought in as plunder from the country round Dyrrachium had been used up already, and the sources from which he [Bohemond] had hoped to get further supplies were blocked by the Roman soldiery who occupied the valleys and passes and even the sea-board itself. Consequently, a severe famine overtook them, consuming both horses and men alike, as the horses had no fodder and the men no food. In addition to this the barbarian army was seized with a disorder of the stomach, apparently due to some unsuitable cereal, that is millet.[39]

None of our sources mentions any serious attempt by Bohemond to take Dyrrachium during the winter period, thus settling in for a protracted blockade of the city until the coming of the spring (1108), at which time the Norman leader decided to burn his ships, as his father had done, and vigorously proceed with the siege. According to the *Alexiad*, the Normans made three attempts to break into the city;[40] first, they brought a battering ram up to the city's walls, on the east side facing the lagoon, which suggests that Dyrrachium lacked a critical element of medieval fortifications technology: a moat. Failing to inflict any serious damage with the ram on the city's walls that were, according to Anna, 'of considerable thickness, so wide indeed that more than four horsemen can ride abreast in safety', the Normans then attempted a slightly less risky but more labour intensive technique: undermining the foundations of the city's walls by digging a tunnel on the northern side of the city. Immediately, however, the defenders dug out a counter-tunnel from which to shoot Greek fire to repel the Normans. Finally, Bohemond resolved upon building an enormous wooden siege tower on wheels, a siege technique that was used for many centuries occasionally by the Romans but often by Persians, Avars and Goths. But because these mobile siege towers were often covered in hides to protect against arrows and incendiary projectiles, in Dyrrachium the defenders also realised that they could not burn down the Norman tower by shooting Greek fire directly at it. Instead, they came up with the idea of filling in the space between the walls and the tower with any flammable material they could find and then proceeding to set it on fire, a tactic that proved very effective.

Sometime in the spring of 1108 Alexios left the Macedonian capital for Dyrrachium, marching through western Macedonia and Pelagonia, pitching his camp somewhere between the southern bank of Lake Ohrid and the river Devol. The only evidence we have about the size of Alexios' army comes from two Latin sources: the *Narrative of Fleuri* records the exaggerated figure of sixty thousand, while Albert of Aachen tells of ten thousand men mustered under the imperial banner, a figure that sounds a bit more plausible.[41] Nevertheless, Anna's narrative gives an idea of the multinational army that the emperor had assembled, which included Greeks (probably from Macedonia and Thrace), Alans, Seljuk Turks, Turkopoles, Patzinaks and Kumans.[42] Finally, the emperor most likely asked for troops from Malik Shah of Iconium, with whom he renewed the old treaties that had been signed by his predecessors Suleiman I (1077–86), Abul-Kasim (1086–92) and Kilij Arslan I (1092–1107).[43]

Alexios' humiliating defeat at Dyrrachium in 1081, and again at Ioannina in the early months of 1082, had taught him an invaluable lesson on how to deal with an invading enemy like the Normans. Twenty-six years later, the emperor adopted the strategy of 'non-engagement', which praised the use of diplomacy, the paying of subsidies, and the employment of stratagems, craft, wiles, bribery and 'other means' to deceive the enemy and bring back the army with as few casualties as possible.[44] This attitude made perfect sense for Byzantine strategists, and had been promoted by the authors of military treatises (known as 'Taktika') for centuries:

> Warfare is like hunting ... To try simply to overpower the enemy in the open, hand to hand and face to face, even though you might appear to win, is an enterprise which is very risky and can result in serious harm. Apart from extreme emergency, it is ridiculous to try to gain victory which is too costly and brings only empty glory.[45]
> [Maurice, *Strategikon*, c. AD 600]

> It is good if your enemies are harmed either by deception or raids, or by famine; and continue to harass them more and more, but do not

challenge them in open war, because luck plays as major a role as valour in battle.⁴⁶ [Leo VI, *Taktika*, *c.* AD 900]

And only when you know everything about your enemy, only then you must stand and fight them, but do not let your army perish for no reason. Fight in such a way by applying tricks and machinations and ambushes to humiliate your enemy, and only when it is the last choice of all, and in the utmost need, only then stand and fight.⁴⁷ [Kekaumenos, *Strategikon*, AD 1078]

Anna Komnena also praises her father's peaceful nature and his placing of a positive value on the minimal use of force, while she condemns the purposeful provocation of an enemy into battle or armed conflict as bad generalship. More specifically, she describes the use of guile and surprise as fundamental aspects of war in Byzantium, especially when the enemy was not 'playing it fair'; for Anna, therefore, it was fair to 'outwit the witty':

He [Alexios] knew Bohemond to be a man of consummate guile and energy and, although he was quite willing to accept open battle with him, as I have said, yet he never ceased working against him by every other possible means and device. For the aforesaid reasons, although he was longing for a fight (for the Emperor, my father, was fond of, and long accustomed to, danger, yet ever let reason be his guide in all matters), he was anxious to overcome Bohemond by other methods. For I hold that a general ought not always to try to gain victory for himself by drawing the sword, but that, when opportunity and circumstances permit, he should occasionally have recourse to wiliness and thus ensure complete victory for himself.⁴⁸

Alexios also had the most suitable troops for this strategy of 'non-engagement', namely the Seljuks, the Turkopoles, the Patzinaks and the Kumans, as I mentioned earlier. These troops were unaccustomed to fighting an enemy with swords and lances in face-to-face combat. Rather, being expert horse-archers, they were much more suited to a war of attrition, and this was exactly the strategy favoured by Alexios in the spring of 1108. Now that the main army had arrived to deal with Bohemond's invasion, it was time to tighten the blockade to a point where the Normans would seek for peace. Hence, Anna reports that her father dispatched four of his most able and trusted officers, Michael Kekaumenos, Alexander Kabasilas, Leo Nikeritas and Eustathius Kamytzes, to take and hold a number of strategic castles in the eastern and southern approaches of

Dyrrachium, including Avlona, Canina and Oricum, Petrula, Deura and Arbanum, while the princess also refers to the *xyloklasiai* – road-blocks made from felled timber that were used to block the passes leading to and from the aforementioned castles.[49]

The emperor's critical strategic decision, however, was to win over Bohemond's senior officers by sending to the Norman's younger brother, Guy of Conversano, who had been in imperial service during the First Crusade, a number of trusted servants, including Richard of Salerno, Richard of Principate and a certain Coprisianus, carrying treacherous letters as though in response to ones supposedly sent to the emperor, in the hope of their falling into Bohemond's hands and spreading dissent in his army.[50] Surprisingly, the Norman took no further action against these officers, even if a number of Latin sources were keen to accuse Guy of having collaborated with the emperor.[51] The fact, however, that Anna does not mention this kind of allegation, although she was always keen to write about Frankish duplicity and avarice, certainly points to the fact that the accusation of treachery and duplicity on behalf of Bohemond's senior commanders was a convenient explanation on the part of the Latin chroniclers for the eventual failure of the campaign and the humiliating Treaty of Devol that followed.

As the blockade of Bohemond's camp was becoming even more effective, the Norman ordered his commanders to try to break it by attacking the imperial units guarding the mountain passes. Anna describes the first clash between picked units of the two armies in the highland passes somewhere between the rivers Vjosë and Devol, where another imperial commander named Kantakouzenos had been besieging a castle identified as Mylos in the eastern approaches to the town of Avlona:

> He [Kantakouzenos] sent the Scythians [Patzinaks] ahead with orders to draw on the Franks by shooting at them from a distance, and at one minute to shoot continuously, at the next to flee backwards and then run forward again. They set off readily but accomplished nothing, as the Franks were drawn up in close order and did not break their line at all but marched on slowly in set order. When the two armies had approached to the right distance for battle, the Scythians were unable to shoot their arrows any longer as the Franks rode down upon them at full speed, so they immediately turned their backs to the Franks.[52]

Here we see, once again, the steppe tactic of feigned flight applied by the Patzinak and (later during the battle) by the Turkish and Alan units in imperial service, and how ineffective it proved to be against a disciplined unit of western heavy cavalry that reportedly drew its ranks together in a mass formation in order to defend themselves against the shower of arrows, before launching a frontal attack at full speed against their lightly armed enemies. This is an episode very similar to the first clash between Turkish units of the imperial army and Guiscard's units of heavy cavalry in October 1081, when the Norman troops had reacted in more or less the same way against the battlefield tactics of the Turkish horse-archers.

After the attacks launched by the horse-archers in imperial service were checked, it was the centre of the Byzantine army under Kantakouzenos himself that made a final frontal attack on the Norman centre, eventually managing to break the cavalry formation and forcing them to retreat back to the castle at Mylos. This victory followed a devastating defeat suffered by Eustathius Kamytzes' men, after they were caught between two Norman cavalry units led by Bohemond's brother Guido and two counts called 'Saracenus' (possibly of Arab origin) and Contopaganus (literally meaning 'short pagan' in Greek).[53]

Following Kantakouzenos' victory, which certainly boosted the Byzantine army's morale, the former officer replaced Kekaumenos as commander of the wider Avlona, Canina and Oricum area to the south of the river Vjosë. He then encountered two attempts made by Bohemond's men to break the tightening blockade. The first was repulsed by one of Kantakouzenos' commanders named Beroetes, while a second expeditionary force dispatched by Bohemond (this time some six thousand strong), which included both infantry and cavalry, was also routed when Kantakouzenos ordered his men to track their enemies' movements and attack them when they were crossing a smaller river in the area, thus being at their most vulnerable.[54]

With conditions in Bohemond's camp becoming increasingly intolerable, Alexios made a critical decision to put Marianus Maurocatacalon at the head of the naval forces patrolling the waters off Dyrrachium, following the failure of the previous naval commander, Isaac Contostephanus, to prevent reinforcements from Apulia reaching the Normans. At this stage of the blockade, the Byzantine units deployed in the highland passes leading to the Norman camp were given orders not just to prevent the Normans from foraging and gathering supplies but to actively harass them by applying guerrilla tactics. Therefore, with the Byzantine emperor not wishing to risk a pitched battle with the Norman army but, rather '[sitting] back like a spectator, watching what was happening on the plains of Illyria', Bohemond was eventually persuaded by his senior officers to seek a way out of this deadlock. The Norman sought permission from the emperor to move his camp to a more salubrious area near Dyrrachium, before being allowed to visit Alexios' tent to open negotiations and to agree on a treaty that would put an end to his designs and ambitions against the Byzantine empire.[55]

The Treaty of Devol

Sometime in September 1108 Bohemond and Alexios agreed on a treaty that effectively ended the second Norman siege of Dyrrachium and brought to an abrupt end the ambitions that the Norman had harboured in the Balkans. Anna Komnena is once more our most detailed and reliable source regarding the documents that were drawn up and distributed between the two parties. We know that Anna had the document signed by Bohemond copied and kept in the imperial archives, which included a statement of Bohemond's obligations towards the emperor. Fortunately, Anna also includes parts of the second document delivered by the emperor to Bohemond that detailed the imperial grants given to the Norman as part of the agreement. These are the points that we need to keep from the Treaty of Devol:

> For since I [Bohemond] declared war against thy divinely appointed Empire and broke the agreement [of 1097], thereby the charges held by thy Majesty against me were cancelled as well. But now as if moved by remorse and like a stricken fisherman I have recovered my sanity and, I might almost say, been rendered more discreet by thy spear, remembering too the defeat and the wars of former years, I come to make this, the second agreement with thy Majesty by which I will become the liegeman of thy sceptre, or to express it more clearly and plainly, thy menial and subject, as thou too hast determined to drag me under thy right hand and art willing to make me thy liege-man.[56]

The term liege-man (*lizios anthropos*) is of great importance in the sense that Alexios was eager to put down in writing Bohemond's obligation to become the vassal of the Byzantine emperor and of his son and designated heir John, and by the terms of this 'feudal' contract he was to provide military support against all the enemies of the Byzantine empire. Critically, the agreement further states that 'I [Bohemond] will never at any time take and hold any country which either now or formerly has been brought under thy [Byzantium] sway ... except only such as are expressly given to me by your divinely appointed Majesties', a point that takes us back to Alexios' agreement with the crusader leaders in Constantinople in 1097.

The second point is about the clause of the treaty that had to do with the future of the patriarchate of Antioch, which was to return to the jurisdiction of Constantinople and have, once more, a Greek Orthodox patriarch, namely John VII the Oxite, who was patriarch from 1090 until 1100, when he was replaced by Bohemond with Bernard of Valence as the new Latin patriarch. Finally, Anna lists a great number of cities and surrounding areas in Syria that either were given to Bohemond as a fief or were introduced into the empire. In brief, Bohemond received Antioch and many of its surrounding areas, while several other territories that surrounded this newly formed principality were incorporated into the empire, namely almost all of Cilicia and the coastal cities of Laodicea, Jabala, Valania, Maraclea and Tortosa in northern Lebanon.

For a leader who had just conceded defeat, the Treaty of Devol seems to have left Bohemond relatively unscathed, and its terms make it perfectly clear that the Norman did receive plenty from Alexios. As Anna reports, Bohemond would also have earned 200 gold pounds as an annual income and the accompanying title of *sebastos* ('revered'), while a point that he would certainly have insisted on was the safety and good treatment of the pilgrims and crusaders travelling through Byzantine lands on their way to Antioch, a demand that Alexios further agreed to guarantee. So what was the reason behind the emperor's 'generosity' towards his nemesis? The answer is surprisingly simple: Alexios was betting on the establishment of a new subservient principality that could have been pitted as a buffer state against the surrounding Muslim states of Mesopotamia and the Fatimids of Egypt, and which could have significantly disrupted Seljuk communications between Iconium, in central Asia Minor, and Mesopotamia. This comes on top of the fact that the emperor would have been fully aware of the overstretched Byzantine logistics for any military operation against the aforementioned Muslim states. Furthermore, it is certainly possible that Alexios would have thought of the likelihood that the Kingdom of Jerusalem would not hold out for long, therefore he could have taken a further step and expanded the vassal state of Antioch further to the south. In short, the recognition of imperial overlordship over the status of the Syrian capital was apparently considered enough, and there was no need to demand the physical possession of Antioch as well. However, the weakness in the agreement was that Tancred, who actually held Antioch, was unlikely to accept it.

Bohemond, after receiving 'an extraordinary quantity and weight of gold and silver, and precious purple ... embarked on a ship and returned to Apulia, cheating those who endured with him the long labours and burdens of war around Durazzo and giving them no reward'.[57] A portion of Bohemond's army would have sailed back home, but others who could afford the additional expenses to continue their journey to the Holy Land would have been allowed to do so. Voices of criticism, however, soon emerged over the purpose of the whole enterprise and the justification of an attack against an empire that was not favoured by God. Writing the main body of his *Ecclesiastical History* between 1123 and 1137, hence with the benefit of hindsight, Orderic Vitalis puts the following words into the mouth of a knight beseeching Bohemond to surrender to the emperor once it had become apparent that the situation outside Dyrrachium was untenable:

> We are paying the penalty of our own rashness in having engaged in a bold enterprise far from our native country and beyond our strength, and having presumed to raise our hands against the holy empire [Byzantium]. We have not been led to join in this expedition to sustain our hereditary rights, nor has any prophet sent by God roused us to arms by divine oracles; but you [Bohemond] are actuated by the ambition of ruling in the territories of another prince to engage in this arduous enterprise, and, as for us, the love of money has led us to undergo the burden of toils and battles. But as God is not mocked, and his judgements fail not, nor does he subvert justice, he has heard with favour the prayers of those who cry to him against us in Greece, and has dispersed our troops, enfeebled not by battle but by famine, and destroyed our force without effusion of blood. We entreat you therefore to make peace with the emperor before you fall into his hands and are condemned to death, and by your loss all your followers are plunged into inextricable difficulties.[58]

Epilogue

Death and Heritage

The death of these invincible princes [Bohemond and Tancred] being known through all the world became the cause of deep grief to the Christians and exultation to the Pagans.
[Orderic Vitalis, *Ecclesiastical History*, X. xxv, vol. III, p. 391]

Death

We know remarkably little about Bohemond after his return to Apulia following the humiliating Treaty of Devol with Byzantine emperor Alexios Komnenos. Constance bore him two sons, John, who died in infancy, and Bohemond (b. 1108 or 1109),[1] who succeeded him in the Principality of Antioch under the guardianship of his mother; Tancred administered the principality until 1111, followed by his cousin, Roger of Salerno, from 1111 to early 1119. A small number of charters issued in Apulia between 1107 and 1109, either by him or in his name, prove, according to Russo, his continuing influence in southern Italian politics.[2] Yet Bohemond's remarkable career met its end when he was taken ill, sometime in late February 1111, and he died shortly afterwards, on 7 March.[3]

Mausoleum in Canosa

Any contemporary or modern commentator would have expected that Bohemond would have chosen to be buried in Apulia. For that reason, cities like Taranto, with its magnificent cathedral dedicated to San Cataldo, and Bari, with its archbishopric see and the shrine of St Nicholas that was consecrated in 1089 by Pope Urban II at the request of Bohemond, were two obvious choices. This expectation could also help to explain Albert of Aachen's mistake in writing that Bohemond was buried in Bari. Nevertheless, in what may look like another proof of his ambiguous nature, the Norman chose as his final resting place the north Apulian town of Canosa with its Cathedral of St Sabinus. But what was the deeper reason behind Bohemond's choice, so far from his domains in southern Apulia?

Gadolin argued convincingly that Bohemond was involved in the (re)building of the Cathedral of St Sabinus in Canosa that was consecrated in 1101, and that the key point in the discussion revolves around the architecture of the cathedral and the place of inspiration for its patron – none other than Bohemond himself. The reason behind Bohemond's involvement in the (re)building of the cathedral at Canosa is directly related to the key role of Elia (d. 1105), the archbishop of Bari (and Canosa) in moving the cult of St Sabinus from Bari to Canosa. St Sabinus (461–9 February 566) was a friend of St Benedict and is credited with saving Canosa from the incursions of the Ostrogoth king Totila in 548. His relics were translated to the early medieval cathedral in Canosa on 1 August in an unknown year of the eighth century, and following the destruction of the town by the Muslims from Sicily the relics were rescued from the ruins by St Angelarius in 844 and taken to Bari Cathedral which, to this day, bears the name *Cattedrale di San Sabino*. However, although the cult of St Sabinus dominated religious life in Bari up to the second half of the eleventh century, Archbishop Elia found himself embroiled in bitter in-fighting between his Bariot clergy and his flock that involved a movement to replace St Sabinus with the cult of another saint.

We saw in a previous chapter that the relics of St Nicholas of Myra were translated to Bari in May 1087, and the magnificent basilica that was about to host them was consecrated by Pope Urban II two years later, in 1089. Yet it should be noted that there is strong evidence of dedication to Nicholas in Bari even before the Norman conquest of the city in 1071; for example, Emperor Constantine IX Monomachos (r. 1042–55) built a church within Bari's walls that placed the city under St Nicholas' patronage well before the translation of 1087.[4] Fully aware that the Bariot tide was turning in favour of the cult of Nicholas, and to avoid any civil strife within the walls of his city, sometime in 1091 Elias had the relics of St Sabinus 'rediscovered' where they most intimately belonged, namely at Canosa, two days' journey north of Bari. But what was Bohemond's role in this process?

Apparently, the town of Canosa needed an elegant cathedral to house the relics of St Sabinus, just like the one that was being built at Bari for St Nicholas. The eighth-century Lombard cathedral at Canosa was evidently an inadequate setting and it had to be significantly improved (or more accurately, rebuilt). Therefore the cash-strapped Elias turned to Bohemond, who since 1086 had been the overlord of large parts of Apulia and Bari. The Norman was quick to grasp the political benefit from being involved in such a venture: he would have resolved the religious in-fighting in Bari, while he would also have earned himself a valuable ally in local politics – Archbishop Elias; the rebuilt Cathedral of St Sabinus was eventually consecrated in 1101.

Finally, it is paramount to refer to what a modern historian has very aptly called Bohemond's 'predisposition towards the "hostile imitation" of Byzantium'.[5] It has been argued that the plan of the Cathedral of St Sabinus closely resembles that of the no longer extant church of the Holy Apostles at Constantinople.[6] The significance of this connection cannot be overstated: the Church of the Holy Apostles was located on the Fourth Hill of Constantinople, and it was first built as a circular mausoleum erected by Emperor Constantine I (d. 337) for his own burial. Next to it a cruciform basilica was built by Emperor Constantius II (r. 337–61), who deposited in it relics of the apostles Timothy, Luke and Andrew. In 548–50 the church was rebuilt, again in the shape of a cross, by Justinian I (r. 527–65), who added a second mausoleum. The two mausolea served as the burial place of emperors until 1028.

After footing the bill for the construction of such a magnificent cathedral in Canosa, it is reasonable to assume that Bohemond would have had a say in the design. For that reason, after having spent almost a month in Constantinople during the First Crusade, he would certainly have been familiar with the design and the Church of the Holy Apostles, undoubtedly an ideal model to imitate back in Apulia and to use as his own personal resting place. On top of that, the cross-in-square chapel added to the south transept of the cathedral, executed after Bohemond's death, probably under the supervision of his widow Constance, is also clearly reminiscent of Byzantium and incorporates several paleo-Byzantine acanthus capitals.[7]

Bohemond's longing, even in death, to equal the glory and prestige of the Byzantine emperors is palpable in his choice of a final resting place in what was, essentially, a copy of the imperial mausoleum in Constantinople that dated back to the first Christian emperor, Constantine. For Bohemond, no doubt, the cathedral at Canosa bore not only 'apostolic' significance, but even the imperial connotations of its prototype. As Gadolin puts it, 'on Apulian soil, there could hardly be any worthier resting place for the bones of one who all his active life had fought for the diadem worn by the eastern Caesars'. Two inscriptions on the door of his mausoleum give us an insight into Bohemond's aspirations (or pretensions?) in the Mediterranean;[8] the first, under the exterior of the cornice of the cupola, reads:

The magnanimous prince of Syria lies under this roof.
No one better than he will be born afterward in the universe.
Greece conquered four times, the greater part of the world
Sensed for a long time the genius and strength of Bohemond.
He conquered columns of thousands with a battleline of tens
by the rein of his virtue, which indeed the city of Antioch knows.

The second inscription is found on the bronze doors which provide access to the tomb from the south:

1. How noble, how valuable Bohemond was,
   Greece has witnessed, Syria enumerates.
   He conquered the former; protected the latter from the enemy:
   Hence the Greeks laugh, Syria, at your destruction.
   Because the Greek laughs, because the Syrian mourns
   (Both justly), this is true salvation for you Bohemond.

2. Bohemond conquered the wealth of kings and the labor of the mighty
   And deserved to be called by his name.
   He thundered over the earth. Since the universe submitted to him
   I can't call him a man; I won't call him a god.

3. He who living was eager to die for Christ
   Earned this, as life was given to him dying.
   Christ's clemency therefore gave this to him:
   That this his faithful champion could be a soldier in heaven.

4. Entering, look at the doors; you should see what is written; you should pray
   That Bohemond be given to heaven and there he should be placed.

The Warrior and the Strategist

Bohemond was, beyond any doubt to my mind, a great soldier with vast experience in fighting overseas. His aggressive strategy in every operational theatre he was active in speaks volumes about his daring character and dynamism that he wished to portray throughout his life. Whether he was in charge of armies in Italy, in the Balkans, in Asia Minor or in the Middle East, his attempt to bring his enemies to battle makes modern historians view his strategy as, clearly, 'non-Vegetian'. Under the term 'Vegetian Strategy' scholars have identified a particular type of warfare in which the commander sought to avoid battle at all costs unless the chances were overwhelmingly in his favour. Instead, he would seek to defeat his enemy by other means, such as the use of fortifications, harassment and blockades.

In the operational theatre of the Balkans, we saw that Alexios Komnenos revised his strategy of confrontation in 1081 into a 'Vegetian strategy' of imposing a tight blockade that would strangle his enemy into submission – a strategy that worked flawlessly twenty-six years later in 1107–08. On the other hand, numerous similarities can be identified between the operational theatre of the Balkans and those of Sicily and the Middle East, where the Normans also appeared as the aggressors. In all of these cases, they operated far from their home bases, with no substantial reinforcements, and had to rely on plundering expeditions in order to supply their armies but also to undermine the political authority of their enemies. The Normans were also very much aware of the political fragmentation of Sicily into three contesting emirates in the middle of the eleventh century, while the civil conflicts in Byzantium that followed the devastating defeat at Manzikert in 1071 would also have been known to Robert Guiscard and Bohemond. Furthermore, in every operational theatre the Normans had clear strategic objectives: the subjugation of the Sicilian capital of Palermo, the second largest city of the empire, Thessaloniki, and the Syrian capital of Antioch.

Considering the above, it becomes obvious why Guiscard and Bohemond wished to engage their enemies in battle. Although numerically inferior to all their enemies, their aim was to achieve a decisive victory in the field that would have significant consequences for their enemy's morale. At Dyrrachium (1081) we could say that Guiscard and Bohemond pursued what modern historians have a coined a 'strategy of annihilation', also known as a 'strategy of overthrow', following Clausewitz.[9] This strategy aims to disarm the enemy by crushing his main armed force in a decisive battle, assuming that the defeated adversary, seeing that he has lost his best chance for victory, will seek peace on whatever terms he can get. This form of strategy thus offers the best hope of a quick end to the war. Manzikert was one such decisive battle with overwhelming geopolitical ramifications for the Byzantine empire, with Doryleum (1097) 'unlocking' Asia Minor to the Latins of the First Crusade, while Antioch (1098) won the strategic Syrian capital for the crusaders and eventually became the capital of Bohemond's principality in the Levant. The Battle of Dyrrachium could also have turned into a decisive battle for the Norman invaders if Alexios had been killed in battle or captured, like the Anglo-Saxon king Harold at Hastings (1066) or the emperor Romanus IV at Manzikert (1071). Alexios' loss would have brought the state to the brink of a renewed civil war, just like the aftermath of the Battle of Manzikert ten years before, but the emperor managed to escape almost unscathed and established a rallying point at Thessaloniki in Macedonia. Instead, during the following two years, between 1082 and 1083, Bohemond and his army were roaming around northern Greece, with the towns of

Kastoria, Ioannina and Arta opening their gates in order to escape devastation. This had clearly become a war of attrition, in which the party that had the greater determination and resources would prevail.

Bohemond had fought with and against Greek, Anglo-Saxon, Patzinak and Turkish troops and had learned to adapt to the geo-political realities of each operational theatre. Both he and his father made effective use of the main tactical weapon of the Norman armies in the period, the heavy cavalry charge, with remarkable results in every operational theatre. At Dyrrachium in 1081 the tactical combination of a feigned retreat and a second heavy cavalry charge resulted in the breaking of the Byzantine army's centre and the eventual annihilation of the units of the Varangian Guard in the field. Yet even though Bohemond further pursued a confrontation with the imperial armies at Ioannina, and even managed to defeat the emperor twice more, one can see the first signs of Alexios' resourcefulness from the early summer of 1082 on. As the emperor did not have any units of heavy infantry to place at the forefront of his army in order to repel the Norman cavalry attack, he instead posted a number of light chariots and caltrops. Alexios' 'Vegetian strategy' became even more apparent during the siege of Larissa in 1083.

Nevertheless, Bohemond showed several signs of tactical adaptation in the field of battle. Both he and his father outwitted the emperor on the night of 17/18 October 1081, when they redeployed their army between Alexios' camp and the Dyrrachian lagoon, with the sea to the right and the lagoon behind them to avoid any possible encirclement by the Turkish troops in the emperor's service. Bohemond outmanoeuvred Alexios again at Ioannina in 1082, after he was somehow informed about the Byzantine stratagem to impede the charge of his knights with wagons, and he swiftly 'adapted himself to the changed circumstances' (*Alexiad*); his answer was to split his forces and launch an assault against the flanks of the imperial army in a pincer move. Finally, the Norman displayed his leadership skills and growing experience in warfare in the Middle East against the nomadic tactics of the Turks at the battles of Doryleum and Harem in 1097, while his keeping of a unit in reserve to prevent any possible encirclement by Kerbogha's units may well have saved the day for the crusaders at the Battle of Antioch in 1098.

Nevertheless, was it Bohemond's restless and unruly character that drew him into chasing after the Danishmendid emir Gümüştekin at Melitene in July 1100, which resulted in him being taken captive by the Turks? I do not believe we could ever give a definitive answer to that question. Undoubtedly, the Norman was a decidedly fallible leader with great successes but also spectacular failures in his military career. For that reason, I cannot find a more fitting end to his biography than a line from the inscription at his own mausoleum at Canosa:

> He thundered over the earth. Since the universe submitted to him
> I can't call him a man; I won't call him a god.

Notes

Introduction

1. Leon Ménager, 'Pesanteur et étiologie de la colonisation normande de l'Italie', and 'Inventaires des familles normandes et franques émigrées en Italie Meridionale et en Sicile (XIe–XIIe siècles)', in: *Roberto il Guiscardo e il suo tempo. Relazzioni e communicationi nelle prime giornate normanno-sueve (Bari, Maggio 1973)* (Rome, 1975), pp. 189–214, 260–390.
2. A modern translation of the work is *The History of the Normans*, trans. Prescott Dunbar (Woodbridge, 2004).
3. William of Apulia, *La Geste de Robert Guiscard*, ed. Marguerite Mathieu (Palermo, 1963).
4. Geoffrey Malaterra, *The Deeds of Count Roger of Calabria and Sicily and of his Brother Duke Robert Guiscard*, ed. and trans. Kenneth B. Wolf (Ann Arbor, 2005).
5. *The Alexiad*, trans. E.R.A. Sewter, revised with introduction and notes, Peter Frankopan (London, 2009).
6. *Alexiad*, XIV, vii.

Chapter 1: Early Life and Kin Dynamics

1. *Alexiad*, XIII, 10.
2. *Alexiad*, XIII, 12.
3. *Alexiad*, XIV, 4.
4. A typical example is, of course, the conquest and keeping of Antioch by the Normans under Bohemond in May 1098, which caused such anguish to the emperor that he felt 'he [Alexios] could not bear it nor restrain himself any longer from returning evil for evil and taking revenge for their [the Normans'] horrible inhumanity': *Alexiad*, XIV. 2; G. Buckler, *Anna Komnena, A Study* (London: Oxford University Press, 1929), p. 441. On the view of the Frankish soldiers as warriors, as depicted in the Byzantine military manuals of the tenth century: G. Theotokis, *The Norman Campaigns in the Balkans, 1081–1108* (Woodbridge: Boydell & Brewer, 2014), pp. 73–5. The faithlessness (φύσει γὰρ ἄπιστον) of the Frankish 'race' (γένος) is repeated by the Byzantine public servant and historian Michael Attaleiates (c. 1022–80) in his *History* (published 1079–80): M. Attaleiates, *The History*, trans. Anthony Kaldellis, Dimitris Krallis (Cambridge MA: Harvard University Press, 2012), XVIII. 5, p. 229.
5. *Alexiad*, V. 6; X. 11; XI. 6; XIII. 8. Compare with Attaleiates, XVII. 6, p. 197.
6. There are innumerable monographs on ethnicity and ethnogenesis in Europe in the first millennium AD. I found the following studies particularly useful: Guy Halsall, *Barbarian Migrations and the Roman West, 376–568* (Cambridge: Cambridge University Press, 2007), ch. 2; T.H. Eriksen, *Ethnicity and Nationalism: Anthropological Perspectives*

(London: 1993); Robert Bartlett, 'Medieval and Modern Concepts of Race and Ethnicity', *Journal of Medieval and Early Modern Studies*, 31 (2001), 39–46; Susan Reynolds, 'Medieval *Origines Gentium* and the Community of the Realm', *History*, 68/224 (1983), 375–90; P.J. Heather, 'State formation in the first millennium a.d.', in *Scotland in Dark Age Europe*, ed. B. Crawford (St Andrews, 1994), pp. 47–70; F. Curta, 'Frontier ethnogenesis in late antiquity: the Danube, the Tervingi, and the Slavs', in: *Borders, Barriers, and Ethnogenesis: Frontiers in Late Antiquity and the Middle Ages*, ed. Florin Curta (Turnhout, 2005), pp. 173–204.

7. *The Etymologies of Isidore of Seville*, trans. S.A. Barney, W.J. Lewis, J.A. Beach, O. Berghof (Cambridge: Cambridge University Press, 2006), p. 197. See also Jordanes, *Origin of the Goths*, 28, 29.
8. *Vegetius: Epitome of Military Science*, trans. N.P. Milner (Liverpool: Liverpool University Press, 2001), I. 1, p. 2.
9. G. Loud, 'The "Gens Normannorum" – Myth or Reality?', *Anglo-Norman Studies*, 4 (1981), pp. 104–16.
10. Hippocrates, *On Airs, Waters and Places*, 24; Tacitus, *Agricola and Germany*, trans. A.R. Birley (Oxford, 1999), I. 4, p. 39.
11. For a translation of these terms, see: *Chanson de Roland*, ed. F. Whitehead (Oxford: Blackwell, 1978), glossary, p. 146. I am grateful to Dr Matthew Bennett for this useful reference.
12. Ovidio Capitani, 'Specific Motivations and Continuing Themes in the Norman Chronicles of Southern Italy in the Eleventh and Twelfth Centuries', in *The Normans in Sicily and Southern Italy*, Lincey Lectures 1974 (Oxford, 1977), p. 6. See also: Eleni Tounta, 'The Norman Conquerors between Epos and Chanson de Geste: The Perception of Identities in Cultural Flows', in *Norman Tradition and Transcultural Heritage: Exchange of Cultures in the 'Norman' Peripheries of Medieval Europe*, ed. Stefan Burkhardt, Thomas Foerster (London: Routledge, 2013), pp. 125–47, esp. 131–7.
13. Orderic Vitalis, *Ecclesiastical History*, VII. 5.
14. Malaterra, II. 24.
15. William of Apulia, IV, p. 52.
16. Malaterra, I. 6.
17. Malaterra, II. 10.
18. Malaterra, I. 3.
19. Malaterra, I. 1; William of Apulia, I, p. 4.
20. K.B. Wolf, 'Introduction', in: *The Deeds of Count Roger*, p. 30.
21. Malaterra, II. 38.
22. *Alexiad*, I. 10.
23. *Alexiad*, I. 14.
24. *Alexiad*, X. 5; XI. 12.
25. Alexiad, V. 4; V. 7; XI. 3; XI. 4; XIII. 4; XII. 9.
26. Orderic Vitalis, *Ecclesiastical History*, vol. III, p. 366.
27. The best study to-date about Norman kin dynamics in southern Italy and Syria is: Francesca Petrizzo, 'Band of Brothers, Kin Dynamics of the Hautevilles and Other Normans in Southern Italy and Syria, *c.* 1030–*c.* 1140' (PhD thesis, University of Leeds, 2018).

28. William of Apulia, I. 4.
29. Theotokis, *Norman Campaigns*, pp. 108–13. I elaborate on the problem of the Norman troop numbers provided by the primary sources for the period of the Norman expansion in the South between 1017 and 1077: G. Theotokis, 'Greek and Latin sources for the Norman expansion in the South: their value as "military histories" of the warfare in the Mediterranean Sea', in: *Warfare in the Norman Mediterranean*, ed. Georgios Theotokis (Woodbridge: Boydell & Brewer, 2020), pp. 11–33.
30. Malaterra, I. 12; I. 16.
31. Amatus of Montecassino, III. 11, p. 89; Petrizzo, 'Kin dynamics', 118–19.
32. Petrizzo, 'Kin dynamics', 40.
33. Menager, *Recueil*, n. 12, pp. 47–55; Petrizzo, 'Kin dynamics', 41. In fact, the sources indicate that Guiscard provided for Alberada after their divorce: Amatus of Montecassino, IV. 23, p. 118; *Chronica Cassinensis*, III. 15, p. 728.
34. Valerie Eads, 'Sigkelgaita of Salerno: Amazon or Trophy Wife?', *Journal of Medieval Military History*, 3 (2005), 72–87.
35. Petrizzo, 'Kin dynamics', 55.
36. Recent studies have shown that in the eleventh and twelfth centuries European attitudes towards illegitimacy were much more fluid and elastic than historians previously thought: Sara McDougall, *Royal Bastards: The Birth of Illegitimacy, 800–1230* (Oxford: Oxford University Press, 2017), pp. 273–9.
37. Amatus of Montecassino, VII. 8, p. 168; VII. 20, p. 175.
38. Yewdale, *Bohemond*, p. 8; Russo, *Boemondo*, p. 19; Loud, *The Age of Robert Guiscard*, pp. 242–3.

Chapter 2: The Norman Invasion of the Balkans, 1081–83

1. Theotokis, *Norman Campaigns*, pp. 108–36.
2. Amatus, V. 4, 27.
3. Kekaumenos, *Logos Nouthetikos*, §87; Tilemachos Lounghis, 'The Byzantine War Navy and the West, Fifth to Twelfth Centuries', in: *A Military History of the Mediterranean Sea, Aspects of War, Diplomacy and Military Elites*, ed. Georgios Theotokis, Aysel Yildiz (Leiden, 2018), pp. 34–5.
4. Georgios Theotokis, *Byzantine Military Tactics in Syria and Mesopotamia in the Tenth Century* (Edinburgh, 2018), pp. 26–51.
5. Anthony Kaldellis, *Streams of gold, rivers of blood: the rise and fall of Byzantium, 955 A.D. to the First Crusade* (New York, 2017), pp. 246–51; John F. Haldon, *The Byzantine Wars: Battles and Campaigns of the Byzantine Era* (Stroud, 2001), pp. 112–27; A. Friendly, *The Dreadful Day: The Battle of Manzikert, 1071* (London, 1981); Jean-Claude Cheynet, 'Mantzikert – un désastre militaire?', *Byzantion*, 50 (1980), 410–38.
6. Georgios Theotokis, 'Rus, Varangian and Frankish Mercenaries in the Service of the Byzantine Emperors (9th–11th Century) – Numbers, Organisation and Battle Tactics in the Operational Theatres of Asia Minor and the Balkans', *Byzantina Symmeikta*, 22 (2012), 126–56; Alicia Simpson, 'Three Sources of Military Unrest in Eleventh Century Asia Minor: The Norman Chieftains Hervé Frankopoulos, Robert Crispin and Roussel of Bailleuil', *Mesogeios/Méditerranée*, 9–10 (2000), 181–207; Jonathan Shepard, 'The Uses of the Franks in Eleventh-Century Byzantium', *Anglo-Norman Studies*, 15 (1993), 275–305.

7. Georgios Theotokis, 'The Norman Invasion of Sicily, 1061–1072: Numbers and Military Tactics', *War in History*, 17 (2010), 381–402.
8. Michael Attaleiates, *The History*, transl. Anthony Kaldellis, Dimitris Krallis (Cambridge MA, 2012), ch. 23, pp. 333–51; Nicephorus Bryennius, *Histoire*, introduction, text and transl. Paul Gautier (Brussels, 1975), bk II, pp. 142ff.
9. Georgios Theotokis, 'The square fighting march of the Crusaders at the battle of Ascalon (1099)', *Journal of Medieval Military History*, 11 (2013), 57–72.
10. Georgios Leveniotes, *Το στασιαστικό κίνημα του Νορμανδού Ουρσελίου (Υρσελ δε Βαιλλευλ) στην Μικρά Ασία (1073–1076)* [Ursel de Bailleul's uprising in Asia Minor (1073–76)] (Thessaloniki, 2004), pp. 144–50.
11. Leveniotes, *Το στασιαστικό κίνημα*, pp. 151–3.
12. *Alexiad*, I. 1–3; Bryennius, II., pp. 184–94; Leveniotes, *Το στασιαστικό κίνημα*, pp. 169–89.
13. Attaleiates, ch. 16, pp. 169–71.
14. Alexander D. Beihammer, *Byzantium and the Emergence of Muslim-Turkish Anatolia, ca. 1040–1130* (London, 2017), pp. 207–15.
15. Claude Cahen, *Pre-Ottoman Turkey* (New York, 1968), pp. 64–74.
16. Attaleiates, ch. 30, pp. 433–41; Zonaras, *Extracts of History*, XVIII. 18, pp. 226–7; Beihammer, *Byzantium*, pp. 218–19; Kaldellis, *Streams of gold*, p. 265; Cahen, *Pre-Ottoman Turkey*, pp. 75–6.
17. Bryennius, IV. 2, p. 258.
18. Norman Tobias, 'The Tactics and Strategy of Alexios Komnenos at Calavrytae, 1078', *Byzantine Studies/Études byzantines*, 6 (1979), 193–211.
19. Marek Meško, 'Pecheneg groups in the Balkans (ca. 1053–1091) according to the Byzantine sources', in: *The Steppe Lands and the World Beyond Them, Studies in honor of Victor Spinei on his 70th birthday*, ed. Florin Curta, Bogdan-Petru Maleon (Iasi, 2013), p. 184; John V.A. Fine, *The Early Medieval Balkans* (Ann Arbor, 1991), p. 210.
20. For the term 'mixobarbaros': 'perhaps the closest equivalent that classicizing authors could find for people who lived within the frontiers of the [Byzantine] *oikumene* and had signed treaties with the emperor, thereby recognizing the rule of law, but who were not Rhomaioi (Byzantines)': Paul Stephenson, *Byzantium's Balkan Frontier, A Political Study of the Northern Balkans, 900–1204* (Cambridge, 2000), p. 109.
21. Attaleiates, 26.2, p. 379; Meško, 'Pecheneg groups', p. 189; Alexandru Madgearu, 'The periphery against the center: The case of Paradunavon', *Zbornik radova Vizantoloskog instituta*, 40 (2003), 50–1; Élisabeth Malamut, 'L'image byzantine des Petchénègues', *Byzantinische Zeitschrift*, 88 (1995), 130–2.
22. 'Skylitzes Continuatus', in: *Georgius Cedrenus Compendium Historiarum* [CSHB], ed. Immanuel Bekker (Bonn, 1839), p. 719; Ioannes Zonaras, *Epitome Historiarum*, ed. Charles Du Fresne Du Cange, Ludwig August Dindorf (Leipzig, 1868), vol. III, p. 714.
23. Meško, 'Pecheneg groups', p. 190; Madgearu, 'The periphery', 51–2.
24. Meško, 'Pecheneg groups', p. 193; Stephenson, *Byzantium's Balkan Frontier*, p. 101; Malamut, 'L'image', 132–4.
25. 'Skylitzes Continuatus', p. 743.
26. John Skylitzes, *A Synopsis of Byzantine History, 811–1057*, trans. John Wortley (Cambridge, 2010), p. 442; Stephenson, *Byzantium's Balkan Frontier*, pp. 117–41; Fine, *The Early Medieval Balkans*, pp. 202–15.

27. Stephenson, *Byzantium's Balkan Frontier*, p. 144; Fine, *The Early Medieval Balkans*, p. 215.
28. Fine, *The Early Medieval Balkans*, p. 215.
29. *Annales Barenses*, ed. G. Waitz, MGH SS V (Hanover, 1864), p. 60.
30. H.E.J. Cowdrey, *Pope Gregory VII* (Oxford, 1998), pp. 425–39; I.S. Robinson, *The Papacy, 1073–1198: Continuity and Innovation* (Cambridge, 1990), pp. 367–97.
31. Loud, *The Age of Robert Guiscard*, pp. 206–8.
32. *Alexiad*, I. xii. Compare with: Malaterra, III. 14: 'He [Guiscard] sweats over the preparations to win Byzantium for himself'.
33. William B. McQueen, 'Relations between the Normans and Byzantium, 1071–1112', *Byzantion*, 56 (1986), 429. On Alexios' letter: Einar Joranson, 'The Problem of the Spurious Letter of Emperor Alexios to the Court of Flanders', *The American Historical Review*, 55 (1950), 811–32.
34. *The Register of Pope Gregory VII, 1073–1085: An English Translation*, trans. Herbert Edward John Cowdrey (Oxford, 2002), VIII. 6, pp. 371–2.
35. R. Upsher Smith Jr, '"Nobilissimus" and Warleader: the opportunity and the necessity behind Robert Guiscard's Balkan expeditions', *Byzantion*, 70 (2000), 507–26.
36. Richardus Pictaviensis, *Chronica*, MGH, SS, XXVI, p. 79.
37. Anna Komnena, *Alexiad*, I. Xiv.
38. Georgios Theotokis, 'Greek and Latin sources for the Norman expansion in the South: their value as "military histories" of warfare in the Mediterranean Sea', in: *Warfare in the Norman Mediterranean*, ed. Georgios Theotokis (Woodbridge: Boydell & Brewer, 2020), pp. 11–33.
39. *Alexiad*, I. xvi; Malaterra, III. 24; Orderic Vitalis, VII, p. 16; *Chronicon Casinensis*, III. 49, p. 429; Romuald of Salerno, *Chronicon*, s.a. 1081, p. 194.
40. *Alexiad*, I. xiv; Malaterra, III. 24.
41. Hélène Ahrweiler, *Byzance et la Mer* (Paris, 1966), pp. 160–3.
42. *Alexiad*, I. xvi; Malaterra, III. 24 William of Apulia, IV, p. 48; Lupus Protospatharius, *Chronicon*, s.a. 1081.
43. Haldon, *Warfare, State and Society*, pp. 51–60.
44. *Alexiad*, III. xii; William of Apulia, IV, p. 49.
45. *Alexiad*, I. xvi; William of Apulia, IV, p. 49
46. *Alexiad*, III. x; McQueen, 'Relations', 443–4.
47. *Alexiad*, IV. ii.
48. Stephenson, *Byzantium's Balkan Frontier*, p. 169; Alain Ducellier, *La façade maritime de l'Albanie au moyen âge: Durazzo et Valona du XIe au XVe siècle* (Thessaloniki, 1981), pp. 71, 105.
49. Donald M. Nicol, *Byzantium and Venice* (Cambridge, 1988), pp. 50–67.
50. Beihammer, *Byzantium*, pp. 221–4. For a different view on Suleiman's control of Nicaea: Peter Frankopan, *The First Crusade, The Call from the East* (Cambridge MA, 2012), pp. 46–8; idem, 'The Fall of Nicaea and the Towns of Western Asia Minor to the Turks in the Later 11th Century: the Curious Case of Nikephoros Melissenos', *Byzantion*, 76 (2006), 153–84.
51. *Alexiad*, III. xi.
52. Peter Frankopan, 'Kinship and the distribution of power in Komnenian Byzantium', *English Historical Review*, 495 (2007), 1–34; idem, *The First Crusade*, pp. 46–8.
53. *Alexiad*, III. xii; IV. i; William of Apulia, IV, p. 49.

54. Stephenson, *Byzantium's Balkan Frontier*, pp. 163–4.
55. *Alexiad*, XIII. iii.
56. *Alexiad*, IV. i; William of Apulia, IV, p. 49; Lupus Protospatharius, *Chronicon*, s.a. 1081; Anonymus Barensis, *Chronicon*, s.a. 1081; Yewdale, *Bohemond*, p. 14.
57. *Alexiad*, IV. ii.
58. Malaterra, III. 26.
59. William of Apulia, IV, p. 51; *Alexiad*, IV. iii.
60. *Alexiad*, IV. v.
61. William of Apulia, IV, p. 51.
62. *Alexiad*, IV. v.
63. Theotokis, *Byzantine Military Tactics*, pp. 31–51.
64. *Alexiad*, IV. iv.
65. *Alexiad*, IV. vi.
66. Patricia Skinner, '"Halt! Be Men!"': Sikelgaita of Salerno, Gender and the Norman Conquest of Southern Italy', *Gender & History*, 12 (2000), 622–41. For a fresh look at Anna's gender models: Leonora Neville, *Anna Komnene, The Life and Work of a Medieval Historian* (Oxford, 2016), ch. 4.
67. Theotokis, *Norman Campaigns*, p. 161.
68. Jonathan Harris, *Byzantium and the Crusades* (London, 2014; 2nd edn), p. 41; Stephenson, *Byzantium's Balkan Frontier*, p. 167; Michael Angold, *The Byzantine Empire, 1025–1204, A Political History* (London, 1997; 2nd edn), p. 130.
69. *Alexiad*, IV. vi.
70. 'Presentation and Composition on Warfare of the Emperor Nicephoros', in: *Sowing the Dragon's Teeth: Byzantine Warfare in the Tenth Century*, ed. and trans. E. McGeer (Washington DC, 1995), II. 69–72, p. 26; II. 124–6, p. 28. See also: Theotokis, *Byzantine Military Tactics*, pp. 220–2, 276–89.

Chapter 3: The Norman Invasion of the Balkans, 1082–84

1. Stephenson, *Byzantium's Balkan Frontier*, p. 167; Alain Ducellier, '*L'Arbanon et les Albanais au XIe siècle*', *Travaux et Mémoires*, 3 (1968), 358–63; Era Vranousi, 'Κομισκόρτης ο εξ Αρβάνων' – σχόλια εις χωρίον της Άννης Κομνηνής (Ioannina, 1962).
2. William of Apulia, IV, p. 54; Malaterra, III. 28. Our only source for the precise date of the city's surrender is: Anonymus Barensis, *Chronicon*, s.a. 1082.
3. Malaterra, III. 29; A. Glavinas, 'Οι Νορμανδοί στην Καστοριά (1082–1083)' ['The Normans in Kastoria (1082–1083)'], Βυζαντινά [*Byzantina*], 13ii (1985), 1255–65.
4. Leo VI, *Taktika*, XX. 36, p. 550. See also: Jonathan Shepard, 'Information, Disinformation and Delay in Byzantine Diplomacy', *Byzantinische Forschungen*, 10 (1985), 233–93.
5. Constantine Porphyrogenitus, *De Administrando Imperio*, ed. G. Moravcsik (Greek text), trans. R.J.H. Jenkins (Washington, DC: Dumbarton Oaks Texts, 4, 1985), pp. 50–2. Compare with the ninth-century treatise: *On Strategy*, 6, p. 22.
6. *Alexiad*, V. iii; McQueen, 'The Normans and Byzantium', 443–4.
7. *Alexiad*, V. ii; A. Glavinas, *Η επί Αλεξίου Κομνηνού (1081–1118) περί ιερών σκευών, κειμηλίων και αγίων εικόνων έρις (1081–1095)* [The Controversy (1081–1095) regarding the Holy Relics and Saintly Images during the Reign of Alexios Komnenos (1081–1118)] (Thessaloniki, 1972), ch. 2, pp. 51–72.
8. *Alexiad*, V. iii.

9. For more about the role of the Vlach populations of Greece in the Norman campaign: Theotokis, *Norman Campaigns*, pp. 168–9.
10. *Alexiad*, V. iv.
11. Kelly DeVries, *Medieval Military Technology* (North York ON, 2012, 2nd edn), ch. 9.
12. For the first battle at Ioannina: *Alexiad*, V. iv.
13. On the importance and complexity of operational and tactical intelligence gathering for the early and middle Byzantine armies, and especially that of the lightly armed cavalry unit of the *prokoursatores* (προκουρσάτορες, Lat. procursor), see: Theotokis, *Byzantine Military Tactics*, ch. 5 (pp. 128–46).
14. Leo VI, *Taktika*, XVIII. 92, pp. 468–70.
15. Leo VI, *Taktika*, XVIII. 91, p. 468.
16. Only Malaterra refers to Bohemond's march to the city of Arta: Malaterra, III. 39.
17. Peter Soustal and Johannes Koder, *Tabula Imperii Byzantini, Band 3: Nikopolis und Kephallēnia* (Vienna, 1981), p. 113.
18. Allan Brooks, *Castles of Northwest Greece, From the early Byzantine Period to the eve of the First World War* (Huddersfield, 2013), pp. 157–66. Myrto Veikou believes that there must have been a Middle Byzantine (Komnenian) construction phase in the Castle of Arta: *Byzantine Epirus, A Topography of Transformation, Settlements of the Seventh–Twelfth Centuries in Southern Epirus and Aetoloacarnania, Greece* (Leiden, 2012), pp. 146–7.
19. Mamuka Tsurtsumia, 'ΤΡΙΒΟΛΟΣ: A BYZANTINE LANDMINE', *Byzantion*, 82 (2012), 415–22.
20. Paul Brown, 'The Gesta Roberti Wiscardi: A "Byzantine" history?', *Journal of Medieval History*, 37 (2011), 162–79, esp. 173.
21. *Alexiad*, V. v.
22. A. Glavinas, 'Οι Νορμανδοί στην Θεσσαλία και η πολιορκία της Λάρισας (1082–1083)' ['The Normans in Thessaly and the Siege of Larisa (1082–1083)'], *Βυζαντιακά*, 4 (1984), 39–40.
23. John W. Nesbitt, Nicolas Oikonomides (eds), *Catalogue of Byzantine Seals at Dumbarton Oaks and in the Fogg Museum of Art, Volume 2: South of the Balkans, the Islands, South of Asia Minor* (Washington DC, 1994), p. 22.
24. https://www.kastra.eu/castlegr.php?kastro=bezesteni (accessed: 08/04/2019).
25. *The Oxford Dictionary of Byzantium*, ed. Alexander P. Kazhdan (Oxford, 1991), vol. I, p. 659 ['doulos'].
26. *The Oxford Dictionary of Byzantium*, vol. II, p. 1122 ['Kephalas'].
27. *Typicon Gregorii Pacuriani*, ed. Mikel T'arxnišvili, Corpus Scriptorum Christianorum Orientalium 144 (Louvain, 1954), p. 49.
28. Leo VI, *Taktika*, XVIII. 91, p. 468.
29. *Alexiad*, XIII. iv.
30. *Alexiad*, V. v. Anna mentions a location named Lycostomium ('Wolf's mouth'), which could be the modern Stomio (Greek: Στόμιο), a village in the Agia municipality, south of the mouth of the river Pineiós, and 37km northeast of Larissa. The sixth-century monastery of Saint Demetrius, situated on the mountain slope above Stomio, was rebuilt in its present form by Alexios Komnenos: larisa.culture.gr/index.php/arxaiologikoi-xoroi-kai-mnimeia-nomoy-larisas/9-uncategorised/116-i-moni-komnineiou-sto-stomio-larisas (in Greek, accessed: 09/04/2019).
31. *Alexiad*, V. vi.

174 Bohemond of Taranto

32. *Alexiad*, V. vi.
33. *Alexiad*, VI. i.
34. *Alexiad*, V. iii.
35. *Alexiad*, VI. v; William of Apulia, V, p. 58.
36. William of Apulia, IV, p. 56.
37. William of Apulia, V, p. 59.
38. Information about the types of vessel employed by the Normans in their amphibious operation is scarce. For more information on horse transports for this period, see: Charles D. Stanton, 'Naval Power in the Norman Conquest of Southern Italy and Sicily', *Haskins Society Journal*, 19 (2008), 120–36; John H. Pryor, 'Transportation of Horses by Sea during the Era of the Crusades: Eighth Century to 1285 A.D.', *Mariner's Mirror*, 68 (1982), 9–27, 103–25; Matthew Bennett, 'Amphibious Operations from the Norman Conquest to the Crusades of St. Louis, c.1050–c.1250', in: *Amphibious Warfare 1000–1700*, ed. D.J.B. Trim, M.C. Fissel (Leiden, 2006), pp. 51–68; John H. Pryor and Elizabeth Jeffreys, *The Age of the Δρόμων, The Byzantine Navy ca. 500–1204* (Leiden, 2006), pp. 304–32; Dionisius Agius, *Classic Ships of Islam, From Mesopotamia to the Indian Ocean* (Leiden, 2008), pp. 321–60.
39. *Alexiad*, VI. v; William of Apulia, V, p. 59; Malaterra, III. 40.
40. *Alexiad*, VI. v–vi; William of Apulia, V, p. 60; Dandolus, *Chronicon*, s.a. 1084, p. 218; Lupus Protospatharius, *Chronicon*, s.a. 1084; Anonymus Barensis, *Chronicon*, s.a. 1085; Romuald of Salerno, *Chronicon*, s.a. 1085.
41. *Alexiad*, VI. v.
42. Malaterra, II. 41, 42.
43. William of Apulia, V, p. 61; *Alexiad*, IV. iii.
44. *O' City of Byzantium: Annals of Niketas Choniatēs*, trans. Henry J. Magoulias (Detroit, 1984), II. 2, pp. 43–5.
45. *Alexiad*, VI. vi; William of Apulia, V, p. 63.
46. *Alexiad*, VI. vii.

Chapter 4: The Interlude Period, 1085–97

1. 'Here lies the Guiscard, the terror of the world [*terror mundi*]. | From the City, the king of the Italians and Germans he hurled. | Neither Parthians, Arabs, nor the army of Macedon could Alexios free, | Only flight: for Venice could prevail neither flight nor the sea.' The epitaph on Robert Guiscard's tomb at the abbey of Venosa, recorded by William of Malmesbury, *Gesta Regum Anglorum*, ed. and trans. R.A.B. Mynors (Oxford, 1998), I, pp. 484–5.
2. William of Apulia, IV, pp. 64–5.
3. William of Apulia, IV, p. 64.
4. Petrizzo, 'Kin dynamics', 33–4.
5. Malaterra, III. 42.
6. Petrizzo, 'Kin dynamics', 34, 117.
7. Léon Robert Ménager, *Recueil des actes des ducs normands d'Italie, 1046–1127. Les premier ducs* (Bari, 1980), n. 47, pp. 171–2; n. 49, pp. 175–6; n. 57, pp. 197–8; n. 59, pp. 203–12; n. 61, pp. 215–19.
8. Orderic Vitalis, vol. II, VIII. 7, p. 464.
9. Malaterra, IV. 4.

10. Malaterra, IV. 4; Russo, *Boemondo*, pp. 45, 50–1; W. Jahn, *Untersuchungen zur normannischen Herrschaft in Süditalien (1040–1100)* (Frankfurt am Main, 1989), pp. 246–8.
11. Romuald of Salerno, *Chronicon*, s.a. 1087, p. 198.
12. Francesco Trinchera, *Syllabus Graecarum membranarum* (Naples, 1865), pp. 65–6. In his recent biography of Bohemond, Russo has cast doubt on the authenticity of this *sigillum* on the grounds that it is missing the lead seal that confirmed it. He believes that the title of prince of Taranto traditionally attributed to Bohemond is a later invention: Russo, *Boemondo*, pp. 50–1.
13. Malaterra, IV. 9.
14. Our only source is: Malaterra, IV. 10.
15. Russo, *Boemondo*, n. 23, p. 54; Flori, *Bohémond d'Antioche*, p. 57.
16. A more detailed definition of the 'Gregorian Reform' describes 'a papally initiated and directed movement of moral and religious renewal. Its overriding aim was to rid the church of the two 'heresies' of *simony* (the sale of holy orders and ecclesiastical offices, and trafficking in them for temporal reward or advancement) and *nicolaitism* (the irregular sexual morality of the clergy)': H.E.J. Cowdrey, *The Age of Abbot Desiderius Montecassino, the Papacy, and the Normans in the Eleventh and Early Twelfth Centuries* (Oxford, 1996), p. xxxiv.
17. Malaterra, IV. 13.
18. Richard Urban Butler, 'Pope Bl. Urban II', *The Catholic Encyclopedia*, vol. 15 (New York, 1912); http://www.newadvent.org/cathen/15210a.htm (accessed: 17 May 2019).
19. Romuald of Salerno, *Chronicon*, s.a. 1089, pp. 198–9; *The Annals of 'Lupus Protospatharius'*, s.a. 1089. See also: Robert Somerville, *Pope Urban II, the Collectio Britannica, and the Council of Melfi (1089)* (Oxford, 1996).
20. Romuald of Salerno, *Chronicon*, s.a. 1089, p. 199.
21. Malaterra, IV. 17.
22. Metcalfe, *The Muslims*, pp. 94–5; Theotokis, *Norman Campaigns*, pp. 122–3.
23. Malaterra, IV. 22, 26.
24. Giovanni Amatuccio, 'Saracen archers in southern Italy'; deremilitari.org/2013/07/saracen-archers-in-southern-italy/ (accessed: 19 May 2019).
25. Romuald of Salerno, *Chronicon*, s.a. 1091, p. 199; *The Annals of 'Lupus Protospatharius'*, s.a. 1091.
26. Flori, *Bohémond d'Antioche*, p. 59 (nn. 36, 37).
27. Yewdale, *Bohemond*, p. 32.
28. Malaterra, IV. 20.
29. Malaterra, IV. 21.

Chapter 5: The Crusader – From Italy to the City

1. Malaterra, IV. 10.
2. Jonathan Shepard, 'When Greek meets Greek: Alexios Komnenos and Bohemond in 1097–98', *Byzantine and Modern Greek Studies*, 12 (1988), 243.
3. Malaterra, IV. 24; *The Annals of 'Lupus Protospatharius'*, s.a. 1096; Romuald of Salerno, *Chronicon*, s.a. 1096, p. 200.
4. Malaterra, IV. 24.
5. Jonathan Riley-Smith, *What Were the Crusades?* (Basingstoke, 2002).
6. *The Annals of 'Lupus Protospatharius'*, s.a. 1095.
7. Malaterra, IV. 24.

8. *The Annals of 'Lupus Protospatharius'*, s.a. 1095; Romuald of Salerno, *Chronicon*, s.a. 1096, p. 200; Ralph of Caen, *The Gesta Tancredi of Ralph of Caen: A History of the Normans on the First Crusade*, trans. B.S. Bachrach, D.S. Bachrach (Aldershot, 2005), ch. 2, p. 23. The account by the anonymous chronicler of the *Gesta Francorum et aliorum Hierosolimitanorum* portrays Bohemond as a shrewd and calculating leader who carefully enquires about the nature of the expedition, the motivation of the participants and their weapons, before deciding to throw in his lot with them: *The deeds of the Franks and other Jerusalem-bound pilgrims: the earliest chronicle of the first crusades*, ed. and trans. Nirmal Dass (Plymouth, 2011), p. 30.
9. Yewdale, *Bohemond*, p. 35.
10. *Alexiad*, X. v.
11. William of Malmesbury, I, p. 356.
12. See Luigi Russo's commendable attempt to tackle this problem: 'Norman participation in the First Crusade: a re-examination', in: *Warfare in the Norman Mediterranean*, ed. Georgios Theotokis (Woodbridge: Boydell & Brewer, 2020), pp. 195–209.
13. Albert of Aachen, *Historia Ierosolimitana, History of the Journey to Jerusalem*, ed. and trans. Susan B. Edgington (Oxford, 2007), II. 18, p. 89.
14. *The Annals of 'Lupus Protospatharius'*, s.a. 1096.
15. *The deeds of the Franks*, pp. 30–1.
16. Russo, 'Norman participation in the First Crusade', p. 5.
17. Francesco Nitti di Vito (ed.), *Le pergamene di S. Nicola di Bari (1075–1194)* (Bari, 1902), [Codice diplomatico barese, 5], doc. 22, pp. 41–2; Yewdale, *Bohemond*, p. 36. Russo believes that Yewdale did not pay this document the necessary attention: *Bohemondo*, pp. 61–2. For more on the funding of the crusades movement, both at national and individual level: Jonathan Riley-Smith, *The First Crusade and the idea of crusading* (London, 2003), pp. 44–7.
18. Alan V. Murray, 'The Middle Ground: The Passage of Crusade Armies to The Holy Land By Land and Sea (1096–1204)', in: *A Military History of the Mediterranean Sea, Aspects of War, Diplomacy, and Military Elites*, ed. Georgios Theotokis, Aysel Yıldız (Leiden, 2018), pp. 185–201.
19. Yewdale, *Bohemond*, p. 36.
20. *The deeds of the Franks*, p. 31.
21. *Alexiad*, X. vii.
22. *Alexiad*, X. viii; Albert of Aachen, *History of the Journey to Jerusalem*, II. 18, p. 89; Russo, *Bohemondo*, p. 63; John H. Pryor, 'Introduction: modelling Bohemond's march to Thessalonike', in: *Logistics of Warfare in the Age of the Crusades*, ed. John H. Pryor (Aldershot, 2006), pp. 1–24, esp. p. 1.
23. *The deeds of the Franks*, p. 31.
24. *The deeds of the Franks*, p. 31.
25. *The deeds of the Franks*, p. 31.
26. Ralph of Caen, *The Gesta Tancredi*, ch. 4, p. 25.
27. Ralph of Caen, *The Gesta Tancredi*, ch. 4, p. 25.
28. *The deeds of the Franks*, p. 32.
29. *The deeds of the Franks*, p. 32. For more about the title of *kouropalates*: *The Oxford Dictionary of Byzantium*, vol. II, p. 1157.

30. Frankopan, *The First Crusade*, pp. 126-7; J. Shepard, '"Father" or "Scorpion"? Style and substance in Alexios' diplomacy', in: *Alexios I Komnenos*, ed. Margaret Mullett, Dion Smythe (Belfast, 1996), pp. 80-2.
31. *Alexiad*, X. ix.
32. *Alexiad*, X. ix.
33. Pryor has argued that the crusaders in 1097 understood their oaths to be oaths of fealty alone, and that to them there was an enormous difference between the swearing of such oaths of fealty and the performance of vassal homage, especially compared to Bohemond becoming λίζιος ἄνθρωπος (liege-man) of the emperor at the Treaty of Devol in 1108: John Pryor, 'The oath of the leaders of the Crusade to the emperor Alexios Komnenos: Fealty, homage', *Parergon New Series*, 2 (1984), 111-41. See also: E. Patlagean, 'Christianisation et parentés rituelles: le domaine de Byzance', *Annales ESC*, 33 (1978), 625-36; Ruth Macrides, 'Kinship by arrangement: The case of adoption', *Dumbarton Oaks Papers*, 44 (1990), pp. 109-18.
34. *Alexiad*, X. ix.
35. On Bohemond's language skills: Shepard, 'Greek meets Greek', 251-8.
36. *Alexiad*, X. xi.
37. Shepard, 'Greek meets Greek', 185-277; Frankopan, *The First Crusade*, pp. 134-6; Jay Rubenstein, *Armies of Heaven, The First Crusade and the Quest for Apocalypse* (New York, 2011), pp. 75-80.
38. Frankopan, *The First Crusade*, p. 134.
39. *Alexiad*, X. xi.
40. *The deeds of the Franks*, p. 35.
41. Ralph of Caen, *The Gesta Tancredi*, ch. 10, p. 31.
42. Ralph of Caen, *The Gesta Tancredi*, ch. 11, p. 32.
43. Raymond of Aguilers, *Historia Francorum Qui Ceperunt Iherusalem*, trans. with intro., John H. Hill, Laurita L. Hill (Philadelphia, 1968), p. 23.
44. *Alexiad*, X. xi.
45. Shepard, 'Greek meets Greek', 185-277.

Chapter 6: The Crusader – Conquering Antioch

1. D.A. Korobeinikov, 'Raiders and neighbours: the Turks (1040-1304)', in: *The Cambridge history of the Byzantine Empire c.500-1492*, ed. Jonathan Shepard (Cambridge, 2008), pp. 707-8.
2. Claude Cahen, *The formation of Turkey: the Seljukid Sultanate of Rum: eleventh to fourteenth century*, trans. and ed. P.M. Holt (Harlow, 2001), pp. 9-11.
3. Haldon, *Warfare, State and Society*, pp. 56-7.
4. *The deeds of the Franks*, pp. 37-8; Raymond of Aguilers, p. 25.
5. For more on Tatikios: *Oxford Dictionary of Byzantium*, vol. III, p. 2014; Charles M. Brand, 'The Turkish Element in Byzantium, Eleventh-Twelfth Centuries', *Dumbarton Oaks Papers*, 43 (1989), 3-4.
6. Rubenstein, *Armies of Heaven*, p. 103; John France, *Victory in the East: a military history of the First Crusade* (Cambridge, 1994), p. 143.
7. Raymond of Aguilers, pp. 25-6.
8. Albert of Aachen, II. 27, p. 107.
9. Albert of Aachen, II. 28, p. 109.
10. *The deeds of the Franks*, p. 37; Raymond of Aguilers, p. 26.

11. *Alexiad*, XI. ii.
12. Albert of Aachen, II. 28–37, pp. 109–25.
13. *Alexiad*, XI. ii; *The deeds of the Franks*, pp. 38–9; William of Tyre, vol. I, III. 11, pp. 165–6; Albert of Aachen, II. 37, p. 126.
14. Frankopan, *The First Crusade*, pp. 145–6.
15. Ralph of Caen, ch. 17, p. 41.
16. *The deeds of the Franks*, p. 41; Albert of Aachen, II. 38, p. 129; *Alexiad*, XI. iii.
17. France, *Victory in the East*, p. 169.
18. France, *Victory in the East*, pp. 173–4.
19. Albert of Aachen, II. 38, p. 129; William of Tyre, vol. I, III. 13, p. 169.
20. France, *Victory in the East*, pp. 157, 174–5; Claude Cahen, 'The Turkish Invasion: The Selchukids', in: *A History of the Crusades*, 6 vols, ed. K. Setton (Madison, 1969–89), I, pp. 135–76.
21. Ralph of Caen, *The Gesta Tancredi*, ch. 21, p. 45.
22. William of Tyre, vol. I, III. 14, pp. 170–1; *The deeds of the Franks*, p. 42; Albert of Aachen, II. 39, p. 130.
23. John France, 'Technology and the Success of the First Crusade', in: *War and Society in the Eastern Mediterranean, 7th–15th Centuries*, ed. Yaacov Lev (Leiden, 1996), p. 165; Anne Hyland, *The Medieval Warhorse from Byzantium to the Crusades* (Stroud, 1994), pp. 140–68.
24. Leo VI, *Taktika*, XVIII. 110, pp. 476–8.
25. Nicholas Morton, 'Encountering the Turks: the First Crusaders' Foreknowledge of their Enemy; Some Preliminary Findings', in: *Crusading and Warfare in the Middle Ages, Realities and Representations, Essays in Honour of John France*, ed. Simon John, Nicholas Morton (Farnham, 2014), pp. 47–68.
26. *Alexiad*, X. ii.
27. William of Tyre, vol. I, III. 14, p. 171.
28. Ibn al-Qalanisi, *The Damascus chronicle of the Crusades*, extracted and transl. H.A.R. Gibb (Mineola, NY, 2002), p. 42. For more on the Turkish reaction following the Battle of Dorylaeum: Beihammer, *Byzantium and the Emergence of Muslim-Turkish Anatolia*, pp. 309–15.
29. *The deeds of the Franks*, p. 46.
30. France, *Victory in the East*, p. 186.
31. Beihammer, *Byzantium and the Emergence of Muslim-Turkish Anatolia*, pp. 285–95.
32. Matthew of Edessa, *Armenia and the Crusades: tenth to twelfth centuries: the Chronicle of Matthew of Edessa*, transl. from the original Armenian with a commentary and intro., Ara Edmond Dostourian (Lanham, Maryland, 1993), p. 166.
33. *The deeds of the Franks*, pp. 48–9; Raymond of Aguilers, p. 31.
34. Albert of Aachen, III. 15, pp. 161–3.
35. Albert of Aachen, III. 8–9, pp. 151–3; Ralph of Caen, *The Gesta Tancredi*, chs 38–44, pp. 61–9.
36. Frankopan, *The First Crusade*, p. 151.
37. Frankopan, *The First Crusade*, p. 152; Albert of Aachen, III. 22–24, pp. 172–77.
38. Albert of Aachen, III. 26, p. 181.
39. Albert of Aachen, III. 29, p. 185.
40. A. Asa Eger, '(Re)Mapping Medieval Antioch: Urban Transformations from the Early Islamic to the Middle Byzantine Periods', *Dumbarton Oaks Papers*, 67 (2013), 95–134,

esp. 103–5; R. Rogers, *Latin Siege Warfare in the Twelfth Century* (Oxford, 1992), pp. 26–30; France, *Victory in the East*, pp. 222–3.
41. *The History of Leo the Deacon: Byzantine military expansion in the tenth century*, intro., transl. and annotations, Alice-Mary Talbot, Denis F. Sullivan (Washington, DC, 2005), pp. 132–4.
42. Raymond of Aguilers, p. 30.
43. France, *Victory in the East*, p. 220.
44. Beihammer, *Byzantium and the Emergence of Muslim-Turkish Anatolia*, pp. 251–3.
45. Bernard S. Bachrach, 'Some Observations on the Role of the Byzantine Navy in the Success of the First Crusade', *Journal of Medieval Military History*, 1 (2002), 83–100.
46. *The deeds of the Franks*, p. 52. See also: Albert of Aachen, III. 60–2, pp. 233–9.
47. *The deeds of the Franks*, pp. 53–4; Raymond of Aguilers, p. 33.
48. Some of the Latin chroniclers understood this difference and used different terms, like Turks and Saracens. See: Albert of Aachen, III. 62, p. 236; and V. 29, p. 374; *The deeds of the Franks*, pp. 53–4.
49. J. Riley-Smith, *The Crusades* (London, 1987), p. 28; Verbruggen, *The Art of Warfare*, pp. 225–7; France believes the number to have been around seven hundred: France, *Victory in the East*, p. 246; Nicolle, rather, puts the figure down to two hundred, see: Nicolle, *Crusader Warfare*, I, p. 137.
50. *The deeds of the Franks*, pp. 58–9; Raymond of Aguilers, pp. 34–5; France, *Victory in the East*, pp. 245–51; Theotokis, *Norman Campaigns*, p. 193.
51. Raymond of Aguilers, p. 37.
52. *The deeds of the Franks*, p. 57.
53. Albert of Aachen, IV. 40, pp. 311–13.
54. Frankopan, *The First Crusade*, pp. 159–61; Russo, *Boemondo*, pp. 93–5; Shepard, 'Greek meets Greek'; John France, 'The departure of Tatikios from the Crusader army', *Bulletin of the Institute of Historical Research*, 44 (1971), 137–47.
55. Ralph of Caen, ch. 58, p. 84.
56. *Alexiad*, XI. iv
57. *The deeds of the Franks*, pp. 66–7.
58. Shepard, 'Greek meets Greek', 187.
59. *The deeds of the Franks*, pp. 66–7; Matthew of Edessa, p. 170; Ibn Al-Qalanisi, p. 45; Raymond of Aguilers, p. 47; Albert of Aachen, III. 61, p. 234.
60. Albert of Aachen, IV. 14, p. 269.
61. *The deeds of the Franks*, p. 67.
62. *The deeds of the Franks*, pp. 67–8; Albert of Aachen, IV. 19–23, pp. 269–85; Frankopan, *The First Crusade*, pp. 161–3; Russo, *Boemondo*, pp. 99–101; France, *Victory in the East*, pp. 263–8.
63. *The deeds of the Franks*, p. 68.
64. Albert of Aachen, IV. 34, p. 299.
65. Fulcheri Carnotensis, *Historia Hierosolymitana (1095–1127)*, ed. Heinrich Hagenmeyer (Heidelberg, 1913), I. 19. 3, p. 243.
66. Frankopan, *The First Crusade*, p. 164; Russo, *Boemondo*, pp. 103–5.
67. Raymond of Aguilers, p. 59.
68. Albert of Aachen, IV. 49, p. 324; Raymond of Aguilers, p. 61; Ralph of Caen, chs 83–90, pp. 105–10; *The deeds of the Franks*, pp. 84–5. For secondary sources: France, *Victory in the East*, ch. 9; Theotokis, *Norman Campaigns*, pp. 194–5; Russo, *Boemondo*, pp. 105–7.

69. Pete Armstrong, *Stirling Bridge & Falkirk, Wallace's Rebellion* (Oxford, 2003), pp. 46–52.
70. Smail, *Crusading Warfare*, p. 173; France, *Victory in the East*, pp. 284–5.
71. Albert of Aachen, IV. 49, p. 326.
72. France, *Victory in the East*, pp. 287–93.
73. Rubenstein, *Armies of Heaven*, pp. 225–6.
74. *The deeds of the Franks*, p. 86.
75. France, *Victory in the East*, p. 285 (n. 53). See also: Ralph of Caen, ch. 89, p. 109.
76. Raymond of Aguilers, p. 65.
77. *The deeds of the Franks*, p. 87.

Chapter 7: Lord of Antioch

1. Raymond of Aguilers, p. 65.
2. Albert of Aachen, V. 2, p. 341; Raymond of Aguilers, p. 65.
3. Shepard, 'Greek Meets Greek', 274.
4. *The deeds of the Franks*, pp. 81–2.
5. Beihammer, *Byzantium and the Emergence of Muslim-Turkish Anatolia*, pp. 315–18.
6. Albert of Aachen, V. 3, pp. 341–3.
7. Malcolm Barber and Keith Bate, *Letters from the East: Crusaders, Pilgrims and Settlers in the 12th–13th centuries* (New York, 2016), letter no. 8, pp. 31–3. Pryor and Jeffreys have dismissed the historical authenticity of the letter: John H. Pryor, and Michael J. Jeffreys, 'Alexios, Bohemond, and Byzantium's Euphrates Frontier: A Tale of Two Cretans', *Crusades*, 11 (2012), 31–86.
8. *The deeds of the Franks*, p. 90.
9. *The deeds of the Franks*, pp. 91–2; Raymond of Aguilers, p. 73.
10. Thomas S. Asbridge, *The Creation of the Principality of Antioch, 1098–1130* (Woodbridge, 2000), pp. 37–8.
11. *The deeds of the Franks*, p. 92. See also: Raymond of Aguilers, pp. 74–5.
12. The siege is recorded in detail in: *The deeds of the Franks*, pp. 93–5; Raymond of Aguilers, pp. 75–9; Ralph of Caen, *The Gesta Tancredi*, ch. 104, pp. 121–2.
13. Raymond of Aguilers, p. 79. We should keep in mind that Raymond is, admittedly, biased in favour of the count of Toulouse.
14. Raymond of Aguilers, p. 79; Asbridge, *The Principality of Antioch*, pp. 40–1.
15. *The deeds of the Franks*, p. 95. Compare with: Ralph of Caen, *The Gesta Tancredi*, ch. 97, p. 116.
16. Raymond of Aguilers, p. 80.
17. Frankopan, *The First Crusade*, p. 171.
18. Raymond of Aguilers, pp. 105–6.
19. Albert of Aachen, V. 26, p. 371; Raymond of Aguilers, p. 105.
20. Albert of Aachen, VI. 55, p. 477. Other sources do not confirm the presence of the Genoese.
21. There is a detailed description of these wooden superstructures by the author of the c.900 Byzantine military treatise: Leo VI, *Taktika*, XIX. 7, p. 504. For these structures in Muslim ships: Vassilios Christides, *The Conquest of Crete by the Arabs (ca. 824): A Turning Point in the Struggle between Byzantium and Islam* (Athens, 1984), pp. 44–5.
22. Matthew Bennett, 'Amphibious Operations from the Norman Conquest to the Crusades of St. Louis, c.1050–c.1250', in: *Amphibious Warfare 1000–1700*, ed. D.J.B. Trim, M.C. Fissel (Leiden, 2006), p. 57. Ioannes Kaminiates mentions the use of

wooden towers against coastal fortifications by Leo of Tripoli during the siege of Thessaloniki in AD 904: I. Kaminiates, 'Για την άλωση της Θεσσαλονίκης', in: *Χρονικά των αλώσεων της Θεσσαλονίκης*, ed. Kh. Messes, intr. Paolo Odorico (Athens, 2009), XXXIV, p. 113.
23. John Kinnamos, *Deeds of John and Manuel Komnenos*, trans. Charles M. Brand (New York, 1976), III, pp. 80–1.
24. Albert of Aachen, VI. 57–8, pp. 481–3.
25. *Alexiad*, XI. vii.
26. Beihammer, *Byzantium and the emergence of Muslim-Turkish Anatolia*, pp. 323–9.
27. Asbridge, *The Principality of Antioch*, pp. 16–21.
28. Ralph of Caen, *Gesta Tancredi*, ch. 40, p. 63.
29. Ralph of Caen, *Gesta Tancredi*, ch. 44, p. 70.
30. Ralph of Caen, *Gesta Tancredi*, ch. 45, p. 70; Asbridge, *The Principality of Antioch*, pp. 22–3.
31. Modern historians have disputed Yewdale's assertion that Bohemond supported Daimbert's candidacy for the patriarchal throne, and even became his vassal, because he desired 'a good title to that which he already possessed' (i.e. that of prince of Antioch): Yewdale, *Bohemond*, pp. 89–92. See: Russo, *Boemondo*, p. 136, n. 16; Flori, *Bohémond*, pp. 204–5; Cahèn, *La Syrie du Nord*, p. 224.
32. Ralph of Caen, *Gesta Tancredi*, ch. 140, p. 156; Fulcher of Chartres, 34.6, p. 341; Russo, *Boemondo*, pp. 134–9; Flori, *Bohémond*, pp. 212–14.
33. Asbridge, *The Principality of Antioch*, p. 51; Yewdale, *Bohemond*, p. 92.
34. Kamal al-Din, 'La Chronique d'Alep', in RHC Or. vol. III (Paris, 1884), p. 589; Matthew of Edessa, *Chronicle*, p. 176.
35. Beihammer, *Byzantium and the emergence of Muslim-Turkish Anatolia*, p. 293.
36. Matthew of Edessa, *Chronicle*, p. 176; Fulcher of Chartres, 35, pp. 344–6; *The Chronicle of Michael the Great, Patriarch of the Syrians*, trans. Robert Bedrosian (Long Branch, NJ, 2013), ch. 168, p. 180 [pdf. page]
37. Albert of Aachen, vii. 27, p. 525.
38. Ralph of Caen, *Gesta Tancredi*, ch. 141, p. 157.
39. Matthew of Edessa, *Chronicle*, p. 177.
40. Ralph of Caen, *Gesta Tancredi*, ch. 143, pp. 158–9.
41. *Alexiad*, XI. ix.
42. Ralph of Caen, *Gesta Tancredi*, chs 144–6, pp. 159–63.
43. Ralph of Caen, *Gesta Tancredi*, ch. 147, pp. 163–4; Orderic Vitalis, *Ecclesiastical History*, X, ch. XXIII, (vol. III) pp. 308–9.
44. Matthew of Edessa, *Chronicle*, p. 192.
45. Matthew of Edessa, *Chronicle*, p. 185.
46. Asbridge, *The Principality of Antioch*, pp. 53–5.
47. Malcolm Barber, *The Crusader States* (London, 2012), p. 82.
48. Christopher MacEvitt, *The Crusades and the Christian World of the East: Rough Tolerance* (Philadelphia, PA, 2010), pp. 84–5.
49. Ibn al-Qalanisi, *The Damascus Chronicle*, p. 60.
50. Albert of Aachen and Ralph of Caen do not mention the Latin attacks against Harran that provoked the Turkish campaign against Edessa, although they both report that Baldwin did send for help to Bohemond. William of Tyre and Matthew of Edessa, however, mistakenly report that Bohemond was called up to participate in the initial

campaign against Harran, before the Turkish combined army arrived to besiege Edessa in early May: Albert of Aachen, ix. 38-9, pp. 689-93; Ralph of Caen, *Gesta Tancredi*, ch. 148, pp. 164-5; William of Tyre, vol. I, pp. 456-8; Matthew of Edessa, *Chronicle*, p. 193. According to M. Barber: 'No Latin chronicler was present, but both Ralph of Caen and Albert of Aachen were well placed to collect information from those who had been.' *The Crusader States*, p. 82.
51. Albert of Aachen, ix. 39, p. 691.
52. Morillo, *War in World History*, vol. I, p. 105.
53. Ibn al-Qalanisi, *Damascus Chronicle*, p. 61.
54. Asbridge, *The Principality of Antioch*, pp. 55-6.
55. Albert of Aachen, ix. 47, pp. 703-5.
56. Ralph of Caen, *Gesta Tancredi*, ch. 151, p. 167; *Alexiad*, XI. xi.
57. Ralph of Caen, *Gesta Tancredi*, ch. 152, p. 168.
58. Fulcher of Chartres, II, 26.4, p. 473.
59. Albert of Aachen, IX. 43, p. 703.
60. Asbridge, *The Principality of Antioch*, p. 59.
61. *Alexiad*, XII. ii.
62. Albert of Aachen, XI. 40, p. 815.
63. Asbridge, *The Principality of Antioch*, p. 64.

Chapter 8: Back to Europe

1. J.G. Rowe, 'Pascal II, Bohemond of Antioch and the Byzantine Empire', *Bulletin of the John Rylands Library*, 49 (1966-67), 165-202, quotation from pp. 179-80.
2. *Tudebodus imitatus et continuatus*, RHCOcc. vol. III, s.a. 1098, p. 208.
3. *Tudebodus imitatus et continuatus*, RHCOcc. vol. III, s.a. 1104, p. 228
4. Flori, *Bohemond*, p. 254.
5. Anonymous Barenses, *Chronicon*, RIS, v. 151, a.c. 1105.
6. Bartolf of Nangis, RHCOcc. vol. III, ch. 65, p. 538.
7. Russo, *Boemondo*, p. 157 (n. 12).
8. Orderic Vitalis, *Ecclesiastical History*, XI. xii, p. 365.
9. Bartolf of Nangis, RHCOcc. vol. III, ch. 65, p. 538. This is the only western source that includes this significant detail, although Rowe expressed some serious doubts about its reliability: Rowe, 'Pascal II', 180.
10. *Chronica monasterii Casinensis*, MGH, SS, vol. 34, IV, p. 438; Suger, *The Deeds of Louis the Fat*, trans. Richard Cusimano, John Moorhead (Washington DC, 1992), p. 45. For Bruno's career: William L. North, 'In the Shadows of Reform: Exegesis and the formation of a Clerical Elite in the Works of Bishop Bruno of Segni (1078/9-1123)', (Ph.D. Diss., University of California-Berkeley, 1998), 66-110.
11. Orderic Vitalis, *Ecclesiastical History*, XI. xii, p. 366.
12. *The Register of Pope Gregory VII, 1073-85*, trans. H.E.J. Cowdrey (Oxford, 2002), 8.6, pp. 371-2.
13. Leonard (d. AD 559) was a Frankish noble at the court of the Merovingian king Clovis I. He was converted to Christianity, along with the king, at Christmas 496, by St Remigius, bishop of Reims. Leonard asked Clovis to grant him personally the right to liberate prisoners whom he would find worthy of it, at any time.

14. William of Malmesbury, *Gesta Regum Anglorum*, ed. and trans. J.A. Giles (London, 1847), IV. 2, a.d. 1123, p. 415. It seems more likely that Bohemond had silver chains modelled on the iron ones that had held him during his captivity.
15. Luigi Russo, 'Il viaggio di Boemondo d'Altavilla in Francia (1106): un riesame', *Archivo Storico Italiano*, 163 (2005) 3–42 (esp. 6–16).
16. Orderic Vitalis, *Ecclesiastical History*, XI. xii, p. 367.
17. Suger, *The Deeds of Louis the Fat*, p. 45.
18. Ekkehardus Uraugiensis abbas, *Hierosolymita*, ed. Heinrich Hagenmeyer (Tubingen, 1877), p. 293.
19. Riley-Smith, *What Were the Crusades?*, p. 2.
20. C. Tyerman, *Fighting for Christendom, Holy War and the Crusades* (Oxford, 2004), pp. 30–1.
21. Riley-Smith, *What Were the Crusades?*, esp. chs 1–3; J. Flori, *La Guerre Sainte* (Paris, 2001), whose work provides an interesting modern treatment of the nature of 'Holy War'; R. Firestone, *Jihad. The Origin of 'Holy War' in Islam* (New York, 1999); I. Stouraitis, 'Just War and "Holy War" in the Middle Ages. Rethinking Theory through the Byzantine Case-Study', *Jahrbuch der Österreichischen Byzantinistik*, 62 (2012), 227–64.
22. Carl Erdmann, *The Origin of the Idea of Crusade*, foreword and additional notes, Marshall W. Baldwin (Princeton NJ, 2019), pp. 193–4.
23. On the 'duplicity of the emperor Alexios' regarding the course of the Crusade of 1101 through Byzantine territories: Orderic Vitalis, *Ecclesiastical History*, X. xix, pp. 288–9.
24. Raymond of Aguilers, p. 90.
25. Brett Whalen, 'Rethinking the Schism of 1054: Authority, Heresy, and the Latin Rite', *Traditio*, 62 (2007) 1–24.
26. Brett Whalen, 'God's Will or Not? Bohemond's Campaign Against the Byzantine Empire (1105–1108)', in: *Crusades – Medieval Worlds in Conflict*, ed. Thomas F. Madden, James L. Naus, Vincent Ryan (London, 1991), pp. 111–25.
27. *The Register of Pope Gregory VII*, I. 49, pp. 54–5.
28. Rubenstein frames his argument on the fact that Pascal and Bruno were both educated theologians who could not possibly have ignored the apocalyptic messages sent by Bohemond specifically to stir anti-Greek sentiments among Latin churchmen in Italy: Jay Rubenstein, 'The Deeds of Bohemond: Reform, Propaganda, and the History of the First Crusade', *Viator*, 47 (2016), 128–9.
29. Rubenstein, 'The Deeds of Bohemond', 130–4.
30. E.O. Blake and Colin Morris, 'A Hermit Goes to War: Peter and the Origins of the First Crusade', *Studies in Church History*, 22 (1985), 79–107.
31. *Alexiad*, XII. i–iv.
32. Anna rarely distinguishes between Latins, Franks or Celts to denote western European soldiers: Buckler, *Anna Komnena*, p. 441. By differentiating between Franks and Celts, she is probably referring to the Franks and the Normans.
33. By her term *Thule*, Anna means all the lands bordering on the North Sea, and because she adds the word 'island' many historians have taken it to mean either Britain or Iceland, although I believe it is the former: Buckler, *Anna Komnena*, p. 438. Hence, Anna's 'men from the isle of Thule who normally serve in the Roman army but had through force of circumstances then joined him' could be a reference to Anglo-Saxon *thegns*, formerly serving in the Varangian Guard where they had long earned a reputation as fearless warriors, who sought the opportunity to join Bohemond's army:

Jonathan Shepard, 'The English and Byzantium: A Study of their Role in the Byzantine Army in the Later Eleventh Century', *Traditio*, 29 (1973), 53–92; Krijnie N. Ciggaar, 'L'emigration anglaise a Byzance apres 1066, Un nouveau texte en latin sur les Varangues a Constantinople', *Revue des Études Byzantines*, 32 (1974), 301–42. Another theory wants Anna's *Thule* to be identified with the northwestern part of the Jutland Peninsula in Denmark, known today as Thy. This assumption makes more sense considering the visit of the Danish king Eric I to Alexios' court on his way to Jerusalem in 1102–03, which must have provided many new recruits for the Guard: Blondal, *Varangians*, pp. 131–6.
34. *Alexiad*, XII. ix.
35. John H. Pryor, 'Transportation of Horses by Sea during the Era of the Crusades, Eighth Century to 1285 AD: Part I to c. 1225', *The Mariner's Mirror*, 68 (1982), 14.
36. Anonymus Barensis, *Chronicon*, s.a. 1107; Fulcher of Chartres, II. 35, p. 521; William of Tyre, p. 471; Albert of Aachen, X. 40, p. 754; *Alexiad*, XII. ix.
37. *Alexiad*, XIII. ii.
38. Dandolus, *Chronicon*, s.a. 1107, pp. 223–4. For more on the treaty of 1082: O. Tuma, 'The Dating of Alexios' Chrysobull to the Venetians: 1082, 1084, or 1092?', *Byzantinoslavica*, 62 (1981), 171–85; M.E. Martin, 'The Chrysobull of Alexios I Komnenos to the Venetians and the Early Venetian Quarter in Constantinople', *Byzantinoslavica*, 39 (1978), 19–23.
39. *Alexiad*, XIII. ii.
40. *Alexiad*, XIII. iii. For more on siege techniques in the Mediterranean world and Byzantium: Leif Inge Ree Petersen, *Siege Warfare and Military Organization in the Successor States (400–800 AD), Byzantium, the West and Islam* (Leiden, 2013), pp. 267–98.
41. *Narratio Floriacensis de Captis Antiochia et Hierosolyma*, RHOcc. vol. 5, p. 361; Albert of Aachen, X. 42, p. 756.
42. *Alexiad*, XIII. v–viii.
43. C. Cahen and P.M. Holt, *The Formation of Turkey: The Seljukid Sultanate of Rūm* (Harlow, 2001), pp. 7–15.
44. Theotokis, *Byzantine Military Tactics*, pp. 31–3.
45. Maurice, *Strategikon*, VII, p. 65.
46. Leo VI, *Taktika*, XX. 51, p. 554.
47. Kekaumenos, *Strategikon*, ed. B. Wassiliewsky, V. Jernstedt (Amsterdam: Hakkert, 1965), pp. 9–10.
48. *Alexiad*, XIII. iv.
49. *Alexiad*, XIII. v.
50. *Alexiad*, XIII. iv. The *Taktika* of Emperor Leo VI recommend a similar stratagem: Leo VI, *Taktika*, XX. 29, p. 546.
51. Orderic Vitalis, XI. xxiv, p. 388; Albert of Aachen, X. 44, p. 758.
52. *Alexiad*, XIII. vi. See also: Albert of Aachen, X. 43, pp. 756–8.
53. *Alexiad*, XIII. v.
54. *Alexiad*, XIII. vi. Vegetius, the fifth-century Roman author of the military treatise *Epitoma Rei Militaris* (or 'Epitome of Military Science'), recognises the danger of an ambush on a river-crossing and urges a commander to place armed guards and even construct temporary timber fortifications: Vegetius, *Epitome*, III. 7, p. 79.
55. *Alexiad*, XIII. viii–ix.

56. *Alexiad*, XIII. xii.
57. Albert of Aachen, X. 45, p. 759.
58. Orderic Vitalis, *Ecclesiastical History*, XI. xxiv, vol. III, p. 389.

Epilogue: Death and Heritage

1. William of Tyre suggests that Bohemond was about 18 years old when he succeeded his father in his principality in early 1127: William of Tyre, vol. II, p. 33.
2. Russo, *Boemondo*, p. 200. For the charters, see: Yewdale, *Bohemond*, p. 132.
3. Falcone di Benevento, *Chronicon Beneventanum*, ed. E.D'Angelo (Firenze, 1998), s.a. 1110; Romuald of Salerno, *Chronicon*, pp. 205–6; Albert of Aachen, XI. 48, p. 825. Italian sources mostly connect Bohemond's death with that of Duke Roger of Apulia, his half-brother, on 21 February 1111. Yet, Gadolin believes the year of Bohemond's death to be 1109, followed by his burial at Canosa two years later, in 1111: A.R. Gadolin, 'Prince Bohemond's death and apotheosis in the Church of San Sabino, Canosa di Puglia', *Byzantion*, 52 (1982), 124–53 (especially 125–31). Gadolin based his assertion on Anna Komnena's account: 'He [Bohemond] lived only six months longer [after the Treaty of Devol, agreed in September 1108] and then paid the debt that all must pay': *Alexiad*, XIV. i.
4. Dawn Marie Hayes, 'The Cult of St Nicholas of Myra in Norman Bari, c.1071–c.1111', *Journal of Ecclesiastical History*, 67 (2016), 492–512.
5. Elizabeth Lapina, *Warfare and the miraculous in the chronicles of the First Crusade* (University Park, PA, 2015), p. 68.
6. Gadolin, 'Prince Bohemond's death', 136–41; Ann Wharton Epstein, 'The Date and Significance of the Cathedral of Canosa in Apulia, South Italy', *Dumbarton Oaks Papers*, 37 (1983), 79–90.
7. Lapina, *Warfare and the miraculous*, p. 69; Epstein, 'The Date and Significance', 86.
8. The translations of both of the inscriptions can be found in: Epstein, 'The Date and Significance', 86.
9. C.J. Rogers (2006), 'Strategy, Operational Design, and Tactics', in: *International Encyclopaedia of Military History*, ed. J.C. Bradford (New York: Routledge).

Bibliography

Primary Sources

Albert of Aachen, *Historia Ierosolimitana, History of the Journey to Jerusalem*, ed. and trans. Susan B. Edgington (Oxford, 2007).
Amatus of Montecassino, *The History of the Normans*, trans. Prescott Dunbar (Woodbridge, 2004).
Attaleiates, M., *The History*, transl. Anthony Kaldellis and Dimitris Krallis (Cambridge MA: Harvard University Press, 2012).
Bryennius, Nicephorus, *Histoire*, introduction, text and transl. Paul Gautier (Brussels, 1975).
Komnena, Anna, *The Alexiad*, trans. E.A.S. Dawes (Cambridge, ON: In Parentheses Publications, 2000).
Constantine Porphyrogenitus, *De Administrando Imperio*, ed. (Greek text) G. Moravcsik, trans. R.J.H. Jenkins (Washington, DC: Dumbarton Oaks Texts, 4, 1985).
Ekkehardus Uraugiensis abbas, *Hierosolymita*, ed. Heinrich Hagenmeyer (Tubingen, 1877).
Fulcheri Carnotensis, *Historia Hierosolymitana (1095–1127)*, ed. Heinrich Hagenmeyer (Heidelberg, 1913).
Guillaume de Pouille, *La Geste de Robert Guiscard*, ed. Marguerite Mathieu (Palermo, 1963).
Ibn al-Qalanisi, *The Damascus Chronicle of the Crusades*, extracted and transl. H.A.R. Gibb (Mineola, NY, 2002).
Kamal al-Din, 'La Chronique d'Alep', in RHC Or. vol. III (Paris, 1884).
Kaminiates, Ioannes, 'Για την άλωση της Θεσσαλονίκης', in: *Χρονικά των αλώσεων της Θεσσαλονίκης*, ed. Kh. Messes, intr. Paolo Odorico (Athens, 2009).
Leo VI, *The 'Taktika' of Leo VI*, Corpus Fontium Historiae Byzantinae, vol. 49, trans. G.T. Dennis (Washington, DC: Dumbarton Oaks, 2010).
Malaterra, Geoffrey, *The Deeds of Count Roger of Calabria and Sicily and of his Brother Duke Robert Guiscard*, ed. and trans. Kenneth B. Wolf (Ann Arbor, 2005).
Matthew of Edessa, *Armenia and the Crusades: tenth to twelfth centuries: the Chronicle of Matthew of Edessa*, translated from the original Armenian with a commentary and introduction by Ara Edmond Dostourian (Lanham: Maryland, 1993).
Orderic Vitalis, *Ecclesiastical History of England and Normandy*, trans. T. Forester (London: Henry G. Bohn, 1854).
Ralph of Caen, *The Gesta Tancredi of Ralph of Caen: A History of the Normans on the First Crusade*, trans. B.S. Bachrach and D.S. Bachrach (Aldershot, 2005).
Raymond of Aguilers, *Historia Francorum Qui Ceperunt Iherusalem*, trans. with intro. John H. Hill and Laurita L. Hill (Philadelphia, 1968).

Skylitzes Continuatus, in: *Georgius Cedrenus Compendium Historiarum* [CSHB], ed. Immanuel Bekker (Bonn, 1839).
Skylitzes, John, *A Synopsis of Byzantine History, 811–1057*, trans. John Wortley (Cambridge, 2010).
The Chronicle of Michael the Great, Patriarch of the Syrians, trans. Robert Bedrosian (Long Branch, NJ, 2013).
The deeds of the Franks and other Jerusalem-bound pilgrims: the earliest chronicle of the first crusades, ed. and trans. Nirmal Dass (Plymouth, 2011).
The Etymologies of Isidore of Seville, transl. S.A.Barney, W.J. Lewis, J.A. Beach and O. Berghof (Cambridge: Cambridge University Press, 2006).
Vegetius: Epitome of Military Science, transl. N.P. Milner (Liverpool: Liverpool University Press, 2001).
William (of Tyre, archbishop of Tyre), *A History of Deeds Done Beyond the Sea*, trans. Emily Atwater Babcock and August Charles Krey, 2 vols (New York, 1943).
Zonaras, Ioannes, *Epitome Historiarum*, ed. Charles Du Fresne Du Cange and Ludwig August Dindorf (Leipzig, 1868).

Secondary sources

Ahrweiler, Hélène, *Byzance et la Mer* (Paris, 1966).
Angold, Michael, *The Byzantine Empire, 1025–1204, A Political History* (London, 1997; 2nd edn).
Asa Eger, A., '(Re)Mapping Medieval Antioch: Urban Transformations from the Early Islamic to the Middle Byzantine Periods', *Dumbarton Oaks Papers*, 67 (2013), 95–134.
Asbridge, Thomas S., *The Creation of the Principality of Antioch, 1098–1130* (Woodbridge, 2000).
Bachrach, Bernard S., 'Some Observations on the Role of the Byzantine Navy in the Success of the First Crusade', *Journal of Medieval Military History*, 1 (2002), 83–100.
Barber, Malcolm, *The Crusader States* (London, 2012).
Barber, Malcolm and Bate, Keith, *Letters from the East: Crusaders, Pilgrims and Settlers in the 12th–13th centuries* (New York, 2016).
Beihammer, Alexander D., *Byzantium and the Emergence of Muslim-Turkish Anatolia, ca.1040–1130* (London, 2017).
Bennett, Matthew, 'Amphibious Operations from the Norman Conquest to the Crusades of St Louis, c.1050–c.1250', in: *Amphibious Warfare 1000–1700*, ed. D.J.B. Trim and M.C. Fissel (Leiden, 2006), pp. 51–68.
Brand, Charles M., 'The Turkish Element in Byzantium, Eleventh–Twelfth Centuries', *Dumbarton Oaks Papers*, 43 (1989), 1–25.
Brown, Paul, 'The Gesta Roberti Wiscardi: A "Byzantine" history?', *Journal of Medieval History*, 37 (2011), 162–79.
Cahen, Claude, *The formation of Turkey: the Seljukid Sultanate of Rum: eleventh to fourteenth century*, trans. and ed. P.M. Holt (Harlow, 2001).
Eads, Valerie, 'Sigkelgaita of Salerno: Amazon or Trophy Wife?', *Journal of Medieval Military History*, 3 (2005), 72–87.
Flori, Jean, *Bohémond d'Antioche: chevalier d'aventure* (Paris, 2007).
France, John, 'The departure of Tatikios from the Crusader army', *Bulletin of the Institute of Historical Research*, 44 (1971), 137–47.
France, John, *Victory in the East: a military history of the First Crusade* (Cambridge, 1994).

Frankopan, Peter, *The First Crusade, The Call from the East* (Cambridge MA, 2012).
Gadolin, A.R., 'Prince Bohemond's death and apotheosis in the Church of San Sabino, Canosa di Puglia', *Byzantion*,52 (1982), 124–53.
Glavinas, A., 'Οι Νορμανδοί στην Καστοριά (1082–1083)' ['The Normans in Kastoria (1082–1083)'], *Βυζαντινά [Byzantina]*, 13ii (1985), 1255–65.
Haldon, John F., *The Byzantine Wars: Battles and Campaign of the Byzantine Era* (Stroud, 2001).
Halsall, Guy, *Barbarian Migrations and the Roman West, 376–568* (Cambridge: Cambridge University Press, 2007).
Harris, Jonathan, *Byzantium and the Crusades* (London, 2014; 2nd edn).
Hayes, Dawn Marie, '"The Cult of St Nicholas of Myra in Norman Bari, c.1071–c.1111', *Journal of Ecclesiastical History*, 67 (2016), 492–512.
Kaldellis, Anthony, *Streams of gold, rivers of blood: the rise and fall of Byzantium, 955 A.D. to the First Crusade* (New York, 2017).
Lapina, Elizabeth, *Warfare and the miraculous in the chronicles of the First Crusade* (University Park, PA, 2015).
Leveniotes, Georgios, *Το στασιαστικό κίνημα του Νορμανδού Ουρσελίου (Ursel de Bailleul) στην Μικρά Ασία (1073–1076) [Ursel de Bailleul's uprising in Asia Minor (1073–1076)]*, (Thessaloniki, 2004).
Loud, G., 'The "Gens Normannorum" – Myth or Reality?', *Anglo-Norman Studies*, 4 (1981), 104–16.
Loud, G., *The Age of Robert Guiscard: Southern Italy and the Norman Conquest* (London, 2000).
McDougall, Sara, *Royal Bastards: The Birth of Illegitimacy, 800–1230* (Oxford: Oxford University Press, 2017).
Ménager, Leon, 'Inventaires des familles normandes et franques émigrées en Italie Meridionale et en Sicile (XIe–XIIe siècles)', in: *Roberto il Guiscardo e il suo tempo. Relazzioni e communicationi nelle prime giornate normanno-sueve (Bari, Maggio, 1973)* (Rome, 1975), pp. 260–390.
Ménager, Leon, 'Pesanteur et étiologie de la colonisation normande de l'Italie', in: *Roberto il Guiscardo e il suo tempo. Relazzioni e communicationi nelle prime giornate normanno-sueve (Bari, Maggio, 1973)* (Rome, 1975), pp. 189–214.
Ménager, Léon, *Recueil des actes des ducs normands d'Italie, 1046–1127. Les premier ducs* (Bari, 1980).
Neville, Leonora, *Anna Komnene, The Life and Work of a Medieval Historian* (Oxford, 2016).
Petrizzo, Francesca, 'Band of Brothers, Kin Dynamics of the Hautevilles and Other Normans in Southern Italy and Syria, c.1030–c.1140' (PhD thesis, University of Leeds, 2018).
Pryor, John H., 'Introduction: modelling Bohemond's march to Thessalonike', in: *Logistics of Warfare in the Age of the Crusades*, ed. John H. Pryor (Aldershot, 2006), pp. 1–24.
Pryor, John H. and Jeffreys, Elizabeth, *The Age of the Δρόμων, The Byzantine Navy ca 500–1204* (Leiden, 2006).
Pryor, John H. and Jeffreys, Michael J., 'Alexios, Bohemond, and Byzantium's Euphrates Frontier: A Tale of Two Cretans', *Crusades*, 11 (2012), 31–86.
Riley-Smith, J., *The Crusades* (London, 1987).
Rogers, R., *Latin Siege Warfare in the Twelfth Century* (Oxford, 1992).

Rowe, J.G., 'Pascal II, Bohemond of Antioch and the Byzantine Empire', *Bulletin of the John Rylands Library*, 49 (1966–67), 165–202.
Rubenstein, Jay, *Armies of Heaven, The First Crusade and the Quest for Apocalypse* (New York, 2011).
Rubenstein, Jay, 'The Deeds of Bohemond: Reform, Propaganda, and the History of the First Crusade', *Viator*, 47(2) (2016), 113–36.
Russo, Luigi, 'Il viaggio di Boemondo d'Altavilla in Francia (1106): un riesame', *Archivo Storico Italiano*, 163 (2005), 3–42.
Russo, Luigi, *Boemondo. Figlio del Guiscardo e principe di Antiochia* (Avellino: Elio Sellino, 2009).
Shepard, Jonathan, 'Information, Disinformation and Delay in Byzantine Diplomacy', *Byzantinische Forschungen*, 10 (1985), 233–93.
Shepard, Jonathan, 'When Greek meets Greek: Alexios Komnenos and Bohemond in 1097–98', *Byzantine and Modern Greek Studies*, 12 (1988), 185–277.
Shepard, Jonathan, 'The Uses of the Franks in Eleventh-Century Byzantium', *Anglo-Norman Studies*, 15 (1993), 275–305.
Simpson, Alicia, 'Three Sources of Military Unrest in Eleventh Century Asia Minor: The Norman Chieftains Hervé Frankopoulos, Robert Crispin and Roussel of Bailleuil', *Mesogeios/Méditerranée*, 9–10 (2000), 181–207.
Skinner, Patricia, '"Halt! Be Men!": Sikelgaita of Salerno, Gender and the Norman Conquest of Southern Italy', *Gender & History*, 12 (2000), 622–41.
Soustal, Peter and Koder, Johannes, *Tabula Imperii Byzantini, Band 3: Nikopolis und Kephallēnia* (Vienna, 1981).
Stephenson, Paul, *Byzantium's Balkan Frontier, A Political Study of the Northern Balkans, 900–1204* (Cambridge, 2000).
Theotokis, Georgios, 'The Norman Invasion of Sicily, 1061–1072: Numbers and Military Tactics', *War in History*, 17 (2010), 381–402.
Theotokis, Georgios, 'Rus, Varangian and Frankish Mercenaries in the Service of the Byzantine Emperors (9th–11th Century) – Numbers, Organisation and Battle Tactics in the Operational Theatres of Asia Minor and the Balkans', *Byzantina Symmeikta*, 22 (2012), 126–56.
Theotokis, Georgios, 'The square fighting march of the Crusaders at the battle of Ascalon (1099)', *Journal of Medieval Military History*, 11 (2013), 57–72.
Theotokis, G., *The Norman Campaigns in the Balkans, 1081–1108* (Woodbridge: Boydell & Brewer, 2014).
Theotokis, Georgios, *Byzantine Military Tactics in Syria and Mesopotamia in the Tenth Century* (Edinburgh, 2018).
Theotokis, Georgios and Yildiz, Aysel (eds), *A Military History of the Mediterranean Sea, Aspects of War, Diplomacy and Military Elites* (Leiden, 2018).
Tobias, Norman, 'The Tactics and Strategy of Alexios Komnenos at Calavrytae, 1078', *Byzantine Studies/Études byzantines*, 6 (1979), 193–211.
Tounta, Eleni, 'The Norman Conquerors between Epos and Chanson de Geste: The Perception of Identities in Cultural Flows', in *Norman Tradition and Transcultural Heritage: Exchange of Cultures in the 'Norman' Peripheries of Medieval Europe*, ed. Stefan Burkhardt, Thomas Foerster (Routledge: London, 2013), pp. 125–47.
Tsurtsumia, Mamuka, 'ΤΡΙΒΟΛΟΣ: A BYZANTINE LANDMINE', *Byzantion*, 82 (2012), 415–22.

Tyerman, C., *Fighting for Christendom, Holy War and the Crusades* (Oxford, 2004).
Upsher Smith Jr, R., '"Nobilissimus" and Warleader: the opportunity and the necessity behind Robert Guiscard's Balkan expeditions', *Byzantion*, 70 (2000), 507–26.
Veikou, Myrto, *Byzantine Epirus, A Topography of Transformation, Settlements of the Seventh–Twelfth Centuries in Southern Epirus and Aetoloacarnania, Greece* (Leiden, 2012).
Whalen, Brett, 'God's Will or Not? Bohemond's Campaign Against the Byzantine Empire (1105–1108)', in: *Crusades – Medieval Worlds in Conflict*, ed. Thomas F. Madden, James L. Naus, Vincent Ryan (London, 1991), pp. 111–25.
Wharton Epstein, Ann, 'The Date and Significance of the Cathedral of Canosa in Apulia, South Italy', *Dumbarton Oaks Papers*, 37 (1983), 79–90.

Index

Abelard, 16, 17, 33, 46, 57
Adhemar, bishop of Le Puy, 74, 114, 115, 125, 130
Adrianople, 32, 37, 77
Adriatic Sea, 2, 19, 20, 27, 29, 30, 32, 34, 56, 57, 58, 63, 68, 77, 78, 81, 143, 149
Aegean Sea, 25, 60, 89, 119
Ahmad ibn-Marwan, 115–16
Alan(s), 152, 154
Alberada of Buonalbergo, 14–17, 65
Alexander II, Pope, 28
Alexandretta, 99, 104, 125–6
Alp Arslan, 20, 24
Amalfi, 34, 69, 74, 75, 143
Amicus II of Molfetta and Giovenazzo ['Amiketas'], 39–41
Amvrakikos Gulf, 49, 60
Antioch, 82, 85, 87, 99, 103–17, 157, 163
  Battle of, 113–16, 142, 164
  Byzantine *dux* of, 21
  Latin Patriarch of, 130, 133, 157
  Norman Principality of, 124–39, 159
  Walls of, 105
Arta, 49, 50, 54, 164
Artah, 104, 126, 137–9
  Battle of, 139
Artuk, 23
Ascanian Lake, 91, 93
Attaleiates, 22–5
Avlona, 18, 31–3, 56–60, 78, 150, 154–5

Baldwin I of Boulogne, 81, 92, 102, 103, 126
Baldwin II of Edessa, 128, 130–6, 148
Baldwin of Hainault, 118, 120
Bari, 4, 17, 19, 27, 57, 66–9, 75, 77, 142, 159–60

Basilakes, Nicephorus, 25, 26, 91
Bengras, Lake, 108
Bithynia, 23, 24, 34, 90, 91
Bodin, Constantine, 27, 40
Botaneiates, Nicephorus, 24, 25, 119
Brindisi, 19, 58, 66, 69, 73, 75, 77
Bruno of Segni, 143–9
Bryennius, Nicephorus, 6, 22, 24
Bryennius, Nicephorus (the Elder), 24–7
Butrint, 32, 59
Butumites, 93, 94, 129

Caltrops, 49, 50, 164
Canina, 31, 59, 150, 154, 155
Cannae, castle of, 57
Capitanata, 4, 19, 57
Cappadocia, 21, 23, 24, 99
Cassiope, 31, 32, 59
Castrogiovanni, Battle of, 5
Cerami, Battle of, 5, 21
Chartres, Cathedral, 145
Charzanes River, 37
Civitate, Battle of, 4, 16, 19, 41
Clermont, Council of, 71, 73, 75, 145
Constance, 142, 144–7, 159, 161
Constantine I, Byzantine emperor, 52, 161
Constantine IV, Byzantine emperor, 20
Constantine VII, Byzantine emperor, 44, 46
Constantine IX, Byzantine emperor, 160
Constantine X, Byzantine emperor, 39
Corfu, 18, 31, 32, 34, 37, 57, 58, 59, 141, 142, 149
  Bishopric of, 33,
  Castle of, 59, 60
  Naval Battle of, 59–60, 124
Crispin, 21
Cyprus, 2, 106, 124, 130

Daimbert of Pisa, 125, 127, 133, 143, 148
Dalassena, Anna, 6
Danishmends, 89, 91, 101, 128, 128, 144
Domenico Silvio, Venetian Doge, 33
Doryleum, 90, 94, 96–9
　Battle of, 56, 94, 98, 108, 163–4
Doukas, Andronikos, 21
Doukas, Constantine, 5, 12, 21, 39
Doukas, family, 21–4, 26, 29
Doukas, Ioannes *kaisar*, 21–4
Drogo Hauteville, 15–17
dromōn, 58
Duqaq of Damascus, 105, 107

Edessa [in Macedonia], 52, 79
Edessa [in Upper Mesopotamia], 102, 103, 126, 131, 133, 134, 136
　Latin Principality of, 126, 131, 133
Epirus, 43, 44, 47, 49, 60, 61, 63, 64
Euphrates River, 23, 89, 101, 135
Excubitae, 39

Fatimids of Egypt, 147, 149, 157
Feigned flight/retreat, 23, 40, 54, 111, 128, 135, 136, 154, 164

Gabriel of Melitene, 101, 128
Genoa, 106, 149
Geoffrey of Conversano, 57, 66
Gisulf II, prince of Salerno, 17
Glycys River, 60
Godfrey of Bouillon, 74, 77, 81, 82, 91, 92–8, 102, 103, 111–13, 121, 127, 129,
Greek Fire, 37, 151, 152
Gregory VII, Pope, 27, 28, 33, 46, 57, 68, 144, 147
Guaimar IV, prince of Salerno, 15, 17, 65

Harem, 107, 126, 164
　Castle of, 106
Harran, 131, 133, 134, 135–8
Henry IV, German emperor, 28, 33, 46, 57, 58
Hermann, 57
Holy Apostles, Church of, 161
Holy Trinity at Venosa, 64

Hugh of Vermandois, 74, 81, 95, 113, 114, 118, 120
Humphrey Hauteville, 16, 17

Ikonion, 22, 90, 99, 118
Ioannina, 47–50, 53, 54, 78, 152, 164
Ionian Sea, 20, 60, 61, 63

Jikirmish of Mosul, 133–8
John II, Byzantine emperor, 6, 8, 82, 156
Jordan I, prince of Capua, 57, 65, 69
Joscelin of Courtenay, 134–6

Kaisarea, 22–4, 89, 90, 99, 102
Kalavrye, Battle of, 25
Kastoria, 44, 52, 53, 56, 78, 79, 164
Kekaumenos, Katakalon, 20, 153
Kekaumenos, Michael, 153, 155
Kephalas, Leo, 53
Kephalonia, 31, 34, 60, 61, 63, 64, 149
Kerbogha, 107, 108, 112–20, 142, 164
Kilij Arslan, 90–2, 95, 96, 98, 107, 152
Kogh Vasil, 130–3
Komnenos, Isaac I, Byzantine emperor, 25
Komnenos, Isaakios, 22–4
Koryfo, 31–2
krites, 60
Kumans, 86, 109, 152, 153

Larissa, 52–6, 164
Latakia, 124, 125, 130, 131, 137–9
　Laodicea, 109, 124, 138, 149, 157
Legnano, Battle of, 48
Leo IX, Pope, 4, 19
Liege-man ('lizios anthropos'), 8, 13, 156

Malagina, 90
Malik Shah I, 23, 90, 101, 105, 152
Mamistra, 109, 110, 126, 127, 131, 137, 139
Manichaeans, 40, 79
Manzikert, Battle of, 21, 24, 25, 26, 42, 163
Melfi, 3, 4, 14, 15, 68–70
Melissinos, Nicephorus, 25, 39, 41
Melitene, 23, 90, 91, 101, 128, 131, 164
Melus of Bari, 4

Michael VII Doukas, Byzantine emperor, 5, 12, 22, 24–6, 29, 39, 144
Misilmeri, Battle of, 60
Monastras, 129, 139, 149
Monte Sant'Angelo sul Gargano, 3
Montepeloso, Battle of, 4, 14
Mopsuestia, 102, 103, 126, 127, 129
Mosul, *emir* of, 107, 108, 111, 112, 117, 133

Nicaea, 24, 25, 34, 89, 90, 119
  Crusader siege of, 91–7
Nicholas II, Pope, 4
Nicomedia, 24, 89, 90, 92, 94

Ofanto, Battle of, 4, 14
Ohrid, 27, 35, 43, 44, 49, 52, 78, 79, 152
Olivento, Battle of, 4, 14
Oricum [Hiericho], 31, 59, 154, 155
Orontes River, 104, 106, 108, 113–15, 120, 125, 136, 138, 139
Oschin, 101, 126
Otranto, 13, 16, 30, 31, 34, 57, 66

Pakourianos, Gregory, 37, 39, 40, 50, 53
Palaeologus, George, 6, 33, 36–8, 56
Palaeologus, Nicephorus, 23
Palermo, 4, 60, 163
Pallia, promontory of, 36
Pandulf IV, prince of Capua, 15
Pascal II, Pope, 143–9
Patzinaks, 25, 26, 46, 55, 80, 86, 91, 109, 152–4
Pelecanum, 94
Peter Bartholomew, 113
Peter of Trani, 15
Peter the Hermit, 74, 91, 94, 148
Philomelium, 99, 118, 119
Pisa, 106, 149
  fleet of, 125, 149
Plaustrella, 48

Rainulf of Aversa, 3, 4, 76
Raymond IV of Saint Gilles, 74, 81, 82, 85, 86, 91–5, 105, 108, 111, 113, 116–18, 120–5, 130, 131
Richard I of Capua, 4, 57, 65

Richard III, Duke of Normandy, 3
Ridwan of Aleppo, 105, 107, 108, 113, 136–9
Robert II, Duke of Normandy, 3, 4
Robert II of Flanders, 74
Roger Borsa, 30, 57, 58, 60, 63–71, 73–5, 143
Roger Hauteville, 5, 64, 68, 73
Romanus IV 'Diogenes', Byzantine emperor, 20, 21, 23, 29, 81, 143, 163
Roussel de Bailleuil, 20–4, 48
Ruj valley, 120–3, 125, 136, 138

St Leonard, 144
St Nicholas of Bari, 35, 68, 69, 142, 143, 159, 160
St Sabinus of Canosa, 142, 159–62
Saint Symeon, port of, 106, 110, 117, 124, 125
Salabrias River, 55
Salerno, 4, 19, 28, 56, 58, 65, 69, 70, 154
Sallust, 12
Samuel, Bulgarian tsar, 53
San Marco Argentano, 13, 15, 67
Santiago de Compostela, 3
Scribla, 15
Seljukid Sultanate of Rum, 89, 114
Serbs of Raska, 149
Shkumbin River, 44
Sigkelgaita, 17, 40, 41, 63, 65, 69
Sophon, Battle of, 23
Stephen of Blois, 74, 81, 95, 118, 119
Suleiman b. Qutlumush, 24, 25, 34, 35, 53, 89, 90

Tacitus, 10
Taktika by Leo VI, 49, 153
Tancred Hauteville, 12, 15, 76, 80, 85, 94, 102–4, 114, 122, 126, 127, 129–31, 134–9, 145, 157, 159
Tarsus, 99, 101–3, 109, 110, 126, 127, 129, 131, 137, 139
Tatikios, 6, 87, 91, 94, 97, 103, 105, 109, 110
Taurus Mountains, 24, 99, 101, 104, 126
Thessaloniki, 25, 32, 37, 42–9, 52, 53, 76–9, 149, 150, 163

Thoros of Edessa, 101, 103
Treaty of Devol (Diabolis), 8, 13, 53, 139, 154–6, 159
Trikala, 52, 53, 56
Troia, 17, 70
Turkoman, 23, 24, 29
Tutush, 23, 90, 101, 105

Urban II, Pope, 68–70, 74–7, 111, 113, 120, 143, 145, 149, 159, 160

Varangian Guard, 21, 22, 39–42, 44, 164
Vardar River, 52, 79
Vegetian ['strategy'], 2, 162, 164

Venice, 33, 34, 36, 59, 106
Vestiaritae, 39
Via Egnatia, 32, 34, 37, 43, 44, 47, 52, 78, 79
Vlach, 47

William I of Burgundy, 148
William II, Duke of Normandy, 3, 4, 39, 147
William 'Iron-Arm' Hauteville, 15

Yaghi-Siyan, 105

Zombou Bridge, Battle of, 22